Johnny West was born into an Anglo-Irish family in London in 1964. He was a Classical scholar at Balliol College, Oxford, joined Reuters as a correspondent, and spent a decade in the Middle East, on and off. After 9/11, he spent three years in Afghanistan, building a network of local radio stations, only one of which has been blown up. In 2008, he translated the first Iraqi account of the Gulf War to be published in English from Arabic, *The Devil You Don't Know*, the memoirs of Zuhair al-Jezairy. He speaks Arabic, Persian and French well and a few other languages badly.

Believing that oil can bring better results for the peoples of the countries where it is produced, he set up OpenOil.net and currently advises the United Nations on public policy and the oil industry. He presently lives in Berlin with his wife and two children. His personal blog is at www.delepaak.wordpress.com

Karama!

JOURNEYS THROUGH
THE ARAB SPRING

JOHNNY WEST

HERON

BOOKS

First published in Great Britain in 2011 by Heron Books,
an imprint of Quercus

Quercus
21 Bloomsbury Square
London
WC1A 2NS

A CIP catalogue record for this book is available
from the British Library

ISBN 978 0 85738 994 7

10 9 8 7 6 5 4 3 2

Typeset by Ellipsis Digital Limited, Glasgow

Printed and bound in Great Britain by Clays Ltd, St Ives plc

For Lecky

Karama /n/ honour, dignity, esteem, standing, prestige

'*Hiya thawrat karama*',
'*This is a revolution of honour*'
Anis al-Shoaibi,
revolutionary in Sidi Bou Zid, Tunisia

Contents

PART THREE
Libya

Karama!

A Prologue

That morning, 17 December 2010, Mohammed Bouazizi rose early as usual, to get to market early. As he had done for the last few years, he picked up fruit wholesale from the depot and pushed his cart a mile and a half to his usual stand near the governor's office in the town of Sidi Bou Zid, southern Tunisia. But on the way policewoman Fetya Hamdi stopped him and accused him of not having a licence to trade. Nobody knows exactly what words passed between them, but a short time later she returned with two male colleagues. They wrestled Bouazizi to the ground and confiscated his scales and produce. One version says that during the altercation, Hamdi slapped him in the face in full public view, another simply that she stood and watched while others did. Bouazizi then went to the municipality, a quarter of a mile away, and asked to see the mayor. A receptionist told him he was in a meeting.

Mohammed Bouazizi then went to a shop, bought some paint stripper and poured it all over himself. Then he struck a match, dropped it, and set himself alight.

'I couldn't believe my eyes,' said Dhafer al-Salihi, a lawyer in the town who saw it. 'He was right there in the street, a human ball of flame.'

Later in the day, his mother Menobia, ailing and veiled, came to the municipality to complain about her son's treatment by the police and demand action. When nobody came out to meet her, she stood outside the building in a one-woman protest.

Her nephew, Mohammed's cousin Ali Bouazizi, came with a handy video camera and took some footage, which he uploaded onto the Internet. The same day a team at Al Jazeera's headquarters in Qatar picked it up and rebroadcast it on their Mubashir – Live – channel. Within twenty-four hours Mohammed Bouazizi went from being a small-town street vendor, one of millions of young Arabs on the breadline struggling to make ends meet, to making international news.

Within weeks, he was to become the emblem of a people-power revolution that toppled a dictatorship in Tunisia that had lasted decades.

In June 2010, Khaled Said, a twenty-eight-year-old Egyptian, was in an Internet cafe in a district of the coastal city of Alexandria called Kleopatra. As he left, plain-clothes policemen outside confronted him in the street in front of several eyewitnesses. They took him into an alleyway and beat him savagely. The story might have ended there, an everyday case of police brutality of a kind that ordinary Egyptians have recognised as routine for decades. Khaled himself might have done no more than grumble to his friends, and worry about whether his tormentors would now watch him to make sure he wasn't going to try and get them into trouble. But Khaled Said died and his brother, fearing a cover-up by the police, posted pictures of his badly mutilated face on the Internet. His case sparked an immediate protest in his home city and reinvigorated an opposition movement in Egypt that had strayed into the doldrums after some high points a few years earlier when it had seemed that it might wreak national change.

A little later, a young Internet executive called Wael Ghoneim anonymously created a page on Facebook called 'We are all Khaled Said'. When he posted a call for protests in the middle of Cairo's Tahrir Square, it got 55,000 subscriptions. Roughly that many actually turned up on 25 January, in a flash making history in Egypt and catalysing street protests that progressed from calls for human rights to be respected, to demanding a change in government, to the resignation in disgrace, just eighteen days later, of Mohammed Hosni Mubarak, the man who had ruled Egypt for thirty years. Some estimates put 3 million Egyptians in the streets that day demanding the resignation of a man whose portrait looked down from every government office, every shop, and most of the squares in Egypt, and who only two years before had captured public sympathy when he was visibly shaken by the death of his grandson.

The spirit of rebellion spread. In the Libyan city of Benghazi a lawyer called Fathi Terbel appealed for a Day of Anger to take place on 17 February to demand human rights and the investigation of an alleged massacre at Abu Salim prison some fifteen years previously in which hundreds were rumoured to have died. He was arrested and when relatives came to protest, some of them were shot. The whole of the east of the country rose up against the forces of Colonel Muammar Gaddafi, Libya's ruler for the past forty-one years.

In Syria a bunch of schoolboys were arrested when they spray-painted slogans on the walls of the southern town of Deraa. In Bahrain, thousands gathered daily at Pearl Square in the heart of the capital Manama, demanding public freedoms. In cities all over Yemen, tens of thousands of demonstrators clashed with the forces of President Ali Abdullah Saleh.

The Arab Spring had begun.

The events triggered by these cases are still in play and, it seems safe to say, will remain so for some time. Nobody knows where, if ever, the fire lit by Mohammed Bouazizi will eventually peter out. But it has turned the Arab world upside down.

This book is in your hands because, sitting in Europe where we had recently moved from the Middle East, I was hungry to see history in the making in a region where I had spent a decade of my adult life. And from late January on, when the protests against Hosni Mubarak reached hundreds of thousands, it was clear that history was being made. Even before Mubarak was forced out, these were already once-in-a-generation events. That's how stagnant the Middle East had been.

Because for me personally, up until that moment the staggering thing about the Middle East since I first set foot there in 1985 had been how grindingly little it had changed. I'm forty-six years old. Of the two Arab autocrats who have gone, Mubarak was already in power as I stepped ashore that June morning in the Syrian port of Latakia, keen to mischannel the funds from my college bursary to study classical ruins into learning Arabic. He had acceded four years earlier, when I was learning Greek, thought I looked pretty cool smoking Gauloises and wondered if I would ever get a girlfriend. Ben Ali was to follow just two years later, in 1987, as I went to grad school. I remember we talked about it in the excited tones of young specialists whose specimen had just stirred inside the jar. Two other autocrats who could be up next, Yemen's Ali Abdullah Saleh and Gaddafi in Libya, were also firmly ensconced, Saleh having seized power in 1977, just about the time I bought my first record, the Stranglers' *Walk On By*, and Gaddafi in 1969, before our house got television.

I framed these events in terms of my own life story because I found the numbers alone didn't really convey the aching longevity of these men's rule – Mubarak 30 years, Ben Ali 23, Saleh 34, Gaddafi 42. But link them to the global big picture and we get concepts like the fact that all of them came to power while the Soviet Union and East and West Germany still existed, when the Internet as we know it today didn't, the European Union numbered ten member states and there were 2 billion fewer people alive on the planet.

Or, in terms of popular culture, Zine el-Abideen Ben Ali, the most recent of them, came to power when Suzanne Vega released her first album *Solitude Standing*, with 'Tom's Diner'. Cool students were enjoying what would later become known as dance music, notably *Substance* by New Order, and John Cougar Mellencamp was king of American rock with *Lonesome Jubilee*. The top-grossing films that year were *Three Men and a Baby*, *Fatal Attraction* and *Beverly Hills Cop II*. I remember devouring Tom Wolfe's *Bonfire of the Vanities* and Bruce Chatwin's *Songlines* when they both came out, and Jose Saramago published *Baltasar and Blimunda*.

Meanwhile, so much happened in the rest of the world. Eastern Europe became eastern Europe, and we rediscovered Mitteleuropa on the terraces of Prague and Budapest. Latin America democratised, Africa too, in parts, India and China emerged as roaring capitalist economies. Goa, Phuket and Machu Picchu went from being adventure tourist destinations you had to save up for to bucket-shop tours. World music brought us first the West Africans and then everyone else, in its own way. Bollywood sneaked up on Hollywood, amusing our jaded Western palates with its vim, and then forcing us to respect its aesthetic through fusion films. Climate change went from being a fringe issue for tree-huggers to the dominant global concern. Globalisation became a fact, first celebrated in the rush after the collapse of communism and then the target of a protest movement, Turin and Seattle, the plush and clever chitter rising from the salons of the World Economic Forum in the Swiss mountain resort of Davos being answered by the World Social Forum, dressed down and indignant wherever – Porto Alegre, Dakar, Mumbai.

The Middle East seemed largely left behind. Its main narratives, born in an earlier time, lived on, unaltered. Israel and the Palestinians were locked in conflict. Iran was trying to export its revolution. The West depended on a cluster of fragile absolute monarchies in the Gulf for oil to keep the global economy ticking. Nostalgia was rife in the Arab world for a system of government, Arab nationalism, which no longer worked and maybe never had. No countervailing progress made up for the wars – Lebanon, Iraq and Iran, Iraq and Kuwait, the US invasion of Iraq – and a crisis of confidence that accumulated over the many failures for anything to shift on the Palestinian issue. There was some fanciful talk, here and there, of liberalisation, usually shorthand for World Bank austerity programmes and brand invasion. But more pervasive were the undercurrents of bitterness, captured in a fundamentalist discourse that framed the West as morally corrupt and, in extremis, infidel. The Middle East's most noted contribution to the globalisation debate was al-Qaeda.

I had started to learn Arabic at the age of twenty while studying Classics, entranced by the idea of learning not just to read but to speak a classical language, determined to get to know a non-European civilisation in some depth. Having something of the obsessive-compulsive, and the spare time of an Oxford undergraduate, I spent several thousand hours at it, then went to Georgetown for a master's in Arab area studies, then joined Reuters. Arabic is a premium language in the news agency world, so I was immediately posted to the region, where I spent six years for them.

I had gone through the almost inevitable attraction-to-Other stage in my twenties and then what I would imagine to be a fairly normal progression, from infatuation with the region and the culture, to mild disappointment, to renewed affection and a deep sense of familiarity. Arab friends gave me an Arab name, Hanna al-Gharbi, the literal translation of my name. It was comfortable. But as time went on, and the rest of the world changed around the Middle East, it all came to seem a little drab. I was tired of being the Other myself now, a role you were often thrust into as an Arabic-speaking Westerner.

I also instinctively distrusted my most obvious career path, to become an Arabist. Not only did I not want to be pigeon-holed, because there was so much more going on out there, but Arabist was just too loaded as an identity and didn't make sense to me. I spoke and read Arabic fluently and had studied and travelled a fair amount. But I have a friend who's done the same with Spanish and lives with his flamenco dancer wife in Valencia. Jason has written five well-received books about Spain but nobody calls him a Hispanist. There's some paradigm not just of knowledge but of inscrutability and power, who knows what about who and does what with it, which underlies the Arabist thing, and I wasn't comfortable with it.

All of which is by way of saying that I had stayed away from the Arab world for more than a decade and had only just returned to the region, working for the United Nations on oil policy and the vexed question of how to make that industry work better for the people of the countries where it is produced.

I spent three years in Afghanistan just after 9/11, building a network of local radio stations for an American NGO and learning classical and modern Persian. Later, when our son was born, we gave him the name Omar, after the poet Omar Khayyam.

And I had continued to follow the Arab world from a distance. In 2007, while living in Paris, I had become incensed late one night when a surf on the Internet revealed that no book written by an Iraqi in Arabic post-2003 had yet made it into English for a Western audience. There were dozens of memoirs by foreign correspondents, some good, many just awful. But nothing by Iraqis. Mesmerised by the image of an undiscovered Shakespeare languishing in Sadr City, I spent six months searching in my

spare time for a text to translate to bring at least one Iraq
to a Western audience, and then, once I had found one, a ye
of to-ing and fro-ing to Iraq to work with its author. The result
was *The Devil You Don't Know*, a memoir by journalist Zuhair
al-Jezairy of his 2003 return to the native land he had to flee
in 1979 and his subsequent years working to bring independent
journalism to Iraq for the first time, as director of the Aswat
news agency.

At the end of 2009, we had moved to Jordan for a year to
reconnect to the region. Jordan is a great place for a family and
it would be nice to think that the desert treks, trawling through
the huge market at Abdali on Friday mornings, and the
unfailing courtesy of the Jordanian people will stay with the
kids into adulthood. But there had been no hint of revolutionary change in the air that year, even up to the days and
weeks preceding the outbreak of protests in Egypt, when we
moved on to Berlin for work reasons.

And yet now here it was: massive, positive change looking
us straight in the eye through the TV screen, the courage and
wit and humanity of the crowds in Tahrir Square. The Arabic
blogosphere fizzed with hope and the right kind of anger, long
impromptu poems and heartfelt pleas. It had taken a long, long
time coming. But now the hold of the Arab national security
state had been broken, it seemed, and a new era was beginning.

I just had to get back there.

But something else struck me. Even as I watched the Tahrir
Square protests, full of admiration, it felt like it wasn't where
I needed to go. I couldn't help thinking about the sparks for

the Tunisian and Egyptian revolutions, and how they came from such out of-the-way places. A small town 200 miles south of Tunis, known for nothing in particular. An old district of Egypt's second city. The final hours of the old regimes might have played out in Tahrir Square and Habib Bourguiba Avenue, the main drag in Tunis. But the game had started on the margins of society, both literally and metaphorically.

Mohammed Bouazizi lived out his life in the underclass, hand to mouth, scrabbling to support a large family in the informal sector, unlicensed and vulnerable, the embodiment of what the French call *la précarité*. Khaled Said belonged to a counter-culture, alienated by the stunning hypocrisy of a regime that preached traditional values and responsibility while pillaging the country's assets and neglecting its young.

I decided to travel to the birthplaces of these sparks, Sidi Bou Zid in Tunisia and Alexandria in Egypt, to see how the world looked from there.

This book is about my attempt to discover what I could of the feel and character of these places and the people who live there.

It is not about the personal stories of Mohammed Bouazizi and Khaled Said, neither of whom saw himself as a revolutionary. It is about their neighbourhoods, their extended families and social networks. Who influenced their lives, and why and how. Where they hung out, where they went to school. It is about their worlds, not their lives, and through them the lives of the millions of young protesters who peacefully brought down two dictatorships in less than two months.

I knew both countries, though Egypt somewhat better. I had

spent a summer studying Arabic in Tunis back in the 1980s, but I'd lived in Cairo as a Reuters correspondent for three years. It was my first posting, in the early 1990s, and like most first postings carries some of that first-love feel for me. The country was like a huge playground, the Reuters card giving me licence to roam and access to almost anyone. It's an intoxicating feeling at twenty-six to interview a minister and then debrief with the cabbie on the way back to the office.

But although I drove all over the country back then, I was also aware of how little time I, like many involved professionally in the Middle East, really spent in the back of beyond, particularly in more recent years. Except when something was happening of course. As journalists we are often drawn to out-of-the-way places, developing intense relationships with places we haven't even heard of the week before. But it's usually because of some conflict or natural disaster, which we follow like moths along a narrow beam, blind to everything else. Reporters spend so much time recounting trips to weird and wonderful places precisely because they are the highlights, not the everyday.

In the two years I was in Afghanistan, immediately after 9/11, I spent a lot of time in the provinces because we were building a network of thirty local FM radio stations. But in the Arab world, especially in recent years with the United Nations, I had frequented capitals and people of authority, close to the epicentre of their political cultures.

The initial game plan was simple. Just get to these places, Sidi Bou Zid and Kleopatra, and hang out, and let whatever story there was come to me, instead of chasing it. As I did so, talking mainly to the young who had taken part in the protests but also to old friends, experts, pillars of society and so on, three broad lines of inquiry emerged for what became, in effect, a street research project: the role of the Internet, the future of political Islam, and the present mass unemployment.

One of the most stunning features of the revolutions to the outside world was how digital they seemed to be. Slogans spray-painted on walls in Tunis said 'Thank you Facebook!', organisers spread word by text and Twitter, and bloggers were part of the revolutionary vanguard. But on the airwaves there was an immediate backlash from analysts saying the Facebook Revolution idea trivialised the real issues – corruption, police brutality, tyranny, mass unemployment – and was some dumb projection of Western levels of computer literacy that had nothing to do with the realities of the Arab world.

Where did truth lie in that debate? What role had the Internet and particularly social networking sites played in the revolution? Much of the debate concentrated on the role the Internet might or might not have played in the days of the protests. That seemed short-sighted to me. What about the before and after? Had the Internet played a significant part in political culture in Egypt and Tunisia in the weeks and months and years beforehand? Most crucial of all, what role would the Internet play now? Was there some way in which, as an acknowledged part of the revolution, it might be integrated into the heart of Tunisia's and Egypt's new democracies?

I had a professional interest in this debate as I had been involved in many projects developing both traditional and digital media around the world, including across the Middle East.

The second question was political Islam, which as the

revolutions went on, seemed to be lurking somewhere in the background, hovering over us and affecting the way we in the West were reacting. Although in both Egypt and Tunisia we were seeing classic people's power, peaceful, huge, witty, and brave demonstrations in favour of all our most cherished public values, relatively few people I knew seemed unguardedly happy about it. 'What about the men with beards?', people would say, or mean, perhaps knocked off balance by the TV images of thousands of protesters prostrate in prayer. Some commentators warned knowingly about how it was not just naïvety but cultural imperialism to assume that crowds who opposed tyranny wanted democracy. Because Arabs aren't like us.

Was that true? Were the Muslim Brothers just waiting there in the wings, rubbing their hands with glee, dusting off their plans for a new caliphate and full *shari'a* law? And if they were, could they achieve it? Did the obvious piety of the protesters in Tahrir Square mean they could be swayed, even if they weren't extremist themselves? Could this be a rerun of Iran 1979, which had also begun with students and leftists, people we recognised as being 'like us', out on the streets protesting against the Shah?

We had just moved to Berlin and I reflected that in 1989, the Berlin Wall Moment resonated way beyond the people who were physically there because you could *imagine* yourself there, stepping through the wall, hugging the people on the other side. But while the Arab world was delirious with joy, there would never be a Tahrir Square Moment of solidarity in the West. What happened if you turned to hug the nearest stranger and it turned out to be a man in shalwar khamis and a chest-length beard, or a woman with a headscarf?

Was it fear of political Islam that kept support and solidarity in check? That prevented a Berlin Wall Moment?

Lastly, there was the issue of mass unemployment. We had heard a lot about the youth bulge, and the fact that the Arab world needed 100 million new jobs. Where could they come from? Unemployment had been the defining issue when I came of age politically, in Margaret Thatcher's Britain, and I was interested to see how it would play here. What were the social effects of this unemployment, particularly when the brunt of it fell so heavily on the young?

What were the expectations of the unemployed now, and the debates around how to address the issue? The protests had been accompanied by a slew of reports on the Arabic satellite TV channels about the corruption of the ruling families. Fabulous sums had been mentioned by Al Jazeera – up to $70 billion stolen by the Mubarak family alone, billions more by their lieutenants.

Corruption was clearly endemic. Catching up with contemporaries, now in early middle age, it is clear that some made life choices that involved a complicity with the system that they would rather have avoided. These are spaces left in our conversations, moments where the journalist in me – So since that doesn't quite add up, what's the racket exactly, how much did you get or pay and why, why couldn't you think of another way of getting ahead? – is bested by the old friend. And the knowledge that in their place I cannot say what I myself would have chosen.

But had the unravelling of corruption scandals now created a straightforward connection in the popular mind between corruption and unemployment – there were no jobs *because* so much had been stolen? If so, what would happen when in one or two years' time so many young people still lacked jobs? How would they use their new-found voices then?

I tried to entertain as few preconceptions as possible, which, if truth be told, is hard when you're dealing with an area you feel you know of old. It became a lot easier when I could keep in mind, as I always tried to, that nobody had seen this coming. Nobody.

From time to time august authorities such as *The Economist* or the Human Development Report published by the United Nations issued earnest warnings about the population bulge and the impoverishment of both natural and human resources in the Middle East. And there was no shortage of scathing op-eds, inside as well as outside the region, slamming the Arab gerontocracy, the domination of nearly twenty countries by men who just got older and older but refused to die or make way. But nobody even came close to predicting these kinds of protests, unfolding in this way, with these kinds of results.

The Arab Spring is not unique in this, of course. Its unpredictability is its right of entry to what might be called, courtesy of Nassim Nicholas Taleb, the Black Swan Hall of Fame, joining the collapse of communism, the ill-fated Oslo peace agreements and the global financial meltdown. But it meant that none of the experts now telling us what it all meant, to be careful about this or pay attention to that, *really* knew what they were talking about.

From the first days, these revolutions had so many threads to them – police brutality, the young without a future, vain old autocrats believing they were indispensable, technology leapfrog. But even before I hit the ground in Tunisia, one word kept cropping up again and again on the Arabic channels when the protesters, singly or in groups, described how they felt, and what they thought they were doing. *Karama* – dignity, or honour, or perhaps even self-respect.

They didn't mean some baroque or epic code of ethics. They meant not being slapped about by some idiot policeman just because he felt like it. Not being denied even an interview for the job because you didn't have family connections. Not being lied to, smugly and repeatedly, by leaders who had ended up believing their own cheap propaganda. Not being told, in a thousand little ways, to accept mediocrity and falsehood and poverty and a perpetual state of helpless emergency.

This revolution is about *karama*, said the young man with the keffiya round his neck. We won't stop now, we just want our *karama* back, said the young woman in hejab.

I wanted to see that *karama*. I set out to find it, at the well-spring of all the Arab revolutions, the town of Sidi Bou Zid, in southern Tunisia, where Mohammed Bouazizi had burnt himself to death.

PART ONE

Tunisia

1

A Revolution of Wit

Sidi Bou Zid has never been a place for the faint-hearted. A mid-sized town 200 miles south of Tunis, it has none of the capital's Mediterranean airs, its tree-lined boulevards and crowded terrace cafes. Many more women wear headscarves here, often on top of baggy, shiny tracksuits, the obligatory stripes down the sides patterned and gaudy rather than white. The town is in the plains, but the mountains of Djebel Salloum loom on the horizon, for generations the last refuge of rebels and brigands.

In the Second World War, the area witnessed a full-on fight between Rommel's retreating Eighth Army and Montgomery's advancing Desert Rats, and a war memorial behind the governorate building lists over 200 men from this relatively small district who died in Tunisia's independence struggle against the French in the 1950s.

I asked a companion about the number, saying I was surprised it was so high. I thought Tunisia's independence struggle had been relatively short and bloodless, certainly compared with neighbouring Algeria's.

'That's true in Tunisia as a whole,' said Aida. 'But not here. Sidi Bou Zid led the war of independence.'

Older townsfolk have described how they felt Ben Ali deliberately starved the region of resources to force its young to migrate towards the softer towns of the coast, Sfax and Sousse and Monastir. Despite a nationwide programme to establish universities in all the provinces, Sidi Bou Zid, seat of a province of the same name with a quarter of a million people, is the exception. What the region lacks in terms of higher education, it was famous for making up for by manning the security forces. Clashes between police and young men, and even between rival gangs of teenagers, were not uncommon. Tough town, tough people.

Nevertheless, when Mohammed Bouazizi immolated himself on 17 December 2010, in full public view on a main street, the news spread like wildfire. An extended clan of Bouazizis lives in the town, ten miles or so from their ancestral village of Gara Benour, and Mohammed was known to a broader section of the town simply because every day he stood at the main junction of the town, by his cart, selling his produce.

I had arrived in the town after a few days in Tunis, keen to understand what had changed. But, only four weeks after the revolution had removed Ben Ali from power, all the talk, not unnaturally, was of the glory days of the protests, when the young men of Sidi Bou Zid had taken on the might of the police state, and won. I needed to find someone who had been in the thick of it.

Anis al-Shoaibi, from the same district in Sidi Bou Zid as Mohammed Bouazizi, went to demonstrate the day Bouazizi set himself alight. He didn't know Bouazizi personally, but in the tightly knit community of Hay an-Noor everyone knew everyone else's family. Like hundreds of his friends and neighbours, he didn't leave the streets for the next four weeks. They faced down everything the Tunisian police state could throw at them until, on 14 January, President Ben Ali fled for Saudi Arabia. The protests had become a revolution and the revolution had won.

He is thirty years old and lives at home with his parents. Although he finally landed a job as a PE teacher in a secondary school last September, three months before the protests, he was unemployed for five years before that. A self-declared 'Internet lad', he spent those years online, eking out the pennies he made from odd jobs to stay as long as possible in the cafes. Espresso and Facebook. Espresso and Facebook. He could make an espresso last two hours.

He wears a Nike-branded sweatshirt and baseball cap, peak forward. He uses his hands constantly, as if he is conducting his own conversation with smooth, graceful gestures.

The hint of a smile often plays at the edges of his mouth and in his big, expressive eyes, even when he speaks of serious things. For although he talks graphically and passionately of the events he was caught up in, at another level you sense a disinterested observer, a raconteur with a fondness for the ironies of life, able to step outside himself.

At the plush cafe where we first met, he teased a young woman for not joining in the conversation. She was right back at him, saying she couldn't possibly get a word in over his booming narrative. 'Yeah I know. I've tried to work on it before,' he replies. 'What can I say? I'm working-class.' He shrugs and smiles and everybody laughs.

He is, in short, the ideal eyewitness. You would not want Anis as an enemy. You would want him as a friend.

'That first day, when the events started, there was absolutely no sign that it would lead to where it did, to a change in regime,' he said. 'If the authorities had reacted differently, I assure you Zine el-Abideen Ben Ali would still be president today.

'The day after Mohammed Bouazizi set himself alight, there was a peaceful gathering in front of the municipality by the people of his neighbourhood, and his work colleagues, the other street vendors,' Anis said.

'His uncle gave a very powerful speech, which many people took to heart. Meanwhile the officials inside sent for reinforcements from the security forces. But up to this point it was still peaceful. Things were calm. The demand was for peaceful dialogue.'

Even at this early stage there was a mood in the wind. Nobody knew for sure why Mohammed Bouazizi, who had endured repeated humiliation at the hands of the police, had snapped this time. Perhaps being forced to the ground, perhaps being dominated by the woman police agent, Fetya Hamdi. But his shocking self-immolation triggered a reaction to meet and protest which was completely reflexive and unconsidered. It was enough for the provincial governor – the town of Sidi Bou Zid is the capital of a province of the same name – to phone his superiors in Tunis to ask them if he could meet with a delegation from the crowd gathered outside. The word came back: absolutely not.

Meanwhile hundreds of police had massed and were milling about. In Ben Ali's Tunisia, there was only one way such a stand-off was going to end.

'Then they used tear gas grenades and sticks to break up the demonstration. And everything exploded,' said Anis. 'This was the nub of it, the denouement as they say in the films. Everything else unfolded from here.'

Trained to regard the people as subjects rather than citizens, the police simply waded into the crowd and laid into them with riot batons, tear gas and abandon. Among those that Anis saw them beat were a disabled woman in a wheelchair and her ten-year-old son trying to protect her. Since police had so forcefully broken up the demonstration in the centre of town, in front of the governorate building, other protests, less orderly, started to break out in the various residential districts immediately nearby, Hay an-Noor and around the Omar ibn al-Khattab mosque.

By nightfall everything had changed. The town had turned into a battlefield. Young men were in the streets shouting with anger, throwing stones and bottles they found lying to hand. Their elders were no longer trying to hold them back. The police were careering through neighbourhoods in patrol cars, picking up whoever they could grab, beating them mercilessly. All semblance of law and order had vanished in an afternoon. Nobody could guess it was never to return, at least not under the rule of the man whose portraits hung everywhere around the town, Zine el-Abideen Ben Ali. Before Anis and his friends were through, those portraits would be ripped down and Ben Ali himself would have fled to a protected compound in the Saudi Arabian port of Jeddah.

What did you think when you went into the streets the first time? I asked. You must have known the risks.

'To be honest, that first time, we weren't thinking at all,' he replied. 'It was an instinctive reaction. Mohammed Bouazizi had burned himself to death and when we wanted to ask questions their only answer was to beat us.

'Then, in the following days, it kept escalating and the feeling developed that there was no way back now. We had risen up because of our *karama*, our honour. After so much fear and humiliation we could not lose that again. It really was victory or death. There was no third path.'

By the time the town woke the next morning, hundreds more police had arrived in the night from Gafsa, Gabes and Sfax, the biggest nearby towns. The streets swarmed with cops in search of a fight.

'Within three or four days the police on the streets reached between six thousand, maybe eight thousand men, from all over the country,' said Anis. (The entire population of the town is maybe 50,000 people.) 'A rapid-intervention force came from Tunis, a special anti-riot squad. As the units came from other parts of the country, the lads showed them a warm welcome. The Tunisian way, and the way of Sidi Bou Zid. With rocks.' The smile flickers again at the edge of his mouth. 'Actually 2010 was supposed to be the official year of youth. They kept talking in the state media about dialogue with the young and how the future belonged to us. Well, this is the dialogue we had. Rocks and tear gas.'

At the same time, though, the noted families of the town invited the newcomers in for tea, which, Anis said, gave the visiting police the impression there wouldn't be much trouble.

'After they had given the police food and drink, it was like they said: "Please, go to your positions, and we'll go to ours,'" he said. You mean, I asked, just to be sure, that it was understood while the police were in the houses of these families that they would shortly afterwards find themselves in combat on opposite sides?

'Oh yes, absolutely. No doubt about it. This is our nature as Arabs and as people from Sidi Bou Zid. That is what hospitality means to us. While he is in your house he is your guest. He should eat and drink. When he leaves, then you can stand up and fight,' said Anis.

Like the chivalry of old, I said, knights with their codes.

'In a way. In a way, yes, that was the mindset, that of the knight, as you mention. And with it, an awareness of traditional values, from our ancestors. For instance, if someone says "Salaam alaikum" to you, you should expect peace from them. No harm will come to you in that interaction,' he said.

The first three days, the protesters hit the streets by day, attacking the town hall and municipality buildings on the main street. 'But we soon realised it was a losing battle,' said Anis.

The police had overwhelming superiority of numbers and equipment. They were photographing all the protesters and picked up something like 200 young men from the town in those first three days. Many of them were tortured, some sent to detention centres in cities on the coast.

So the protesters decided instead to retreat into their own districts, where they knew the backstreets and alleyways, and to fight by night. That way they couldn't be photographed and it would be hard to round them up.

'The lads would wait for five o'clock with the utmost

impatience,' said Anis. 'Why five? Because it was the start of protest time. From five in the afternoon until three or four o'clock in the morning.

'In that first week, we went into the streets with a mixture of anger and joy. The anger you know about. The joy? Because lads who had had nothing to live for for years now had a fascinating challenge in front of them. It was gripping. Addictive, almost.'

The same pattern of careful rules and some sort of spontaneous, unarticulated code continued. The night was for street fighting but there was a truce by day. Anis had some work to do by day and would pass through half a dozen police checkpoints.

'I would greet them and they would greet me – "Salaam alaikum" – as if there wasn't a problem in the world. At night, returning home, it was the same. I'd pass through the checkpoints and then, after 100 metres, I'd slip into the crowd and be back at them, throwing stones.'

By day, police and protesters even sat side by side in the same cafes, sipping their espressos.

'You've been in this town a few days, you've seen how it is. There's nothing to do except cafes. And between one cafe and the next, there's another cafe. Well it was common to see police in the same cafe as the lads. They would exchange pleasantries about football, or TV – anything but what was going on.

'Once I saw a lieutenant come in and sit down next to an old man. Pointing to a group of youngsters chatting peacefully, he said: "Is that them?" "Is that who?" replied the old man. "You know. The group who are burning tyres and dropping rocks on us every night," the policeman said. "Yes. Of course," the old man said, evenly. "Lord have mercy!" replied the policeman. "We always thought they were so puny. We thought they were just the Internet lads."'

For twelve days the youth of Sidi Bou Zid fought virtually the entire apparatus of the police state alone. Al Jazeera had found Ali Bouazizi's video and rebroadcast it, along with others from the town, but the protests didn't spread in force to other towns until 29 December.

'What the authorities never got was that, particularly for the unemployed, this became a revolution of *karama*. You take a man thirty-five years old, unable to marry or work. Day by day he was getting stronger, losing his fear. We were also starting to fight smarter. Keep away from the centre of town, the main installations. Always keep just below the line that would let them use live ammunition on us.'

The fighting in Sidi Bou Zid was brutal but rarely lethal, reminiscent perhaps of the first Palestinian intifada against Israeli occupation of the West Bank and Gaza at the end of the 1980s, which I remembered well. The sheer theatre of the *shebab*, or young men, dancing out into open view to throw their rocks or Molotov cocktails against tanks and armour, danger enough to make the adrenalin pump but not enough to kill all dissent. The compulsive nature of the clashes, the heady mix of danger and moral righteousness drawing you to it rather than turning you away. Once or twice back then it had taken as much discipline as I had not to simply join in, the experience of being there just so compelling.

There were only four deaths in Sidi Bou Zid out of some

200 across the country. Later, as the protests spread, police under pressure to quell protests that were turning into a nation-wide revolution frequently used live ammunition, most notably in the neighbouring city of Kasserine, where on 10 January some twenty people were killed in a single day.

Gradually, the slogans and demands were evolving. From the specific case of Mohammed Bouazizi, it broadened into demands to solve the issue of unemployment. From there, to removing the corruption that riddled all levels of the Tunisian state. And from there, to changing the rulers who presided over this mess. There was a primal, perhaps even inarticulate logic to the sequence. There weren't enough jobs because of corruption. Corruption flourished because of dictatorship.

But *karama*, honour or dignity, remained the underlying motif.

'The fiercest day of fighting was when the state TV, Channel 7, carried its first piece about Mohammed Bouazizi. They treated it like it was just some individual incident, a young man who had killed himself, like it was sad but it was his fault. And the whole piece was just thirty seconds.

'They were mocking us. We were shocked watching it. The lads went mad with anger, and the police became the object for that. That was the fiercest day,' he said.

He recalled an incident he saw on his own street. Police were constantly breaking into houses, violating the sanctity of the home which is so deep a part of traditional values. When they went into one of his neighbours' houses a young man hurled a burning car tyre down from the first floor, taking down one of the riot police coming through the front door: 'We don't know what happened. If that policeman lived or died. But there were moments in the fighting when you just lost your reason and reverted to instinct.'

But although the protesters, many of them high-school or college kids on winter break, may have fought with heart and, at times, blinding anger, they had an innate sense of limits even to combat. Anis is proud of the fact they steered clear of atrocity.

'There was this policeman who got lost in the backstreets and was surrounded by the lads. They closed in on him and started to hit him. But when they lifted his riot helmet off they found he was old and bewildered. So they released him,' said Anis.

Another time, when a policeman was separated from his colleagues and surrounded, the young protesters dowsed him with petrol. And then let him go.

'We used to tell each other: "Do whatever you have to do in the street. Whatever is necessary. But don't attack or damage public property,"' he said. As elsewhere in Tunisia, and indeed Libya and Egypt, the protesters targeted only symbols of the regime, such as the headquarters of the ruling RCD party. What little looting there was could not be clearly laid at the protesters' door, as the regime used agents provocateurs and their own militias from the first hours of the conflict.

I asked Anis about his family's reaction to his new life as a revolutionary. 'The overwhelming feeling from my parents was anxiety. But they knew why we had to do it. They'd lived with the regime longer than we had.

'For twenty-three years there had been non-stop propaganda. On the TV, in the newspapers. All that time there was no freedom. You could talk about anything except politics and the president. The media made him out to be a god who never made mistakes.

'And there was an extremely strong intelligence apparatus, very much in control. They knew how many cups of coffee you drank a day, how much sugar you put in it. They had complete information – who your friends were, where you went, who you met, the colour and make of your car, the number plate. And that meant we weren't connected as a society. We didn't talk to each other or have solidarity because of the fear.

'So my parents understood. In my own case, for five years I had been supposed to be employed by the state as a sports teacher. A programme was announced, they were hiring thousands of teachers every year, they said. But for five years, nothing happened. There were men of forty-five who were unmarried, still effectively suspended in an age where they couldn't grow up.'

I asked if this state of suspension between youth and adulthood, as it must have been experienced by hundreds of thousands of Tunisians, affected family life.

'I was unemployed for five years and went through a lot,' he told me. 'When I woke up there would be coffee, cards and the Internet. And that was it, from nine in the morning until midnight. I had no purpose. What does it mean when you're thirty years old that you wait for your father to give you pocket money? To buy coffee, or cigarettes? It definitely created a sort of tension in my relationship with my parents. I know I got short-tempered with them. It was all hope for a job, and then despair when it didn't happen. And then tension with my parents. I tried. I won't hide from you I tried to get a job many times. Just to get pocket money.'

He recalled at one time considering trying to get an RCD party card for his mother, who is functionally illiterate, and at another time debating whether the family could pay 8,000 dinars, $6,000, as a 'consideration' to a distant relative in return for getting a party recommendation for one of the precious teacher jobs being allocated. Both times they pulled back, under the realisation that to go ahead would commit them to a lifestyle of corruption simply to recover what they had already invested.

For four years, Anis helped out as a volunteer instructor in a karate club. When he had proved his worth by working several months for free, the club paid him an occasional stipend. By the time he left the job several years later that had risen to a monthly 'consideration' of 300 dinars a month, or about $220. In a middle-income country like Tunisia, where prices are little short of southern Europe's, that just about counts as pocket money, disposable income for a young single adult providing he's careful.

There were also internship schemes introduced, where the state would pay 100 dinars a month for youngsters to be taken on by private companies, a kind of Youth Opportunities Scheme. But, as Anis tells it, you needed connections even to get one of these spots. And in any case Sidi Bou Zid, in Tunisia's traditional hinterland of the southern interior, had no industry and few companies of any size that this scheme could apply to in the first place.

As in environments of low economic opportunity the world over, drugs and crime began to be attractive. In Sidi Bou Zid, petrol smuggling from neighbouring Libya achieved a certain kind of street cred. Good money, fast, with a degree of risk from defiance of big power, and popularity for providing a much-needed service – fitting work for young men seeking to prove their mettle. But even the smugglers were to become a key part of the uprising, furnishing a limitless supply of old car tyres to burn in street blockades, relayed in shifts.

In as much as they needed structure, Sidi Bou Zid's protests were self-organising.

'The lads divided up responsibilities spontaneously. It was a war of attrition. Some would go up to the front line and attack. When they got tired, they would fall back to defence and others would take their place. Then there were the cameramen, and those whose job was to bring tyres to burn,' said Anis.

For sure, existing institutions played a role. Tunisia's trade union movement had been nobbled at national level but retained a certain kind of activism in the regions. In Sidi Bou Zid and other towns across the south, new groups had sprung up in recent years to represent the chronically unemployed. Activists in the PDP, one of the officially sanctioned opposition parties, joined in the protests early. But these were supporting roles. These institutions endorsed, justified and explained the protests. They did not plan or run them in Sidi Bou Zid, cradle of the revolution.

The glue that cohered this spontaneity, according to Anis, was social media. He himself was well versed in digital media, having started a Web radio station with a small group of friends when he was unemployed. But he describes a situation in which awareness of and participation in social media is a given among the young men of this small town, marginalised in just about every way from the mainstream of Tunisian society. Channels and hash tags arose spontaneously, a new one opening each time the regime infiltrated or closed an old one.

'I would be on the streets fighting from eight until eleven. Then I would go home and the battle on Facebook would begin. The battle in the virtual world was just as fierce as on the street. First, the lads took scenes from the fighting on video, just on their mobile phones, and we had to upload them. Second, there was a lot of operational information being exchanged in real time, in chat rooms or by text.

'"Where are the police concentrating now?" someone would ask. "Over in Hay an-Noor," someone else would reply. "No they've moved to the main street," a third person would say.'

The struggle online was cat-and-mouse, just as in the streets. Tunisia's security services had their own hackers who hijacked Facebook accounts and created mined links that removed admin privileges from pages, or simply destroyed user accounts altogether, if you clicked on them.

'In the first days we would use proxies,' said Anis. 'Then they would close the web servers the proxies were on. You couldn't use the http's secure protocol. You couldn't get on to Facebook. But we didn't stop. If they closed your account, you opened a new one. If they shut a page, you opened a new one.'

The number of Facebook accounts among Tunisia's 11 million people had doubled in the previous twelve months from 1 million to 2 million, a higher proportion than in most European countries. Some individual pages had over 100,000 subscriptions when the protests started.

The revolutionaries of Sidi Bou Zid in those weeks experienced two parallel information ecosystems.

The first was their own social and personal media networks. At its rawest, rapportage direct from the streets, but also the next level up, an unpaid army of collators and editors, synthesising and summarising the revolution as it spread. These networks were fast gaining recognition from international satellite TV stations such as Al Jazeera and the Arabic language services of France24 and the BBC, which fed back into the impetus of the protests themselves. If you're risking your life, it helps to know, and to know other people know, that you're a hero.

'You could go into the street and burn one or two tyres, create a lot of fire and smoke. And there was the chance that could end up on satellite TV,' said Anis. 'That was serious motivation to keep on protesting.'

The second ecosystem was the old world of state media, where the protests, once they could no longer be ignored, were being painted into the same old, tired set pieces of political theatre the Arab world has known for the past fifty years. Curiously, by the time the protests began, this may even have been a contributing element to the revolution. State media had long lost any credibility to persuade, but they retained the ability to offend and goad with the pap they disseminated about the protesters: uneducated elements bla bla bla, armed gangs bla bla bla, foreign interests bla bla bla. The main terrestrial channel, TV7, was so disgraced that it had changed its name, to National Tunisian TV, within a week of Ben Ali leaving power.

In 2008, industrial unrest at some mines in the town of Gafsa had created a stand-off that lasted for months. People died, parts of the town were under siege, and the government cut off Facebook across the entire country for two months.

So why hadn't the authorities simply closed the networks down again, I asked Anis. If they had done it before, and had enough skill to sabotage individual accounts and pages, surely they were aware of the power of these platforms. Why didn't they just pull the plug?

'They simply didn't expect anything from us, the Internet lads, and by the time they did it was too late,' he replied.

'There were two main differences between Gafsa in 2008 and Sidi Bou Zid in 2010. The first was that we were able to get the story out, and keep getting it out. The second was that our demands were public and national: freedom of speech, the right to work, elections. Whereas Gafsa was a particular issue affecting a particular group.'

They might get sympathetic talk around the dinner table, in other words. But not feet and voices in the streets.

The spreading of the protests from Sidi Bou Zid to Tunisia's other towns and cities meant the unravelling of the regime. The security forces no longer had the resources to play cat and mouse. The units which had thronged the streets of Sidi Bou Zid were dispersed to fifteen other towns at once. These other places experienced much less of the delicate dance of repression and defiance, tiptoeing around the line of lethal force, which had characterised the protests in Sidi Bou Zid. In Kasserine, Gabes and eventually Tunis, the security forces opened fire with live rounds, killing people. Every time they did the funerals of the martyrs escalated the scope of the demands and the ferocity of the protests. It took only two more weeks for the regime to fall.

So, I said to Anis, you won. This revolution which you didn't even know you had inside you succeeded, the tyrant fled, and it's a new era. What impact do you think it will have on your life? If we were in 2030, what would you expect to say about the Tunisian revolution?

'I was born in 1980. But I feel like I was born in 2011. The last thirty years have been wasted. Not even the basics were there. And at the same time, I feel as though the revolution has only been half achieved.

'In the media and the new political players, they have addressed some of the side issues of the revolution. But not its core. They're still not engaging us, the young people, in proper dialogue. Instead they're mucking about in wage negotiations with people who already have jobs.'

His comments reflect the major fault line that has remained in Tunisian society – those with jobs and those without them. Straight after Ben Ali fell, unions and workers in public and private institutions caught the revolution bug. Older on the whole than the mainly teenage and twenty-something protesters who had faced down the regime, they began to stage sit-ins and marches and other forms of demonstration about working conditions. The new government, faced with an immediate barrage of wage and other demands, threw itself into issues it knew how to react to even if not to solve, delegating the task of figuring out a new constitution, elections, and possible transitional justice to special committees that sat separate from the ministries.

Anis is frustrated with this self-interest: 'Now is not the time to demand higher wages. If we fix our political system, then we will see justice, and these kinds of social problems will start to be addressed.'

Mass unemployment does not fall into this category of secondary, social issue. For him, and many of his peer group, it is a fundamental question of rights. Graffiti on walls all over town proclaim it to be a matter of metaphysical dimensions, alongside freedom and dignity. Left on the scrap heap for what was going to be for ever, Anis's generation believes the state should provide not just the opportunity, but the right to work. He even has his own pragmatic policy for the central issue of unemployment – reduce working hours in official positions to create new jobs.

'Give us a real and honest dialogue. If you come to us and say I can offer ten new projects for employment, we'll understand. We have waited so long we can wait a little longer if we see credibility in the process,' he said. 'But if you come like the old president did, from one day to the next, waving his magic baguette and saying "I can create 300,000 jobs," we will laugh. You couldn't create these jobs in the last twenty-three years and now you're going to create them in two years? It's impossible.'

And yet, like many of his peers, Anis defines himself as apolitical – strange for a group of young people who have just overthrown a tyranny, until you realise that their definition of politics is interest in the mechanics of political power, parties and personalities and bums on seats.

'We have no affiliation to any political party or movement.

We were leaderless. Or rather, leadership was fluid and happened in the streets through force of personality, not through position and title round a table. And we thank God for this, because the regime could not understand this and wasted time trying to find our leaders,' he said.

So if it was not political, what, in his view, was the revolution about?

'This was a revolution of wit. Every night, the lads would compete with each other as to who could make up the best chanting rhyme,' he said.

Some of the chanting rhymes were scrawled over walls around the town square. Others were, in the days and weeks after the revolution, still on everyone's lips, just waiting for a moment in the conversation to come out. *Hay! Hay! al-hajama fi dubai* – 'Rejoice! Rejoice! The hairdresser's gone to Dubai' – a disparaging reference to Ben Ali's wife Leila Trabelsi. *Ya shahid irtaah irtaah, ihna nuwasil al-kifaah* – 'Be at peace, martyr, for we will continue the fight'. *Bi rooh, bi dam, nafdeeka ya alam* – 'We sacrifice our blood and lives for you, O flag', a play on the traditional shouts of allegiance to a particular charismatic leader, like Saddam Hussein, or Yasser Arafat, replacing the personality with the institution of the flag.

'We'd be laughing as we threw stones,' said Anis. 'This was not a jasmine revolution. We can't call it a jasmine revolution. People died and too much blood was spilt. It was a revolution of *karama*, of honour. We got our honour back.

'But you won't understand it until you know that it was also a revolution of jokes and laughter. This kept us going through it all. That, and the fact that the authorities left us no way out.

They escalated all the time, so we knew it was either victory or death.'

As he spoke, it was hard to tell which he thought was more important in the end.

2

Small Town, Big Shots

When Mohammed Bouazizi's mother Menobia came to protest at Sidi Bou Zid municipality in the hours after he had set himself alight, her nephew Ali Bouazizi, Mohammed's cousin, brought along a camera, filmed her, and uploaded it onto the Internet. The rest has already become instant folklore – Al Jazeera broadcast it, the lads took the police on in the streets, the protests snowballed from just Sidi Bou Zid to the rest of the south, to nationwide, people died, the riots spread, the regime faltered, Ben Ali left for Saudi Arabia.

But the video, and the fact the world heard of Sidi Bou Zid, was no fluke home video gone viral. Ali Bouazizi is a committed leftist militant in his thirties, older than Mohammed, who had been active against the Ben Ali regime for many years. The video was the first stage of a concerted campaign he and a close group of comrades conducted over the next ten days, uploading more videos, calling anyone they could find in the Arab satellite networks and across the international media. It was also simply the latest in a number of previous campaigns they had run since at least 2008, from this small town, trying to mobilise protest and opposition through spreading word of injustices across the Internet.

'This is where I uploaded the video of Mohammed from,' said Ali. We were walking along the street and had reached a tiny corner shop, a counter and three chairs, which sold mobile phones and credit, including data access via wireless receivers. 'I knew the interior ministry in Tunis would trace the IP address, but not to me. I have a number of spots all over town with different IP addresses. You need to use and throw IP addresses like SIM cards. It takes twenty-four hours for them to track it down.'

A motorcyclist puttered up the road the wrong way, lurching a little as he balanced some produce on the back. We were by the town square, which was laid out just like the *place* of a small French town, lines of trees and well-managed dirt so you almost expected to see old men stooping over their *boules*. A bunch of fat geezers in leather jackets stood around outside a tyre shop waiting for repairs, and straight opposite, almost inevitably, some tight-jeaned men in their early twenties were sprawled, two chairs apiece, outside a cheap cafe like they had nowhere else to go. Meanwhile family men and women hurried to and fro with large shopping bags, as it was late afternoon before a public holiday. This was the backdrop to the digital activism of Ali Bouazizi.

I had found Ali behind the till of his large groceries shop in the centre of town. A couple of employees moved in and out of the back store, restocking the shelves, and there was a constant queue at the checkout. It was one of those shops in the Middle East where there are a thousand lines and no fresh produce. You can't buy anything unprocessed, the fruit and veg is canned, the meat all deep-frozen, and fifty different types of biscuits, most of them unfeasibly sweet. A modernist shop, known in most dialects of Arabic as a supermarket however big or small it is.

He must be considerably better off than his cousin Mohammed had been. This is not uncommon in the Arab world, where there can be large discrepancies of wealth and education among extended families, a world known to us only through the neurotic preoccupation of the middle classes in the Brontës and Dickens and Jane Austen with holding their station in life. Mohammed's immediate family suffered two blows that must have made their struggle even harder. First his father, a construction worker who went to Libya in search of work, died when Mohammed was three years old, depriving the young family of a breadwinner. Second, his stepfather – who was also his dead father's brother, another not uncommon practice – fell too ill to work normally. That is why Mohammed had to start working at the age of ten, and leave formal education at the age of nineteen, before he could go to college.

Ali, meanwhile, used his relative wealth to allow him to spend time on his political activities. He is a member of the Progressive Democratic Party. Politicos had described the PDP as being tolerated, just about, by the old regime. A little-known detail in mature democracies is that dictatorships, more often than not, adorn themselves with some cosmetic opposition. Although they were in reality one-party states, even East Germany and Romania had 'historic' opposition parties right through communist rule. But Ali belongs to the radical wing of the party, already harshly critical of its leader, Ahmed Nejib Shebbi, for taking a ministerial post in the transitional government.

'There are manoeuvrings. Preparations.' He spoke with the assurance of the professional conspirator. 'Everything we see is a prologue. What do they want?' he asked me with a smile that was more challenging than relaxed. He had already refused to let me film him and wondered aloud if I belonged to an intelligence service.

'Who?' I asked.

'*Who*?' he repeated incredulously. 'The capitalists. The Americans and the French. They want what they wanted out of Ben Ali. A political discourse which is progressive, and an economic policy which is neo-liberal.'

I gathered, loosely, that he meant the foreign powers were grooming his party head, clearly a sell-out, to stand in the elections and provide, essentially, continuity of the capitalist system. A situation which, I gathered from his description of his campaigning life to date, he would not take lying down.

'We always knew the regime was weak,' he said, explaining his years of campaigning. 'They could not reconcile their conflicting interests. The Trabelsis' – the family of Ben Ali's second wife Leila – 'the Ben Alis themselves, sometimes the security apparatus itself must be regarded as an interest group. The regime seemed to be everywhere, but its core commitment was weak, do you see? We knew if we could just find the cause to push, we could harry them out by media campaigns.'

Ali's discourse was Assured Left of the kind I hadn't heard since the ferocious debates in the common room of my Oxford college. But he was far from a student politician. He experienced the reality of a dictatorship, which made his activism very live. Not for the first time in my life, I envied the dogmatism that allowed him to know why he was taking risks, why it was all worthwhile. It was impossible not to admire his courage, intelligence and efficiency even as his world view seemed remorselessly reductive, and his confidence at times shaded into superciliousness.

People were approaching him for advice of one kind or another every few minutes as we stood in the street. A man in his mid-twenties called Saleh, dressed American squeaky clean, fresh jeans, baseball jacket and very white sneakers, came up. He said he had been caught praying while on campus, for which he was tortured for eight months, then imprisoned for two and half years on trumped-up charges of terrorism. If this sounds absurd, nobody batted an eyelid. It was entirely plausible in Ben Ali's Tunisia. In a sign of how little confidence Tunisians have that the revolution is really transformative, Saleh wanted Ali's help to expunge his record, afraid that his prison term meant he could neither get a good job nor carry on his education.

'So you know who I am?' Ali said, somewhat redundantly. 'Listen, the right response to repression is not backwardness, OK?' he said. He laid an avuncular arm on Saleh's shoulder and proceeded to give him a friendly short lecture, to make sure he understood that true progress lay elsewhere than on the path of political Islam. Then he suddenly turned to me, his arm still on Saleh's shoulder, and said:

'Look at this young man. He is the flower of this country, a fine young man. They throw him in prison but what is his crime?' He smiles challengingly again. 'He prays. This is our tradition, this is his right. And not just prison. Torture.' Saleh is staring straight ahead with the look of someone trying not to cry. It occurs to me that maybe he has not told anyone, including his family, what he has really been through, until now. People often don't. I look away.

Ali gives him the names of some people in Sidi Bou Zid who are shadowing the national committee set up to investigate human rights abuses under the old regime, and Saleh walks away. Ali darts back into his shop, where the queue at checkout is never less than four deep, then across the road to a group of four young men who get out of a car to chat for five minutes, then they drive off, then he is back in the shop. He had already accomplished the first challenge of a real politician, to be genuinely useful to people. I wonder if he will enter the system, stand for parliament, make a stir within his own party, or join or even form a new one. Because there is no doubting that, even if he might not be the perfect dinner guest, real democracies desperately need people like Ali Bouazizi.

Since Ben Ali had fled, Sidi Bou Zid had become iconic for the whole country. Twice or three times a week people's convoys came down from Tunis to thank them for their revolutionary courage, and in fact I had arrived in the town with one of them, maybe 100 cars and coaches with a thousand or more middle-class students, doctors, lawyers, journalists and so on from Tunis. An earlier convoy had run into trouble when it brought humanitarian supplies. This touched a raw nerve for the people of the town, who may be hard up but are not exactly Biafra or southern Sudan, and they refused to receive their guests from the capital until it was understood they did not need any aid. Subsequent 'convoys of gratitude' learnt from that mistake and brought chocolate and flowers. The day I had come, the main streets were decked out with banners and thousands of people on the street. Cafes were filled to overflowing, there was a rally and concert in a stadium on the edge of town, and the guests had departed raving to each other about the great-hearted generosity of these simple folk.

But the town felt uneasy in the evenings. Driving round it on a Saturday night, a young man with cropped hair, stripped to the waist, holding his T-shirt in his hand, ran up and down a main road while police cars tried to catch him without causing a fuss. A drunken yob, we assumed. Once, as we cruised slowly, a man practically hurdled over the bonnet right to left, pursued by a small posse. We followed and found he had disappeared into some alleyways 100 metres further on. A police car turned up and some of the pursuers got in to continue to hunt him. Who was he, I asked, what has he done? Nobody seemed to know. Most of them were chasing him because the others were. Everyone assumed he was an agent provocateur from outside the town. But nobody could say how he had been spotted and how they knew for sure.

A few days before, the police station had burned down overnight with two prisoners inside it who died. In the revolutionary environment, this made national news instead of being smothered and the town came out in protest again for the first time since Ben Ali had fled. I first read about it in a newspaper in Tunis, 200 miles away. A formal investigation had been launched and four local officers had been summoned to the capital to explain themselves. Nevertheless it was a murky story and testament to the fact that powerful and lethal undercurrents still swirled around Sidi Bou Zid. A prominent lawyer, Dhafer al-Salihi, said he had been approached by a relative of one of the two men to take the case on but had declined.

Adel Hamami had been an ordinary clerk in the municipality. But the word was that for some time he had been freelancing his services as a go-between to arrange for local gangs to act as muscle for local grandees, both in and out of government posts, in pursuit of their interests. The nature of these deals wasn't clear. Intimidation to facilitate business deals, perhaps. Once the protests started he negotiated rent-a-mobs for the regime to break up demonstrations. But when the revolution succeeded he was arrested for incitement, and, unwisely, threatened to spill the beans on all the deals he had been party to. So one or more of the many powerful people he could expose decided to kill him. They somehow arranged for the police station to be unmanned at night, set fire to it, and made sure help didn't come in time for Hamami to make it out alive. His badly charred corpse was recovered the next morning.

The other victim, Reda al-Bakari, just happened to be sharing the same cell. A habitual drunk, unemployed and living at home at the age of thirty-seven, his own father had committed him to the lock-up overnight, under a law that several people said was commonly used in Tunisia. He had expected to pick him up hungover in the morning. The father's anguish must have been unbearable.

Salihi related this story, and many others, chain-smoking French cigarettes in the town's only posh cafe. He could have been a character from Stendhal, the clever lawyer in a town too small for him, burning to make his way in the world. He had well formed and withering opinions about almost everything, the revolution, the coming elections, his fellow lawyers. He laid out on the table the cards of other journalists who had interviewed him, from *Vanity Fair*, a French magazine called *Le Pèlerin*, and Japanese TV, and insisted on speaking unintelligible English. He was mid-thirties perhaps but his face looked ravaged by hard liquor.

It was clear that the patronage networks forged under the old regime were still very much in place at local level. Maybe a hundred people had fled the country when Ben Ali did, but beneath them were networks of thousands of governors, mayors, police chiefs, businessmen and others who got and maintained their positions by a mixture of obeisance and bribery, kiss up and kick down. They hadn't gone anywhere.

Standing on a street corner, a huge, shiny four-by-four motored smoothly down the road, conspicuous against the tatty pickup trucks and tooty mopeds. The smoked-out windows were up apart from a crack through which music pumped from a $500 sound system. 'That's so-and-so, back from the Gulf,' said Aida. On second glance, the car had number plates from Dubai.

Later, we drove past a large villa on the edge of town. 'That's Taher al-Agabi's,' she said, and told his story. Agabi was a regular greengrocer but had somehow managed to strike some deals with a former governor, Fawzi Ben Arab. Now he owned a chicken farm, a milk collection point, some olive groves and a chicks' hatchery, all on extensive pieces of land that he'd bought off the state for next to nothing. One presumes the normal range of kickbacks, minority shares and sub-market prices, but nobody had access to the documentation.

She and Mahjoob were becoming animated so I said, OK then, why don't we turn around, go back to his villa, and ask him about his holdings? Ask him if he feels there are any adjustments that need to be made, if he wants to state anything for the record about how he fashioned his business empire? They looked a bit taken aback, but didn't object as I wheeled the car round.

The villa stood proud and alone, with high walls surrounding it, on farmland close to the highway to Tunis. The main residential building was set at the back of the compound with a strange kind of watchtower, servants' quarters. I made sure to park far enough away from the walls so the car could be seen from the windows of the house. It seemed unlikely anything of substance would emerge from this encounter, but it would be nice to think it sent a message of things to come. The polite request, the car outside, the business card proffered, the doorman embarrassed into small talk at the gate for ten minutes before the answer comes back that now is not the time for a meeting.

And so it turned out. Aida brightly explained our mission. Old guard stayed at the gate. Young guard in plastic flip-flops shuffled up the pathway to the main house. And then came back to say Mr Agabi was out. Even though that old guard had said he was in just five minutes before, we were standing at the only exit, and we could see his car parked inside. There wasn't an intercom system to play with so our Michael Moore moment had come to an end. We beamed smiles at the guards, explained that we'd happily come back at another time of Mr Agabi's choosing, and slowly, nonchalantly, got back into the car. Where we chatted for a couple more minutes, and I pointedly took some flipcam footage of the villa, before moving off slowly. No hurry after all.

Later we had lunch at a friend's house. His father had recently retired from the Tunisian Gas and Electricity Company, where he had worked all his professional life. When we mentioned Taher al-Agabi, Mizouni said he had had a couple of run-ins with him. On one occasion Taher had tried to jump the queue to get the new agro-industrial facilities he was building on former state land connected to the grid at a knockdown price. Mizouni, the number two in the company's branch for the province, refused. Then Taher had pulled his strings, found someone in the ministry in Tunis to issue an order down to the local branch. Mizouni's boss, the local number one, came into his office and told him he had to lay on the grid extension as Taher had requested. Not unless you countersign, Mizouni said. After some huffing and puffing, the boss relented and signed.

'I've got a copy of it in here, along with all the others,' he said, pointing to a large cabinet in the living room. He was surprised when I was surprised that he kept his own archive. 'Every official of integrity in Tunisia has his own archive. It's the only way you can sleep at night. I still consider that decision was against regulations. But I have proof that it wasn't my decision. A man just wants to work in an honourable way, and do his duty by his family and by God,' he added, prosaically, as if this were the most natural thing in the world to say.

50

Days after the revolution, a website called Tunileaks had shot to prominence. In the beginning, it was republishing Wikileaks cables, but it moved later to publishing documents submitted locally. On the Prophet's Birthday, a holiday, youngsters took over the town square with huge speakers blaring Tunisian rap. They also brought a notice board to post printouts of leaked documents, such as a list of employees that were to be barred from government service indefinitely, and photocopies of a sale of state land near Tunis for 2 Tunisian dinars ($1.50) per square metre. I wondered if any files related to Taher al-Agabi would make it up there soon, or any of the other files from Mizouni's store.

But it wasn't just security jobs and local businessmen who were part of the old regime and beholden to it. A few days earlier, I got word of a high school where the students were on strike against the headmaster because he was from the ruling party, and implicated. During my reporting career, I have always been drawn to schools because so much of a society is gathered there – its archetypes in the textbooks, its social conditions in the teachers, its future in the children. Perhaps for that very reason access to schools is often hard in the Arab world. When I had first arrived as a Reuters correspondent in Cairo, I was all fired up to get inside Egypt's school system. But the dean of the foreign correspondents club, an old BBC hand, bet me I wouldn't be able to manage it in less than a year, such was the protocol and tight control attached to the system. He won the bet.

Everything seemed fairly normal at the Martyrs High School. There was the obligatory portrait of Ibn Khaldun at the entrance, possibly history's most famous Tunisian, a fourteenth-century author credited by many with creating the rudiments of modern sociology. In the computer lab, IT teacher Mohsin Ali was teaching three girls the rudiments of HTML during the break because they were particularly keen. 'Only static pages for the moment,' he said, almost by way of apology. Later they would get onto databases, an image manipulation program called the GIMP, and some programming in Pascal. One of the two deputy headmasters, Mohadhab al-Hejlawi, took me into an Arabic language class where a peroxide blonde teacher was going through the dual forms with a group of politely bored teenagers. The sports field looked a bit ropey. No nets in the goals, the pitch muddy and uneven and the lines worn away in places. But none of the players seemed to care. Meanwhile, the boarders sat outside their dorms. Like many developing countries, Tunisia's public high schools have a system of boarding for pupils from the surrounding countryside.

But the headmaster's office was closed and Hejlawi couldn't tell me when it might open again. We made discreet enquiries as to where the headmaster, Ali Youssefi, was. On leave, Hejlawi said in an even tone. He clearly wouldn't be unhappy if Youssefi never returned to work. Equally clearly, he wasn't going to make any public comment.

Ali Youssefi lived in a tied house. It was on school grounds but only accessible from a separate entrance on the street, so that from the school you had to go out into the road and walk round to reach the front door. On the way, one of the school secretaries caught up with us, eager to give us her version of events. Youssefi was a pig, she said, who harassed female staff.

He didn't have a kind word for anybody, was arrogant and rude and incompetent. He came to work drunk sometimes, wearing shorts, she said, which in the Tunisian context both of social conservatism and respect for authority figures is little short of turning up in your undies. She was still bending our ear when a young woman opened the front door to Mr Youssefi's compound. A graffito message on the side wall proclaimed 'Ali Youssefi: wanted by the people'.

We'd like to understand what's going on with the school, we said, pressing our cards into the young woman's hand. She closed the door again and told us to wait. Five minutes later, Youssefi came to the door itself and opened it a crack. Who? What? Really? We kept talking and the door opened wider. I handed him another card to add to the first one, and he let us in.

'Forgive my appearance,' he said, his arms waving to his checked dressing gown and blue pyjamas. 'I'm on sick leave.' What's wrong? we asked and he mumbled something about a stomach bug. 'Come in, come in.' He ushered us up a path through the large but untended garden, into the salon of the house.

A television was on mute. Youssefi lit a cigarette and the young woman, his daughter, arrived with coffee in cups on a silver tray. Craggy face, bushy moustache, hoarse voice. A copy of the independent newspaper *Shorouq* lay on the coffee table, folded and read, several days old. You got the feeling he'd spent most of the last two weeks he'd been off school watching TV, staying up late, and perhaps drinking too much.

So you studied in Baghdad, I said, pointing to a degree

certificate on the wall, addressing him in French as he had me.

He broke into a smile. 'Yes, indeed. The Golden Age!' he replied. When was that? I asked. He had gone there in 1979 and stayed until the end of his master's in 1984, he said. It seemed an odd phrase to use, I mused, for the years in which the Iran–Iraq war broke out, Baghdad was put on a war footing and the city came under direct rocket attacks. Well there was the war, he said, but it wasn't like later, with the sanctions and then . . . he trailed off but I understood the fall of Saddam Hussein and the Baathist regime was probably still mourned in the Youssefi household. His wife was Iraqi and ran a local girls' school.

So what do you make of the revolution here? I asked him. He was prepared. 'We are with the revolution, of course.' I wasn't sure where the *we* had come from. 'There were certain necessary corrections that were inevitable. But the problem is, there are deviations.' His language could have been taken from any of the textbooks used to support secular dictatorships across the Arab world for the last half-century. Corrections, deviations, necessary developments, objective circumstances, the party and the Leader and the Revolution. What's more, he meant it. I hadn't heard anyone mean it in a long time. *Il n'y a pas d'encadrement*, he said, disapprovingly, there is no structure to it. What did he mean? I asked.

Well, he said, and entered into a long peroration about the new minister of education, Tayyib al-Bakoush. Culminating in the fact that he himself was *insurrectionnel*, Youssefi exclaimed, offended. The other day he allowed some college students to come and see him and put their demands to him, I saw it on

TV, he said. When we looked impassive, he felt obliged to spell it out for us: 'He was being interviewed by the students live on TV!' That sounded pretty good to me but I said nothing. I was waiting to ask him about the school. 'He's a human rights activist!' Youssefi expostulated, as if that explained everything.

So tell us about what's happening at the school, I said. Well, he replied, calming himself right back down, there is a breakdown in discipline but it's nothing serious. We'll get back to normal soon.

But the students want you to leave. They say you are linked to the old regime. That's nonsense, he scoffed, all the students love me. And went on to explain that there were 'outside hands' stirring up trouble. So you're not a member of the ruling party, the RCD? I asked him. I am a member, yes, but so were thousands of others. It doesn't mean I'm part of the regime. It didn't help me get the job, he replied. How long have you been headmaster here? I asked. Seven years. And before? Youssefi had held two previous headmasterships in other towns in the south, the first in 1987, when he was just twenty-seven years old. That's pretty young, I observed.

'I suppose it is,' he said, smiling as if in fond remembrance. It felt like those were the days when he was a promising young man with a future. Not that he'd done badly as things turned out. He had achieved solid middle rank in the technocracy and had the revolution not happened would doubtless have walked an untroubled path into comfortable and respected old age. But back then, the sky was the limit.

He was giving nothing away. He saw the best way forward as a certain degree of cordiality combined with minimal disclosure – and absolutely no admission of anything, ever. The Baathist way.

There was a minimal pause in the conversation and he turned to address Aida for the first time, in Arabic: 'You know the girls are now beginning to wear veils to school?' he asked, shaking his head. Aida is unveiled.

What's wrong with that? I asked him. School should be a sacred place, a protected place, he replied. No politics and no religion.

'*L'école républicaine*?' I suggested – the Republican School, the French articulation of strident secularism in the education system. *Exactly*, he replied, sighing as if relieved to be understood. He was selling secularism to me, the European, but I felt sure he would have been equally capable of selling xenophobia to a fellow Tunisian. Youssefi comes from a world where political correctness long ago married opportunism, with ferocious results.

We took our leave, as it was clear that little more would come from the conversation. I couldn't tell whether Youssefi thought he stood a serious chance of returning to his post, was holding out for a payoff, or simply didn't know what to do. He was definitely a piece of work, though.

Mohammed Bouazizi's primary school stood nearby, and we dropped in. Some of the teachers were a delight: a woman called Gamra Manawwar took us to her fourth-grade classroom where she made me give a short speech about Britain and what people there thought of the revolution. Two ten-year-old girls were bursting to put their hands up, question after question. Tasneem wanted to know about the Channel Tunnel.

Karima wanted me to know about the Solidarity Bank, a Ben Ali project to alleviate poverty. Even though the bank had collapsed, we still have our solidarity, she said, delivering the punchline she'd heard from her dad, most likely, with aplomb. Even the sluggish boys wanted to know how Manchester United were getting on without Ronaldo. There was that wonderful feeling of kids blossoming under a gifted teacher, of order maintained through respect rather than fear.

And other classes and teachers were just a nightmare. In Irshad Hamdouni's class the kids were all terrified. He was never not angry. He made them recite their English songs and then told them to ask me questions. Go on, ask him questions, he shouted. It was embarrassing. He was so tense that when I touched him lightly on the forearm to try and earth him a little he nearly jumped out of his skin. The boys at the back, sniggering, gormless and defiant, looked headed for trouble.

The school was run down. They bought their own chalk, and their own light bulbs. In every class teachers pointed out a handicapped child who was in there as part of a policy decision some years back to integrate – but without the necessary support. In one class we all stood round a beautiful deaf girl sitting at her desk, a knot of teachers explaining at some length how she didn't have a clue what was going on and didn't stand a chance. She smiled sweetly. At the same time, both the will to organisation and institutional knowledge had remained. The staff room was full of complex logistical charts fitting two entirely different shifts of pupils into five time slots each day. Several of the teachers, such as Abdel-Qadir al-Mansouri, the deputy head, were truly devoted and had spent twenty or more years there, having long ago made their accommodations with crappy salaries and the lack of a career and just got on with doing their best.

Nobody I spoke to at the school remembered Mohammed Bouazizi. The symbol of the revolution had passed through these classrooms fifteen years ago, waited in the lunch queue and played tag in the playground. But he had left no trace.

The Bouazizi family had been catapulted to international fame on the back of a deep personal tragedy and their lives were now being shaken by forces way beyond their control. The phenomenon of instant celebrity had reached Sidi Bou Zid.

A few days before I had seen crowds at a march pick up Mohammed's half-brother, Ziyad, no more than ten years old, and carry him on their shoulders shouting the slogans of the revolution. He looked overwhelmed. His sister and mother were rumoured to be on their way to Paris, where the mayor, Bertrand Delanoë, had declared a square would be named after him.

With the fame the family had become public property. Some students in Tunis I had spent the day with freely criticised their patriotic credentials because they said the mother had accepted 50,000 dinars – $35,000 – from Ben Ali to keep quiet. Others said the families of three other men who had died had been due to receive hush money but the regime had changed its mind for some reason, so then the relatives of the other men had put the Bouazizis under pressure to pass around some of the money they had received. Yet more reports in the media quoted the mother as saying Ben Ali had handed her a cheque in front of state media, only for his aides to swipe it back off her immediately they stopped filming, and that she never saw a penny.

One narrative made the Bouazizi family direct victims of the Ben Ali regime's rapacity. They had been thrown off the land and moved to town when one of the state-owned banks had repossessed a farm owned by Mohammed's uncle, which five or six families within the clan had been working on. The uncle had fallen behind with payments on a debt, the bank had snapped up the land in the twinkling of an eye and sold it on to one of what are known here as the *Qawadda*, the Pimps who build instant fortunes by pillaging state assets. That would make Mohammed Bouazizi the victim not just of petty abuse but of the grand larceny that had hit the country these past twenty years, making his story more directly a narrative of all Tunisians who had been disinherited, in one way or another, by Ben Ali and his kleptocrats.

Others said the sequence was wrong. Mohammed and his family had moved into town years before the uncle had been forced to sell the farm.

One of the most shocking stories is about Ben Ali visiting Bouazizi in hospital. The day he immolated himself, he had lain an hour and a half before an ambulance fetched him to the local hospital. From there he was moved to a larger unit in Sfax, seventy miles away. As the protests spread, he was moved again, to the burns unit at Ben Arous Hospital just outside the capital. It was there that Ben Ali took a photo opp on 28 December, eleven days after the original incident.

The official picture shows Bouazizi lying in bed, propped up by pillows and swaddled in bandages with only a minimal opening for his mouth. Ben Ali is standing, earnest, hands folded, the solicitous leader come to enquire after one of his citizens.

Except that Mohammed Bouazizi was already dead, this version says. The president of the country was putting himself on the evening news bestowing bedside manner on a man whose third-degree burns had already killed him.

Sometimes, in the maelstrom of myth and counter-myth, a gut instinct just hits you. The body language of the doctor and nurses in the photo opp makes this story feel right. They are standing apart from Ben Ali, arms folded, pointedly staring not at Bouazizi in shared concern but at Ben Ali himself, in what looks like a gesture of defiance. It's striking for the time, because this is still December. Protests had reached Tunis the capital the day before, but small-scale, maybe a thousand people. There is still no question in anyone's mind that the regime will fall. They are in the presence of the undisputed ruler of their country, a man who ruled an apparatus that day by day was rounding up opponents and sending them for torture. The staff at Ben Arous knew this. If they held this posture of anger, my gut instinct says, it was not as a conscious political act but because Ben Ali was doing something so repellent at a normal human level that they could not help themselves.

This macabre stardom, visited on a simple family who seemed already to have said everything they had to say, made me reluctant to visit the family home. If truth be told, I had not done day-to-day reporting for a decade or more and had lost the reflex of wading in there to ask the same questions as everyone else, to how-do-you-feel them, just because I needed my own quotes.

No, in fact, real truth be told, I had never had that reflex even when I worked as a Reuters correspondent. What I loved about being a reporter was the opportunity and excuse to be curious about everyone and everything so that life was work and work was life in the most positive sense. What I had always hated was doorstepping. Luckily, as a news agency Reuters didn't really do celebrity or tabloid. If you had to do it, it was a legitimate public interest story, almost always with players, putting ministers, guerrillas and tycoons on the spot about their policies, operations and deals. I could do that. I just couldn't find it in me to care enough to jam a microphone in the face of a civilian when it felt like nothing new – literally no news – would come of it. It is undoubtedly a professional weakness that I can only confess because I'm no longer in the breaking-news business.

But when Aida pointed out that we were in Hay an-Noor, Mohammed Bouazizi's district, we couldn't very well not go there. Neighbours directed us to a modest dwelling in a side street, an unbolted metal door leading into a small, concreted front yard and a small house at the back of it. I parked in front and Mohammed's little brother Ziyad came out and waved. He knew who we were and what we wanted, and if I had to guess I'd say that in his ten-year-old world the fact his completely unremarkable home had suddenly become a shrine, the object of bizarre pilgrimage by colourful strangers from all over the world, was a whole lot of fun. But I thought of his mother and imagined her struggling with grief and perhaps also inarticulacy, determined to preserve the sanctity of her eldest son by talking to whoever demanded it, and yet her grasp on the real

Mohammed somehow diminished a fraction with each new, purposeless interview. I decided to visit his grave instead, started the car again, and moved off. Through the rear-view mirror I could see Ziyad, out on the street now, watching us leave.

A large Tunisian flag stands over Mohammed Bouazizi's fresh, unmarked grave but otherwise there is nothing to distinguish it from the hundred or so others lying on open, stony ground, a plain stretching away to the Djebel Selloum to the west, a hundred olive groves in between swaying in the steady winter wind. For we are not in the town of Sidi Bou Zid itself but the village of Gara Benour, about ten miles outside it, where Bouazizi was born and grew up.

We parked the car next to the village school that Bouazizi had attended. A small schoolhouse stood on the edge of the cemetery where they say Bouazizi learnt his letters. There was a fresh graffito that read: 'To the honour of the martyrs, and the glory of the Leaders'. The Arabic word *zaeem* carries the connotation of charismatic leadership, giddy and powerful. Gamal Abdel Nasser and Saddam Hussein were both *zaeem*. I asked Aida and Mahjoob what they thought of it. 'We don't need any more *zaeems*,' said Aida. 'We need a parliament.'

At least half the other graves are Bouazizis. A few have professionally worked inscriptions, Qur'anic verses and precise dates of birth and death, such as Mohammed bin Mohammed bin Mohammed bin Jada Bouazizi, showing his status by the four-generation lineage. But many more either have no inscription at all or ones that seem to have been scratched with a stick or other ready instrument, sometimes in the cement as it was setting. Near Bouazizi's end of the graveyard lie a couple of smaller graves for children, Hosni bin Ammar and Ulfa bint Salem, who died at the age of three in 1986, making her almost an exact contemporary.

As we walked round the unenclosed cemetery, we teased out the immensely delicate question of Bouazizi's status as *shaheed*, or martyr. The story was, after all, that he had set himself alight. This remained unchallenged for weeks. But when his death was announced his family insisted that he had never meant to drop the match. If Mohammed Bouazizi had committed suicide, far from being a hero, he could not even be buried in a normal graveyard. Many clerics would say he had gone straight to Hell, since suicide is considered as serious as murder in Islam. Your life, just like everyone else's, is not yours to end.

I was gently probing the point with Aida and Mahjoub, two recent graduates, who had accompanied me to the grave. We can't ever really know, can we, I said, but let's face it, if he had committed suicide the family would have to say it was an accident anyway. Aida said that Youssef Qardawi, a televangelist sheikh who has a weekly show on Al Jazeera, had suggested that all good Muslims should pray to God to forgive him.

'In any case, it is God who decides if he is a martyr or not,' she said, as we reached the grave.

She and Mahjoub both held their hands out to recite the Fatiha, the first chapter of the Qur'an. Then we picked some wild flowers from around the graveyard and put them on his tomb.

3

The Great Expectations Gap

Back in town, the slogans were spray-painted in black on the white walls all down the street. 'Work is Honour'. 'Where is Our Right to be appointed?' 'Equality, Dignity, Work'. Sidi Bou Zid is a great place to go and get a sense of perspective if you're feeling jaded in your job.

Inside a government building a group of perhaps twenty people were gathered. They'd been staging a sit-in for a week now, forcing all the employees in the building, the higher education directorate, to stay at home. They were from the Committee in Defence of Unemployed College Graduates and they wanted the government to give them jobs.

'How many people know Tunis?' asked Abdel Mottaleb, a man in his mid-thirties who seemed to be leading the group, planning a trip to the capital to make the authorities there sit up and pay attention. Three or four did, it turned out. 'Maybe we can split up into groups and the people who know Tunis will go one in each party.' They planned an hour in the higher education ministry and then to hit the media, Al Jazeera, France24, the BBC. 'We'll demo on Habib Bourguiba Avenue and get the cameras there,' he said.

I was filming them so it was obvious I was a journalist. He

asked me about their media strategy. Should they call a press conference, or try and engage the major international media one by one?

This put me in a bit of a spot. As gently as possible I said that having just come from Tunis, there were about a dozen small demonstrations a day going up and down Habib Bourguiba Avenue right now. Actually it had become a regular afternoon diversion, what high-school lads did after school and, who knows, to show off for the cute girls that were always hanging around, but I didn't say that. What exactly did they want to achieve? I asked.

We want jobs, said Abdel Momin, an older man, a little surprised. Well you do have a certain cachet here in Sidi Bou Zid as the guardians of the revolution, I said. Why don't you try and persuade a film crew to come down here and make a feature of you on the march? You know, the revolution succeeded and the deposed Ben Ali fled but the cancer of unemployment still remains in the cradle of the revolution, something like that, I said. Then your journey is part of the story. Coming up through the country by minibus, maybe you can make common cause with other groups of unemployed in the towns you pass through. Something like that?

This met with an impassive response around the room. Abdel Mottaleb asked if I could 'arrange' a film crew to come down here from Tunis. I had few contacts among the residual crews now in Tunisia and in any case the story didn't seem to have any legs to me even as a feature. From my days as a breaking-news journalist it seemed like the kind of thing you would only do if you already had a connection with a particular leader or group, and knew you could make the story work through their character. There were hundreds of thousands of unemployed young men and women all over the country. Why them? Plus, the transitional government had a thousand priorities and limited resources. Was this kind of special interest demand the best way to kick-start a meaningful debate on economic policy? I tried to convey a little of this without hurting their feelings.

The walls behind them were plastered with posters and scribblings about unemployment. 'We want Sidi Bou Zid's quota of jobs', 'Eleven, twelve, thirteen years of unemployment. We're still waiting', 'There have been enough promises' and 'We are decision makers. Listen to us!' 'We are afraid we might die before we get the chance to work'. 'Trembling hands do not forge history nor do deaf ears hear the call of duty'. Many of these slogans used the Tunisian colloquial word for work, *khadama*, more literally, 'to serve', which gave their demands more poignancy. They were only asking for the right to serve.

The group, crammed in the foyer of the small building, ranged in age from early twenties to fifties. They soon forgot about me and my hesitant media advice and plunged back into their internal debates about tactics, not just for the Tunis trip but the sit-in. One of them quickly wrote a draft declaration to the head of the office they were occupying, offering to end the sit-in in return for guarantees that there would be serious progress in their legitimate demands. Then they spent half an hour editing it en masse, taking it apart, putting it back together again, criticising each other's grammar and sentence construction. Then the room went quiet as Abdel Momin phoned the director on his mobile asking him to come and meet with them. Another debate about whether they should appoint a deputation to sit with the office director before or after the sit-in ended. And so on and so on.

Throughout the morning I remained unclear whether they had any actual policies to suggest for Tunisia's unemployment problem, beyond the notion that they themselves should get government posts of the kind that college graduates used to expect all over the Arab world: teachers, a post in a ministry, a regional inspector of something. There were vague references to the principle of seniority. The government should lower the retirement age and then use a matrix of seniority and qualifications to appoint the long-term unemployed. But it looked like they weren't that engaged with the big picture.

Eventually the meeting broke up. 'What do you think our chances are?' Abdel Mottaleb asked me on the steps outside, where everyone was smoking. 'Do you think we'll get jobs in a month or two?' I struggled for a couple of seconds to find the right words, but he broke back in answering his own question.

'Of course not. We're not naïve, you know!' Well, that was a relief! 'This is about organising, making people feel they can do something. Look at this! Even three months ago we would never have dared to think about occupying a government office. And now here we are. We'll develop our own organisational power and then let's see.'

Fair enough, I thought. It all seemed pretty harmless, and if people felt empowered by it then that was all to the good. But it all felt a lot more political than actually focused on the result of getting jobs. A man called Reda wanted to know how

I would compare the Tunisian Revolution with the French Revolution. An elderly woman called Najla showed me the documents from a lawsuit she was launching claiming some form of abuse of human rights from the Tunisian government as a result of so many years' unemployment.

What, I wondered, were the realistic chances of tackling Tunisia's great unemployment problem, shared also by Egypt and even oil-rich Libya?

The World Bank cited unemployment at just over 14 per cent in Tunisia in 2008, the most recent data available at the time of the revolution. Other figures showed it fairly constantly between 12 and 15 per cent over most of the past decade. This is of course very high compared with Europe and North America, where even after the global financial crisis unemployment has climbed to 8 or 9 per cent from much lower levels that obtained in the boom before it. At the height of Margaret Thatcher's austerity programme in the United Kingdom, when unemployment hit 3 million in 1982, the national unemployment rate crept up to 12 per cent, enough to spark inner-city riots in Liverpool, London and elsewhere.

But the real figure is probably considerably higher, with a lot of disguised unemployment. Economists say that women are typically under-counted in the workforce, and the tricks and procedures of registration discourage many from being formally counted. Local union officials had estimated unemployment in Sidi Bou Zid could be as high as 30 per cent. And then again, that's before you get to age variations. The significance of unemployment wasn't just in how many people were unemployed but what their profile was, how long it had been going on, what chance there was that it would change. In Arab countries, high population growth combined with higher unemployment rates among the young created a labour market in which it seemed unemployment was the core problem of the base of the population pyramid.

Abdel Mottaleb's meeting in Sidi Bou Zid was not unique. All over Tunisia loose associations for the defence or protection of the unemployed, usually concentrated on college graduates, sprang up in the past ten years. The fact they were able to achieve little on the core issue, or even to mobilise much in Ben Ali's police state, is beside the point. Unemployment was no longer an economic issue. It was a social and cultural one, perhaps even one of identity.

Larbi Sadiki, a lecturer at Exeter University, wrote an article for the Al Jazeera website in which he called unemployment 'the Bin Laden within'. Unemployment had become an ideology among the young and mainly urban poor across the Arab world, he wrote.

Millions of young men and women lived lives without hope or purpose on the periphery, in cramped, featureless housing, nobodies from nowhere. The men aspired simply to a regular job, with the government if possible, which would allow them to live on their own, get married and have children. The women largely aspired to marry those of the men who managed this. For these millions, in the prime of their life, there was nowhere to go, nothing much to do, no way to even be sure you existed in the real world beyond the fact that you got up, got dressed, ate breakfast and carried on. Mere subsistence year after year.

I met college graduates in their thirties who had never had

a job that used their qualifications. Abdel Mottaleb himself, for example, a graduate in accounting, had only worked as a guard in security firms, and then only intermittently. Aida had spent years without working. Anis al-Shoaibi, five years. Abdallah al-Souissi, leader of a similar group in the town of Kairawan, nine years.

It was embarrassing. When I asked a class in Mohammed Bouazizi's old school if anyone in their family was unemployed, nobody said father, mother, brother. It was all uncle, cousin, neighbour. And yet statistically in a class of thirty-five kids, that couldn't have been true. The crime pages of newspapers were filled with incidents involving people identified as unemployed in the headline. In neighbouring Algeria, the intelligentsia coined a new word to describe social strata driven desperate by the search for settled employment: *khobziste*, a cute Franco-Arabic hybrid meaning, roughly, 'Breadist'. As in – you've got some and I haven't.

The Tunisian revolution had started by asking for jobs and ended by demanding Ben Ali's head. The progression had seemed logical and the issue of corruption became hard-wired to unemployment in people's minds.

And that was before Al Jazeera got going.

Day after day in January and February, during the protests in Egypt, they broadcast stories about corruption. Mubarak and his family were said to have stolen a staggering $50–70 billion in Egypt. This was an outrageous figure in an economy that had a GDP of only two and half times that, and clearly they came under some pressure because a few days later they ran a story that didn't say so directly but seemed designed to answer off-air criticisms about hyperbole. Some think tank somewhere estimated that a reasonable number to account for losses to the Egyptian economy from corruption was $6.8 billion a year over the period 2000 and 2008. That would be over $50 billion right there. Other stories said democracy was the 'magic ingredient' in economic growth, quoting experts saying that foreign investment was bound to increase as Tunisia moved towards democracy and even that the markets in New York had risen in expectation that the revolutions would be good for business.

The Tunisian press reported that an American firm was interested in opening a factory in Sidi Bou Zid, investing a couple of hundred million dollars and creating possibly thousands of jobs. Details were short but it was the talk of the town for a couple of days. I wondered how many of these kinds of straws in the wind would land in Sidi Bou Zid and other places in the months and years to come, how many would materialise into real jobs, and what the reaction would be to that ratio.

I watched the satellite TV channels build these morality tales about the scale of stolen wealth in restaurants, hotel salons and people's homes across North Africa through February and March. Al Jazeera wasn't alone. The Tunisian media chipped in with daily exposés about new palaces and villas, vaults, and missing gold and more dodgy arrangements in large companies. But Al Jazeera was the most prominent, particularly because it was the channel everyone was glued to for coverage of the revolutions. And I watched their impact. The waitress in Cairo who remarked she'd just heard the government could give every single person in the country $400 back from the corruption, as if she were expecting an announcement at any time. The numbers of people in Tunisia and Egypt who said, oh, the answer to the economy is just to get the funds back from abroad and reinvest them, as though the Swiss bank accounts alone could create all the jobs Abdel Mottaleb and his group were demanding. The union officials in Tunis who believed that now they should be in a position, courtesy of government funding, to offer personal loans to all their members.

A dangerous gap in expectations is growing. Ben Ali had issued a last-ditch promise to create 300,000 more jobs in two years and was ridiculed. But now everyone expects the transitional government, or the one that would come after elections, to do the same or more. And in Egypt you can multiply those problems in both scale and intensity.

The linkage of unemployment to corruption is potentially explosive. Because logically, if you expect, or 'know', that the stolen funds can solve all the economic problems then when, after a year or two, those problems still remain, it stands to reason that the new government is just as corrupt as the last one. Cue a second set of protests without the same innocence and sense of joy as the first.

And it wasn't just the numbers, it was the way jobs were imagined. All the emphasis, both from officials and among the people themselves, was on *wazifa*, the position, the post, at a large institution, most likely the public sector. That was what counted. Which ignored the fact that it was the informal sector that had done most of the job creation in the past decade or more in Tunisia, Egypt, and elsewhere across the Arab world. It was government jobs that Ben Ali was referring to, just as it was to public-sector salaries that Hosni Mubarak's government announced a 15 per cent raise across the board in his last days in an attempt to stave off the revolution. The government sector is what matters, what is proper.

Not that the private sector is entirely absent. Osama al-Chebbi opened his own cafe in Sidi Bou Zid at the age of twenty-seven. La Phalène is the town's only upmarket joint, lounge chairs, tasteful art deco on the walls. La Phalène is the only cafe in the town, and therefore probably the province, where women come freely and sit together with men.

'I was worried when I started it last year,' he said. 'I thought that people wouldn't accept it. But we have had great acceptance, thank God.'

But Osama, who graduated in IT, comes from a well-off family whose network provided start-up funds for his business. Very few youngsters have the same opportunities.

Esmat sat in his office in Tunis, smoking in the dress-down style of a young Euro-businessman: jeans and navy blue jacket, dress shirt open at the collar. He'd come back from France, where he gained a master's in business studies, to see if he could get foreign investors interested.

'I had a group of Spanish investors here the other day,' he said. 'In the long run there's plenty of opportunity.' What in? I asked. Tourism, he said. But tourism isn't such a great job creator, dollar for dollar, I said.

Well there's only so many sectors foreign investment is naturally interested in, he replied. For job creation the other thing we really need is entrepreneurship in the informal sector.

That means micro- and what are known as SMEs in the

jargon, small and medium-sized enterprises, employing 100 people, or fewer. In the tired old game of foreign assistance played between Arab regimes who were strategic allies and Western donors like the United States, the European Union and the World Bank, the donors have put increasing emphasis on job creation in the informal sector in recent years. Both Tunisia and Egypt had seen numerous projects, grants and loans to help create the preconditions for small and micro-businesses, and I had even seen terms of reference for similar projects in the provinces of Yemen, where, when up to a third of the population are malnourished and water is running out, you might think that entrepreneurship was going to be challenging. The upbeat language in these project documents always talks of entrepreneurship and innovation. That's code for self-employment, which the masses of the Arab world know mostly as pushing a street cart like Mohammed Bouazizi, or shining shoes, maybe running a small food stand or a taxi, if you can come by the capital to buy one.

But talk to any cabbie and you quickly realise how hard even that is. When I reached Cairo and Alexandria, later, I conducted my own business interview among half a dozen cabbies. Estimates for buying a cab in decent condition varied between $15,000 and $20,000, there being some complicated licensing system. Nevertheless, as cabbies typically pay as much as $15 a day to rent the cab now, the investment would pay for itself in a thousand work days, or five years roughly. At the end of that period, the cabbie – and there must be 100,000 in Cairo alone – would have acquired a fair-sized asset to add to his security, even accounting for depreciation, and once he passed the payback on it could increase his income very significantly.

There was a founding premise to all the aid talk of entre-preneurialism that nobody ever spelled out plainly. All the people who read these kind of documents know it anyway and it might offend the regime. Namely: no government will ever solve the problem of unemployment in these societies. The aid industry has spawned a cluster of NGOs that proselytise for the free market, such as the one I later tried to hook up with in Alexandria, who write papers and attend conferences and talk the good talk, in the tepid hope that they can infuse something of the glory of entrepreneurial life into Arab youth. An inter-national network acronymed as YES, the Youth Employment Summit, held a founding conference attended by Bill Clinton back in 2002. But it all seems too glossy, not quite weathered enough by the real world to make you think it can solve the problem.

Microfinance had come to Tunisia, as it had to a hundred or more countries since Mohammed Younis first pioneered it in Bangladesh, but the government had regulated it from a position of almost total ignorance. The Solidarity Bank, later famously pillaged by the Ben Ali family, created nearly 300 micro-credit associations across the country, but then a law imposed a 5 per cent annual cap on all charges for loans, including administration and interest. This prevented any of these outfits from becoming sustainable in the normal way, which is to use the revenues they received from clients paying back loans to lend to new clients. An international microfinance group called Enda incorporated a local affiliate which, not subject to these restrictions, became the main lender in the country. By the end of 2010 they had 165,000 active clients, most of them women, and sixty-five branches around the country.

But as elsewhere, microfinance is geared to, and taken up by, people who are largely on the margins of the labour market, especially women. It would need to be massively expanded, both in terms of the numbers of clients and the size of the loans, for it to make a dent in Tunisia's jobless figures, to take significant numbers of young men like Anis and Abdel Mottaleb off the streets.

Meanwhile, the mindset of the *wazifa*, the salaried position, won't go away. Abdel Mottaleb and the associations for the defence of unemployed college graduates are one small example. People want government jobs even with unfeasibly low salaries because they could get promoted, because there are other entitlements and, in the last period at least, you couldn't get your slice of the cake unless you achieved a position.

And the problem is that the ideology of letting the private sector do it is already tainted because in the public mind it was given an outing in the last ten to fifteen years in both Tunisia and Egypt. There is therefore little differentiation in many Tunisians' and Egyptians' minds between free-market economics and crony capitalism. From the 1990s, IMF programmes and World Bank structural reforms were in play in both countries, along with the rhetoric of the free market, albeit with some wobbles. I remember asking an Egyptian minister then why the local currency had not fluctuated by so much as a single per cent against the US dollar in over a year since it had been freely floated, only to be told: 'If free markets require fluctuations, we will fluctuate it.' In Egypt, the English word 'businessman' entered normal parlance among people who spoke no English, like 'football' or 'rap', to denote the coterie of multi-millionaires around the Mubarak family, especially around President Hosni Mubarak's son Gamal.

Crony capitalism advanced at just the same time as liberalisation programmes and the result was pretty much the worst of all worlds. Lots of people lost their jobs, and what there had been of a social welfare net all but disappeared, yet there was no fundamental change at the heart of the economy, apart from private rapacity replacing institutional self-interest as the main seeker of economic rents. This meant that to many looking in from the outside, the old idea of a national economy with commanding heights guided by the government, with jobs for every college graduate, was not discredited. On the contrary the timing meant it was the newfangled ideas of free market and job growth in the private sector that were seen to be self-interested pap. And now the revolutions, with their tales of fabulous corruption, have reinforced that narrative.

Mass unemployment is the real time bomb for the Tunisian and Egyptian revolutions, and will be in any other Arab country where regime change happens as a result of people power, even oil-rich Libya. No high-profile leader has come close to spelling out the truth yet, that resolving it will take a decade or more, and that's with the right policies and plenty of investment, neither of which is certain.

The stakes are high. The outflow of economic migrants from Tunisia sped up in the weeks after Ben Ali left as the revolution engulfed the country's maritime authorities, disrupting their previously smooth working arrangement with Italy to intercept illegal migrants on boats. Thousands arrived on the outpost island of Lampedusa which, 200 miles south of Sicily, lies less than 100 miles off the Tunisian coast. There were the usual stories of boats capsizing and dozens drowning before the coastguard could reach them.

That could be a prelude to what would happen if either Tunisia or Egypt descended into chaos.

'Can you help me get a visa?' is still a common refrain among the Arab young. Perhaps a dozen people asked me outright in these journeys – university graduates, workers, unemployed and, in one case, a successful lawyer. Almost everyone I met had a brother, a cousin or a friend in Europe. Going to join them was always on the list of options perpetually revolving through the minds of the young and unsettled. They were well aware of the risks – of drowning on the high seas, of the boat not turning up, of losing their life's savings. And of what might await them if they got through – months possibly years working for next to nothing on the black market, graduating maybe onto driving minicabs or running a small business. But many still prefer that to the dead-end lives they are caught in.

4

A Tale of Two Checkpoints

While driving down to Sidi Bou Zid, by chance I got the opportunity to experience a little of the police intrusiveness that Mohammed Bouazizi suffered his whole life. I had been in Tunis for a few days and hired a car in case any interesting detours cropped up on the way back down. I was to get more than I had bargained for.

It all started when I picked up a hitcher on the road from Kairawan as the sun was just starting to dip in a cloudless pale winter sky.

Mourad, about my age, was returning home from Tunis, where he had been to plead his case for reinstatement at the state television and radio station. He was not a happy man.

'I'm back in the village where I was born. Every day I have to ask my father for pocket money. It's embarrassing,' he said.

Mourad turned out to be a non-stop bundle of need. There was a long and involved story, which I have to confess I only caught the gist of, about how he had been kept freelance at the station and never given a proper contract, with the dates of particular injustices recited from memory like historic events – 'On November 12, 2003, the station director informed me that my services were no longer needed . . .' Once he knew I was a foreign journalist, he wanted me to go to the TV station and intercede. He rummaged in his battered briefcase, found some papers, and waved them across my line of vision as we sped down the road. I must come and drink tea, stay the night, review his CV, work out an employment strategy, sing him Irish folk songs. He needed me and I was brilliant.

We arrived at a crossroads. I was supposed to turn left to Sidi Bou Zid but Mourad asked me to drop him in his village, down the road straight ahead of us, so we continued on. The paved road ran out and we were on dusty track now. After a mile or two, he caught sight of a minivan rumbling along the road in front of us.

'That's him! That's the man who was supposed to pick me up! I was standing right there and he went straight past me. Go on, catch up with him!' he said.

What better way to get the feel of a place than a brief car chase? I jammed my foot down and settled into the tailwind of the minibus, which was clocking considerable speed up the gentle slopes that led off the central plains into the mountains, towards the Algerian border. We pulled alongside some five miles later and Mourad flagged him down. He got out and went over. For a couple of minutes I could see the driver waving his arms palms out, shoulders pushed back, the global 'that's life' gesture. He was sorry but not very. Then Mourad got back in the car.

'He said he didn't see me. I don't believe him,' he growled and told me to turn round. At this point I thought Mourad must live in one of the two villages behind us and had just wanted to catch the driver to teach him a lesson. But once we had passed through those villages and come all the way back to the main road, it turned out he was taking me to some cafe many miles further down the road, where his idea was we would drink tea – because Tunisians are hospitable people! – before I took him back to his village, further up into the mountains, along the same road that we were now coming down. Confused? Imagine how I felt! The light was fading and I wanted to be at least off the side roads before dark. So, amid much protestation, and promises of future cups of tea, back we went up the track.

I had expected his village to be just beyond where we had caught the minibus. But we kept climbing and climbing, through one, two, three more villages. I kept thinking about the route back. It was turning dark and I turned the headlights on.

We came not so much to a police station as to a police camp, a huge square compound whose perimeter lights we saw from miles away, sitting on the main road, monitoring all traffic further up the valley. But the road was tree-lined, it kept popping in and out of view and I had not quite expected to run into it so soon when I turned the corner, and still had the headlights on full.

It was a fatal breach of checkpoint etiquette. Later, I remembered a Lebanese friend whose father had miraculously recovered from being shot in the head at a checkpoint for a similar mistake during the civil war. You turn the headlights *off* and the lights inside the car *on*, so *they* can see *you*, Wissam said. Doesn't matter if you can't see where you're going.

'Why did you have the lights on full?' the old policeman snarled. Mourad explained I was just a stupid foreigner but he was not assuaged. 'Wait here,' he barked as he took our IDs and disappeared inside the barracks. He was gone for a quarter of an hour. His embarrassed younger, junior colleague tried to make small talk. Meanwhile, we could hear drill in the parade ground, a new cohort barking, their joint voice clanging into the empty, echoey valley. The sign outside read 'School of Keepers of the Peace'.

The older man came out, ordered us out of the car and told me to lay all my bags out on the stony ground and open them.

'What is your name?' I asked him. 'Could you tell me your name, please? In Europe, all policemen have numbers on their shoulders.' He just walked away. I followed him. Mourad became so agitated by this he chest-bumped me to stop me. I realised the only way in and out to the villages was through the check-point and, revolution against police brutality or no revolution, he was shit-scared. I had gone too far and had to back off.

I was beginning to feel I should have paid more attention to the reports of unrest that had come in from other parts of the country at this time, in the first month after Ben Ali fell. A couple of days before I had been sitting in a bloggers' conference in Tunis when Omar Mestiri, a veteran dissident and organiser of the conference, suddenly strode up to the front and grabbed the mike off a speaker to announce, breathless: 'I just wanted you to know that there are ongoing protests in Le Kef, the police are using live ammunition and four people have been shot dead.' The late afternoon conference calm had been shattered as the audience erupted, first standing up, then standing on their chairs chanting the slogans of the revolution again, the speaker at the mike shouting herself hoarse, saying: 'What are we doing here? What are we doing here?'

Nobody knew the cause but several people said the town, close to the Algerian frontier, was still in the grip of the same families and forces that had made an arrangement with the Ben Ali regime. I got the impression there might be many outlying parts of the country, like Sidi Bou Zid itself, where nobody really knew who was in charge. In some places where the army was on the streets, everybody deferred to them. But that was partly because they had positioned themselves as neutral and their promise not to enter politics was believed. So it still left the question of who was in charge, really. Meanwhile, a lot of the people most closely associated with the old regime at local level were still around and had skeletons to hide and scores to settle. A climate of insecurity would suit many, not least senior policemen who might need time or chaos to cover the tracks of whatever.

In that kind of environment, the danger is less that you might be directly targeted, as a foreigner or a journalist, for example, more that you might be detained, attacked or worse as a pretext, or a cover – a play – in some tangled local dispute. It seemed like this kind of unrest was simply an aftershock of the revolution rather than a concerted counter-attack, but it was too early to know for sure.

Another ten minutes passed outside the police training camp and the commander came out, explaining there had been a misunderstanding, that his subordinate had thought I was going to stay the night in the village. I was not sure what difference that made, but by this time was past caring. The elder policeman gripped my hand in a shake and pulled me forward to kiss me on the cheeks. There had been some interaction inside, he was under pressure from his boss now, and he needed to square me.

'We are all brothers,' he said, as he leant in to peck me on the cheek.

'No we're not!' I said, pulling back. 'It doesn't have to be like this, either sharp and rude, or the brother routine. You could try just being civil.'

'Brothers,' he repeated, pulling me in to him again with some force. I could not hold out. We air-kissed. It lent a whole new dimension to the iconography of Arab leadership photo opps, Saddam and Arafat, Hussein and Asad. And I had thought the power handshake of Western politics was complicated enough!

I took back my passport and we got in the car and carried on to Mourad's village – another 5 km beyond the checkpoint. Is this the only way in and out for all the villages, this road? I asked. He said yes. I pondered the implications of that, how you will live your life when every day, to go to work or school, or shopping, you have to stop at two police checkpoints. And they know where you live.

It was pitch-black by the time I returned from Mourad's village and crossed back through the checkpoint – all smiles and waves now. I carried on the bumpy road until I came to the next village but had to pull up sharply. There was a barricade of rocks which had not been there an hour before.

A boy, no more than sixteen, came up. 'Show me your ID card,' he said.

'If you are police or army I will show you my ID card,' I said. I was probing him. It's a fine balance. I'm a firm believer that often the best way to get through situations where nobody knows what the rules are is to pretend that you do, and act authoritatively. On the other hand that can go badly wrong.

It got ugly fast. His friends arrived. Five, six, seven of them crowded round my side of the car. One or two others were on the other side and one of them tried to open the passenger door. It felt like I could be seconds away from something pretty nasty. They were mostly teenagers, but there was an older man with them, early thirties, who leant in through the window. He was so drunk he could not actually articulate, though it was only seven o'clock. He stuck his head through the window, inches away from mine, repeating the same phrase which I couldn't understand.

What happened if they told me to get out of the car? My gut screamed that would be suicide. Could I just plough into reverse and break out of the cordon back to the police camp, which seemed a good deal more appealing now than it had a mere five minutes ago? But there were too many of them to be sure of getting out of the crowd without running someone down. I knew my limits: I couldn't drive through someone as though they weren't there. Whatever the situation and rationale, I just didn't have it in me. And if I clipped someone, even by accident, and then crashed, or didn't make it back to the station, these boys would probably finish me off with rocks or anything else that came to hand. Talking was my relative strength. Find a leader and talk to him. All of this passed through my head faster than you've read this last paragraph. But it still seemed like there was plenty of time. Time slowed down. I wasn't scared. That came later.

Just then, one of the young men in the crowd apologised, explaining the police had empowered them to act as a militia in the neighbourhood because of a spate of recent robberies. He was calm and sober.

An apology. A better nature to appeal to. I zeroed in on him, ignoring the others. I needed to hand my passport to someone to get through this, so I stretched my arm out of the car window, twisting it through a thicket of outstretched hands, swaying like a sea anemone. He looked at it with the screen light of his mobile phone. As he did so, I tested the ground again.

'I appreciate you need to do this. But you should sort your boys out. They shouldn't be drinking,' I said. He nodded without looking up from the passport.

He had shown he wanted respect and recognition for what he saw as real public service. He had also shown leadership. I was acknowledging both, at the same time as trying to estab-lish my own moral authority. I was trying to make him leader. I had no way of knowing if that meshed with their group dynamic, but I needed a leader to deal with, right there and then, that second. Any leader was better than none.

'You know I've come a long way to Tunisia, as a guest,' I said. 'I know you don't want your country to get a bad repu-tation.'

He looked up, handed my passport back, and told some of the other boys to shift the rocks and open the road for me. It took an aching ten seconds for the boys to move their rocks in front of the bumper. As I drove off, I caught his tone, telling them off. It took all my self-discipline not to jam the accelerator down to speed away as fast as I could. And then I was out of it as quickly as I had been in it.

The entire incident took probably a minute.

But for the rest of the trip, another two hours south to Sidi Bou Zid, I was as razzed as I can remember being in a long time, including my years in Afghanistan. A car nosed up behind me. Anxiously, I slowed down, hoping it would pass. When it did, I swung out behind it and for the next fifty miles used it as my checkpoint shield, keeping a steady hundred metres behind it. Close enough to speed up towards it for protection in numbers if, say, there was a problem with another car. But far enough away that if it got into trouble, or was surrounded at a checkpoint, I would have space to turn round and get the hell out of there. I had no idea whether the reasoning was sound, I just needed to take some action to not feel completely at the mercy of events. Somehow a road safety sign saying: 'Why hurry? We'll still be waiting for you' had me laughing till it hurt.

In the space of an hour I had tasted the Arab police state, and anarchy on the streets. It was a sobering experience. I realised that, for all my liberal enthusiasm, if I had to choose between them, I would choose police state. For perhaps the first time, I could not just intellectualise but feel in my bones why the police states had endured so long. An old Arabic proverb says: 'Rather sixty years of tyranny than one day of anarchy.'

Any reasonably analytical view, of course, says different. Not that the proverb is wrong but that it only tells part of the story. The police state promotes itself as the devil you know and somehow, organically, fosters anarchy and extremism as the alternatives to itself. Those kids at the checkpoint were not revolutionaries. If you could attribute any political impulse at all to why they were there, in that state and attitude, it is more likely to be closer to counter-revolution. Why them? Why blind drunk? What 'spate of robberies'?

But when it comes to the crunch, we human beings are not reasonable and analytical. Sitting in pitch-darkness in some village I didn't even know the name of, seconds away from serious trouble, I was down with the police state if it would let me see my family again, keep me alive for another day, or even the next ten minutes.

My experience with the two checkpoints was a short, acute attack of tyranno-anarchitis. Tens of millions of Arab men and women have suffered its chronic form, day in and day out, these last fifty years. I suddenly felt a little more sympathetic to the hedgers and the doubters in the Arab Spring.

5

The Repression Industry

It occurred to me, deep into a day of discussion about torture, with torture victims, in the town of Kairawan, in the centre of Tunisia, that sometimes the most striking things about profound subjects are the trivial, almost casual details. I was there because the week before I had met Hamed, a blogger and activist who studied in Kairawan, at a bloggers' conference in Tunis. Was there anything the blogging community needed help with, I asked his group, always on the lookout for opportunities for action research. Sure, he said. You can help us document torture cases, so we can start to get justice for them. His group, he added, was comfortable blogging the revolution but felt they could do with a hand when it came to assembling and presenting these testimonies so that they were media-friendly.

So here I was down in Kairawan, on my way to Sidi Bou Zid, talking to three young men who had been picked up during the revolution, when protests were spreading nationwide and the security apparatus wanted to find the ringleaders. Abdallah, Ali and Yassin had been taken from a friend's house, where they had been watching the news on Al Jazeera, transported to interior ministry headquarters in Tunis, Torture Central, some 100 miles away, and beaten and tortured for two weeks. In retrospect, they had been saved, magically, by the victory of the revolution. Otherwise, who knows?

I was interviewing them, as gently as possible, one by one. The recordings took place in the local branch of the trade union federation that somebody had an in with, itself a nest of conspiracy in the days after the revolution, with lots of good old-fashioned smoke-filled conference rooms. We were constantly interrupted by people sticking their head round the door, rounds of tea and coffee, and all the normal bustle of a crowded administrative building in the Middle East.

The fact that, weeks later, some of them were only just holding it together, trying to hide the shake in their hands by fiddling with an endless cigarette, embarrassed to pick their teacups off the saucers in case you heard the clatter, was hard enough to see. But the truly disturbing stuff came out as small talk.

There was the doctor all three talked of from their time at Torture Central, who came in between sessions. He was a real doctor all right, white coat and stethoscope and little brown bag, who took their pulses and blood pressures. And then gave the torturers medical advice on whether they could carry on or not, for all the world as though they were examining sports injuries as a match went into extra-time.

There was the badinage of the torturers, often reported by the victims without any particular sense of resentment, as if it were natural conversation. When you were hung, naked, in chains, on a metal bar laid across two tables, it was called *arroti*. 'The spit' is the closest word in English, the image being of a trussed chicken on the roast. To be beaten on the top of the head with two sticks is *darb ad-dabboukeh*, a local percussion instrument like the tabla, the intelligence man an enthusiastic drummer. The torturers not only used code names to avoid being identified, but applied a certain wit to it. You could be strung up naked and beaten by a man named Tito, or electrocuted by another called Camera. If you were particularly uncooperative they would take you out of the standard torture chambers for a special encounter with *Ammar Zabda*, 'Ammar Butter', the department's most accomplished maestro of pain.

But most shocking, because most banal, was Yassin's chance encounter with an old classmate in the interior ministry.

He, Yassin, was in a heap of prisoners collapsed in the middle of a reception area and recovering from their official welcome to Torture Central, an orgy of beating by the plain-clothes policemen standing round them in a ring. They were about to be hauled off one by one for interrogation with whips, chains, electricity, the works.

His friend was a plain-clothes policeman – torturer – who happened to be passing by. They greeted each other warmly – Salaam alaikum, how are you, how is your family. Then the classmate made the mistake of asking what are you doing here. Not by way of provocation, just as part of the normal exchange of greetings. They both knew it was a booboo as soon as he blurted it out. But it fell to Yassin to correct the situation. A comedy of manners so exquisite as to be almost baroque. He might be an innocent victim but his first instinct was not to want to embarrass his torturer friend by spelling out why he was there. He shrugged and gave an awkward smile. You know. Least said . . .

The building was bulging with hundreds of politicals, bussed in from all over the country by central order of the ministry in the previous few hours, enraged that its regional intelligence services had failed to spot the conspiracies obviously being hatched by the usual suspects, they felt, in front of their dumb eyes. They were not as yet fully attuned to the faceless conspiracy that is Facebook. Yassin and his friend shook hands, through the ring of agents guarding the heap of prisoners, all of whom had blood on their faces. The friend went on his way, to what kind of workload we can only imagine. But it is unlikely he went home that day without someone else's blood on his hands.

What all this tells us is that torture in Ben Ali's Tunisia was schooled.

Abdallah al-Souissi is perhaps the strongest of the three I informally deposed. Yassin and Ali were both hesitant. Yassin particularly had shaky hands and squinted because he needed glasses but wouldn't get them. Hamed told me later that one of the group of thirteen had tried to commit suicide after being released, perhaps more of a cry for help than a determined attempt. But Abdallah was tall, well-built, smart and highly articulate. Since graduating a decade ago, he had become active in the provincial branch of the Committee to Defend University Graduates, a growing organisation in Tunisia in recent years as unemployment rose and became more entrenched. He thinks that is why he was on the list of people to be picked up in the interior ministry sweep. He has pronounced leftist views, including the conviction that the USA and Britain had played a key role in maintaining the Ben Ali dictatorship.

'They picked us up at 8.30 p.m. on 9 January. We were at a friend's house watching the news. There were thirteen of us and they must have been tipped off because they hauled us out into at least three police trucks that I saw,' he said.

The group was held overnight in the police station on the edge of Kairawan. There was a lot of brutal beating and name calling but it was less systematic than what was to come. Some of the local plain-clothes political police had identified the targets and they supervised the beatings of the prisoners, who were all herded into one building overnight. I asked Abdallah if he knew their names and where they were now. Yes, he said, Moez and Makram and Waheed. They're still in town and as far as I know still on the force.

The next day, 10 January, they were transported, manacled and blindfolded, to Tunis, Abdallah said, to the main interior ministry building. How do you know that? I asked, intent on reaching maximum clarity for the sake of future justice. They made a mistake with me, he said, they opened the door of the police van and helped me down while we were still in the street. They took off my blindfold, and after a few seconds I realised we were on Habib Bourguiba Avenue, just opposite a cafe I had spent many hours in as a student. Then they bundled me back in the truck, hitting me to cover their mistake.

After their joint 'welcome', the prisoners were then taken off to torture one by one. The rooms were ordinary but for the fact they had no light. Abdallah faced one interrogator and two or three enforcers. For hours they suspended him from an iron bar set between two tables and beat him with a cosh. All the while the interrogator, whose real name, Nabil, he found out when one of his men inadvertently called him it, asked leading questions. Any silence was treated as further provocation. Finally, they stripped him naked and made him stand most of the night in freezing January temperatures before taking him down to a cell in the early hours.

What did they want to know from you? I asked him. 'Anything,' Abdallah replied. 'In the beginning it was rhetorical questions, "Why did you plan the revolution? Who was in it with you?" But that didn't get them very far and by the end they just wanted any information they could get out of you.'

He thinks he slept for four hours before he was woken by another interrogator coming into his cell. He had pulled his file and wanted him to know it, citing where he had studied, who he was friends with, what he had said one Tuesday eight years ago. A quarter of an hour later he was hauled off to another torture chamber – beatings with implements, suspension, 'the usual', as he put it. The doctor came into the chamber four times during all this to examine him: tongue out, look at the swinging pendant, say 'ah', flex your arm for the blood-pressure reading. Each time the doctor told the torturers they could carry on. Abdallah was strong and still had mileage in him.

But he was beginning to lose track of time. Both the torture chambers and his cell had no natural light and his watch had been taken with all his possessions on entry. He was taken for two or three more sessions. The techniques were becoming more diverse, in both torture and interrogation. Major Nabil, clearly a college graduate, would sometimes play nice cop, now, saying he knew Abdallah wasn't really 'one of them'. If he would just sign some papers saying he made some small mistakes, they could let him go. After a few days the beatings became less severe, the interrogations less frequent, the treatment in the cell marginally better.

But that was actually the scariest time. He could hear the rat tat tat of automatic gunfire very close and shouts of 'Allahu Akbar'. He thought the regime had managed to quell the uprising, and was now executing prisoners en masse.

What Abdallah didn't know, because his captors hadn't told him, was the fight was over and his side had won. The change in treatment a few days earlier was because Ben Ali had already fled the country. The gunfire he had heard had betokened first the regime's final hours, as the regular army staged a show-down with Ben Ali's Republican Guard and won, and then cele-bration, as rebels rode shotgun down the main boulevards of the city. All this time he had been held, along with hundreds of others, while his captors tried to figure out what to do with them.

On Monday 17 January, a uniformed policeman came to his cell and took him to a large hall. He was handed back the possessions he had surrendered, nothing missing, and told to sign a declaration not to demonstrate again. Then he was released through a throng of people in the hall and corridors.

It was only when he got to the street that someone told him Ben Ali had gone.

'It was the best moment of my life,' he said.

What did you do? I asked. 'I smoked a cigarette and watched life. Just normal life on the street,' he said, a big smile creasing his face.

He found his colleagues and they travelled back together to Kairawan on the train, arriving late that night. Back home, some of the local policemen involved in picking them up, and in beating them that first night before they were sent to Tunis, have approached them since the fall of the regime. In cafes where they sat drinking coffee, or calling them anonymously on their mobile phones, using that peculiar mixture of instant camaraderie and self-pity common to the bully revealed. Come on, man, we were just doing our jobs, we had to do it you know, and anyway it wasn't me it was Moez, Makram, Waheed – each of them incriminating the other. There may be honour among thieves but not among torturers. Be reasonable. *Illi faat maat* – what's gone is gone, no? No point dwelling on the past.

At the point he told me his story, nearly a month later, no action had been taken. To be fair it's not as though the transitional government had nothing else to do and the new interior minister, Farhat Rajhi, had a healthy reputation as an independent-minded judge who had tried to resist the incursions of the Ben Ali regime into the sovereignty of law. But Abdallah, Ali and Yassin are faced with the bizarre situation where the men who beat and tortured them are still on the streets, maybe still working, unpunished, and know where they live and their mobile phone numbers. Abdallah is also sure he could recognise Major Nabil from Tunis if he saw him. His torturers felt enough impunity to not wear masks. But it's far from clear that justice will be done.

With each of the three – Abdallah, Ali and Yassin – I interviewed them twice. Once at the trade union branch, on audio for something like ninety minutes each, with all the meanderings and the missing time sequences, and the details that didn't quite add up. And then a second time on camera for ten to fifteen minutes, once the story was straight and we'd rehearsed the order of questions that would come, in the back room of an Internet cafe. We put the videos up on YouTube.

It was actually the day Mubarak left power in Egypt. Hamed and I were itching to be there, but nobody else in the small Internet cafe seemed much bothered. A young man at the entry sat playing a video by local rapper Psyco M streamed on a Facebook page. Three headscarved, teenaged girls huddled over Skype video-conferencing options on the screen in front of them.

It was turning dark and lights were beginning to come on in the concrete monstrosity apartment blocks opposite. Hamed pointed out the blocks that were police perks, row upon row of entry-level box flats. Perhaps some of the men who had tortured our friends lived in them. Perhaps they were watching the collapse of the Egyptian regime on Al Jazeera just like us, wondering what on earth had happened to their world.

Ali and Yassin's stories had enough commonalities with Abdallah's to begin to sketch out the general elements of how the repression industry worked. The same sequence from the 'warm welcome' in the reception area to the solitary interrogations. The first torture session the longest, sleep deprivation in the cells, the good-cop bad-cop routine, the smart interrogator and stupid muscle, the doctor, the 'chicken' suspension between two desks, the stripped naked and cold water routine, the sleep on the floor in your own filth technique. Naturally there were some minor differences. But they were minor. Generally, it seemed the cogs moved fairly standardly in the machine.

But I was still mesmerised by Yassin's chance encounter with his old classmate at Torture Central. Just how much of a coincidence was it? I wondered. The night before, I had been prompted by some coverage on Al Jazeera to scribble down some very rough calculations of the political economy of the police state.

In Egypt the security state employed something like 1.7 million people, all in all, armed forces, regular police, traffic police, general security, state intelligence, uniformed and plain-clothes informers, and *baltagiya*, officially sanctioned thugs called in as the occasion required, in networks that tentacled down to neighbourhood, if not street level. They were nearly all men. Of the 82 million population, there were somewhere between 20 and 25 million men of workforce age. That made for roughly one in every fifteen Egyptian men of working age working for, or with the security state. Multiply that out by five or six for the families and there were something close to 10 million people with a direct material interest in the continuity of the regime. That would help explain some genuine, if painfully small, demonstrations in favour of Mohammed Hosni Mubarak that we were seeing in those last dying days of the Egyptian regime.

In Tunisia the numbers were strikingly similar, proportionally. Some 165,000 men worked full-time or part-time with the security apparatus out of a male workforce of perhaps 3 million. That made for roughly one in every sixteen men of working age. This compares with roughly one in thirty-five in each of Britain and the United States.

Hamed and I were at lunch with Yassin after we'd finished

the interview, eating a tuna piquante omelette that was much better than I had feared. How many boys were in your class at high school? I asked him.

He surprised me by saying thirty-five, about the same as in the grammar school I had gone to in England. But then middle-income Tunisia is not imploded Egypt, where classes of forty or fifty are crammed into classrooms with barely enough space to put chairs for them all, despite the fact that the schools still have to work in two sessions to accommodate all the pupils, and your kids will probably never even get to decent literacy unless you somehow find the money to pay their state school-teachers, on the sly naturally, for private lessons.

'So apart from the friend you saw in the interior ministry, how many of them later went into the security services?' I asked.

'Most of them!' he replied with a sweeping gesture of the arm. Hamed's wry smile next to him implied this could be poetic licence.

'And how many in your class, Hamed?' I asked.

'Oh not so many,' he replied. 'But then I come from Monastir, on the coast. It may be only a forty-minute drive from here but it's a different world. More people go to college, there are more jobs. It's more like the Mediterranean. Actually, what am I talking about? It *is* the Mediterranean.'

He had a point. Hamed was one of a group of bloggers who had been instrumental in spreading word of the growing protests, helping them to grow some more. He was also an archaeology student involved in a project for the virtual recon-struction of multi-storeyed houses in Pompeii. We had spent the previous evening discussing the difficulties of ancient Greek epigraphy, since they used too many acronyms and neglected punctuation, comparing the first line of the *Iliad* as found on the Perseus classical collection website with how it would have been in the original manuscript. His conversation divided its time between Arabic and French, with occasional forays into English and the odd flourish in Spanish, from some cherished time spent in Barcelona.

Whereas Yassin came from Kairawan. Although it is one of the earliest seats of Islamic civilisation, with a seventh-century mosque and a medieval walled town, now pedestrianised and on UNESCO's roster of World Heritage sites, Kairawan today is an inland town in a developing country, holding little in common with the Mediterranean feel of Tunis and the coastal towns. Tunisia's interior is famously less developed than the coast.

Like Clydeside in the UK or Chicago South Side in the USA, there are a lot fewer options than national averages suggest. An ambience of deprivation, marginalisation and torn social fabric means more people go to prison. And more people go into the army, or some other wing of the police state.

The '*zéro huits*' of the Tunisian interior, as the Tunis bourgeoisie once called them, proving that social classification by telephone code is not unique to class-ridden Britain, have disproportionately supplied the rank and file of the security apparatus. General Ali Siriati, the head of the presidential guard, who instantly entered folklore when he placed snipers on the roof of the presidential palace and frogmarched Ben Ali to a waiting helicopter with a gun to his head, is from this part of the country. The head of the traffic police nationwide, apparently an enormously influential position, is from Sidi Bou Zid.

So the national average of one in sixteen could easily be doubled in the region of Kairawan. And doubled again in Yassin's school, depending on the precise neighbourhood and degree of relative privilege or deprivation. The high-school class he graduated in could feasibly have had four, five, or six boys who became security men, the 'sons of Ben Ali', while he became a student organiser and oppositionist. But they all lived in the same town and would see each other on the streets.

I tried to imagine what that was like.

When I was a teenager, the hardest boy in the whole school was Fint Krieven, a couple of years older than me. He was fighting Irish, flaming curly red hair, not particularly tall but broad sloping shoulders and a kind of fizz about his eye and step that made you stay out of his way.

Fint was not a bully but he had a temper on him and knew how to step up to a fight. I was once on the top deck of the bus on the way to school when six boys from the secondary modern school across the road cornered him in the back seat. He conceded nothing, stared them down and when the blows started just threw himself forward and gave it all he had. Just before he was overwhelmed he bolted, diving headlong rather than stepping down the winding staircase and jumping straight out of the open door at full speed. I just had time to see him tumble over, pick himself off and dust himself down before the bus turned a corner. When I saw him in the playground at morning break, he winked at me, with just the flicker of a smile.

Fint Krieven left school at sixteen, but I will never forget the last time I saw him. It was a couple of years later and I was out in Bromley town square at about ten o'clock on a Friday night, walking past the new McDonald's, where the exciting rumour had it they had to install blue lights in the toilets to stop people shooting up. There was a commotion. A couple of policemen were grappling with a couple of lads my age. As I walked past I saw that one of them was Fint. He appeared to be holding one of the suspects off the ground with a single arm and threatening to hit him with the other.

I hasten to say – in case he reads this book! – I have no particular reason to think that Fint Krieven has ever done anything wrong. It's about the numbers. St Mary's Grammar School Sidcup may well have supplied a few more policemen. But nobody from my class, and not anybody that I was aware of from my whole year.

If I try to understand what it has been like for Yassin and Abdallah and Ali to live in the Arab national security state these past fifty years, I try to imagine five boys from my class, and Fint's class, and every other class in St Mary's Grammar School Sidcup joining the police or the army, or the secret police, or just being informers.

Who would they have been? Paul Legett, because he was just so physically imposing? Peter Todd, because he was class boss for a while? Paul Draper because he liked being officious? Not me, of course. I am too bookish and argumentative, as anyone will tell you. Not Simon Elvin or Quentin Darcy, whose backgrounds were too refined. John Sweeney? Mark Ostrowski? Andrew Preece as a chief constable one day because he was both smart and practical and disciplined?

And then we need to try and imagine a different kind of police. One in which thuggery is encouraged, obedience must be blind, and Daddy is always on the wall. Because – with the spectacular exception of Libya, which we will come to – it is Daddy not Big Brother, this iconography that has pervaded the Middle East for the last generation, the endless posters of Mubarak and Ben Ali and Saddam and Asad and the kings Abdullah.

In a way George Orwell did us a disservice with *Nineteen Eighty-Four*, fixing our meme of a police state so well that it endures to this day, past its time. In the novel, there is a veneer of egalitarianism because Oceania is a modern industrial state, fully mobilised, which not long ago went through an ideologically driven revolution. Citizen Smith, Citizen O'Brien. Orwell perfectly captured the Soviet Union, the looming totalitarianism of 1948, when he wrote it. Stalin as Big Brother.

But the ideology of the Arab national security state, if it ever was tight, became flabbier and flabbier as time went on.

Perhaps it is because we were used to thinking of police states as having some purpose, some ideological integrity if you like, that we in the West were very slow to grasp what was so obvious to the people who live there. Egypt and Tunisia were police states, even if you could go on holiday there and sunbathe and windsurf and drink espresso and eat at Thank God It's Fridays and get on the Internet and the locals wore jeans claiming to be the same global brands, and Manchester United team shirts, and fiddled with their mobile phones just like we do. Dimly perceived through the membrane of tourist resorts, hire cars and luxury apartments, the bumbling, badly-dressed, often barely literate police seemed like Keystone Kops. If you were an ordinary Tunisian or Egyptian they were a lot more sinister than that. Because, with five boys each class, it's a lot more intimate.

So take these five toughest boys. Remove them at an early and impressionable age from any real learning environment. Put them in a world where they learn, at the outset of their careers, how to serve Daddy and the Homeland but progress on to how to get what's theirs. Because at the end it was mostly about 'the cake'. Then let them loose on the rest of the class as police, judge, jury and prosecution all in one, full of contempt if you, for whatever reason, ended up poor, or spite and envy if you were smarter than them but didn't translate that into pecking order. That's what it might be like to be Yassin.

But with the special twist, if you were Yassin or Abdallah or anyone else who had gone to the street, that they hated you personally – for your disloyalty to Big Daddy.

Because it's just too flat to dismiss ideology in a police state, even in a failed one like Tunisia, as mere conscious hypocrisy. Maybe the more enduring contribution of *Nineteen Eighty-Four* is doublethink, to portray how passionately human beings can be made to believe something they simultaneously know not to be true. That is what O'Brien shows Winston Smith when he teaches him to believe that two and two are five. If interest and ideology were no longer fused, as they had been in the tight autocracies of communism and perhaps early-stage Arab nationalism, they remained inextricably intertwined. And at the end, when earlier dreams of social and economic progress had withered to become mocking memories, the last fragment of anything left to believe in was simply veneration of *ar-Rayyes*, the President.

'Why do you hate the President?' Major Nabil asked Abdallah again and again, in his darkened chamber off Habib Bourguiba Avenue, often enraged, occasionally genuinely mystified. 'We are all the sons of Ben Ali. We will always defend him.'

As he relayed this conversation to me, Abdallah just shook his head slowly from side to side. Under torture he had answered these questions again and again, he told me, with whatever sequence of words he thought most likely to postpone his next beating. But now he was free, it seemed he could answer how he really liked. Which was to say nothing at all.

6

'The Language of Lies and Talking Down'

I drove back up to Tunis without incident, but with a fresh appreciation for just how more comfortable life was in the capital. Habib Bourguiba Avenue was a non-stop fashion parade for young men and women, beer freely served on the terraces, lit as the evening set in by ornate wrought-iron lamp posts and with its Italianate facades kept a fresh white apart from cute blue window frames. Long rows of neatly groomed shop windows ran down its avenues, banks and designers and bookshops. Tunis was a city apparently at ease with its identity, far from the dust and drabness of the towns of the interior, *zéro huit* territory. That identity had been formed in stages.

First it was a classic *madina*, a traditional Islamic city that oscillated for centuries between local rule and integration into the Ottoman Empire, then a European *ville*, peopled by communities from all over the Mediterranean as it fell under French colonial rule in the nineteenth century. Finally, in 1956, it became an Arab capital, one of a score that popped up in the era of Third World independence.

The city expanded physically at each new stage in its evolution, the Europeanised present-day centre of the city, focused on Habib Bourguiba Avenue, formerly known as Jules Ferry, engulfing the casbah during the nineteenth century, around Parc Du Belvédère, and, after independence, large public housing projects that resembled the French *cités* on the western periphery – Hay at-Tadhamen, Le Kram, Wifaq and Borj Shakir. Each new stage was also accompanied by a cultural and linguistic shift, French under the protectorate moving to classical Arabic with independence. Almost as if different gauges of language overlaid different parts of the city and the social segments they were identified with, in modern times, French for the city as it once was, within its European confines, and Arabic for the city as it is now, with its sprawling suburbs.

This makes Imad Ktata, manager of Shams FM in Tunis, a man with an unusual mission.

'I want to remove all *fusha*, classical Arabic, from this radio station. I don't want to hear a single word of it,' he said as we sat in the hospitality suite of the station, all orange sofas and big screens.

Shams, started by Ben Ali's daughter, was one of two private stations to get licences under the old regime as music-driven entertainment FM stations. Over the previous weeks, they had developed a news operation as the revolution unfolded, discarding the terms of their licence, which had banned them from broadcasting anything related to current affairs. Now they were trying to find their place in the country's newly freed, and soon to be crowded, media space. I was there to assess their needs as part of a report I was preparing for Internews, the media development NGO I had worked for in Afghanistan and then later run the European branch of out of Paris, to see if there was anything technical assistance could bring now to the task of helping Tunisia's media play their role in the democratic transition.

'I don't just mean they write their scripts in classical Arabic and then we translate them into dialect by swapping in words here and there. I want people to write their scripts as they talk, naturally, in Tunisian dialect. That's not what they learn right now in college. We need to teach them from the beginning,' he said.

It's hard to exaggerate the significance of this. In many societies, a radio station's new language policy might figure as an interesting development in the perpetual and irresolvable conflict between high and popular culture, debated by scholars and shock jocks accusing each other of elitism and dumbing down. But in Tunisia and most of the contemporary Arab world it's a seismic shift. And it's all the more subversive for being merely incidental to Imad's main purpose. He didn't set out to be shocking. He just wants to serve his listeners without preaching to them.

Language is at the heart of most cultures, but the relationship may be unique, and uniquely intense, in Arabic. To abandon classical Arabic as a formal policy, not just to quietly reduce or supersede it but to ban it from the airwaves, is nothing short of cultural revolution.

It's not as though popular culture has just arrived in the Arab world. It's been around for as long as mass media, and folk culture for centuries before it. And some, including myself, believe the explosion of Arabic popular culture, through satellite TV and the Internet, has been the single most important change in the region in the last twenty years, dwarfing mere events such as wars, peace talks, terror campaigns and regime change. Not only was there more popular culture but more of it was produced in the Arab world, which now had its own music channels and talk TV. Some of the most popular foreign programmes were Turkish soap operas whose themes, set against modern urban life in a Muslim society, struck a chord with viewers. Without a shot being fired, it ended the autocracies' ability to impose a monopoly on thought and brought the beginning of the end of such legitimacy as they had been able to fashion. The rest was just a matter of time.

But what Imad Ktata's policy means is that popular culture no longer knows its subservient place. Shams FM won't run chatty DJs in between songs and then revert to 'correct' news bulletins at the top of the hour. Quite the opposite. He is trying to make the news 'go Tunisian' so that the bulletin itself blends into the thousands of conversations in taxis and workplaces that he hopes it sparks each hour and the phone-ins that might precede or come after it. In this new world, classical Arabic persists, but it is optional and no longer authoritative. And in market terms, if Imad has his way, it will become niche.

Shams FM is not an isolated occurrence. What kind of Arabic you speak has become a direct political issue in Tunisia, and to a lesser extent in Egypt.

In the month of protests that ended his rule, Ben Ali gave four addresses in an unprecedented bid to show that he understood the importance of public communications. The first three were in standard paternalistic autocrat. I speak to you now at a difficult time. We can't say that Tunisia's perfect of course, but don't worry, we're going to fix those few things we haven't already fixed after we restore order and crush the drug-crazed foreign hands who are using these slight concerns, which in any case we were on top of, as pretexts to undermine everything we have achieved together. Just as important, all three were delivered in lugubrious, cumbersome classical Arabic, Ben Ali's glasses perched on the end of his nose, apparently still struggling with the autocue after all these years.

His last throw of the dice, delivered on 13 January, was more conciliatory. But if he now understood the fix he was in, the way he chose to try and get out of it was disastrous. For the first time since he came to power twenty-three years before, he went man of the people and used Tunisian dialect for a public occasion. It was striking, coming from him, but had the opposite effect to the one intended. He couldn't carry it. It made him look insincere, and therefore weak and opportunist. He had never been loved. Now he would no longer be feared.

'I got you. I got you,' he repeated, almost like a nervous tick. 'I got all of you. The unemployed and the poor, the politically active and those who want more freedom. I got you.'

A rap song hit YouTube the next day with the title: 'No you didn't get us'. It was an instant hit. But by that time Ben Ali was on a plane to Jeddah.

The first foreign minister in the transitional government, Ahmed Ounaies, lasted two weeks before his first major news conference, in Paris with his French counterpart Michèle Alliot-Marie, brought him down. He made two mistakes. The first was to fawn on Alliot-Marie instead of roasting her for her connections to businessmen close to the Ben Ali regime. This was already a scandal in France, and one that was to bring her down shortly after, and yet the man representing the new Tunisia could only say he had always dreamt of meeting her. The second was to speak in classical Arabic in a way that adumbrated, expounded, vaticinated, opined and prognosticated instead of just telling it like it is, that was inebriated with the exuberance of its own verbosity, prolixity, oratorical legerdemain, and long-windedness.

Many Tunisians watching live on TV were embarrassed. A Facebook page calling for his resignation which opened within a few minutes of the start of the press conference had garnered 9,000 likes by the time it ended an hour later. The next day 300 workers in the foreign ministry, not normally the most restive of folk, staged a sit-in demanding his resignation, and a week later he was gone, having never fully resumed his duties after the fatal gaffe.

Meanwhile, the first TV appearance of the new interior minister, Farhat Rajhi, was a raging success. As with Ounaies, his gauge of language wasn't the only determinant. He was direct, self-effacing, something that was bound to knock the socks off many Tunisians, and on top of his brief. But as with Ounaies, language was a big part of the overall package. Rajhi answered in the same gauge he was being questioned in, Tunisian dialect.

'I swear to you, if he'd spoken *fusha* we'd have been down into the streets again demanding his resignation,' said Ayman, a medical student in Tunis. Why, I asked, what is it with *fusha*, classical Arabic? '*Fusha* is so far from the people,' he replied. 'It is the language of lies and talking down.'

Ayman himself is completely fluent in *fusha*. He had just

spent half an hour singing beautiful classical *mawals* in it, haunting dirges of doomed love between Laila and Qays, two mythical figures, explaining that he had developed his singing talent from Qur'anic recitation which he had been taught as a boy.

So what is it that can connote so powerfully about using one scale of language rather than another, powerfully enough to make or break a political career? And how could it become a defining issue in the Arab Spring?

The Englishman in me suggests that the first thing to say is that the difference between *fusha* and the various Arabic dialects is not one of accent.

There are certainly undertones of social class. It is unlikely, for example, that many people in Gara Benour, the village where Mohammed Bouazizi was born, are comfortable in *fusha*, and a safe bet that you would find a considerably higher proportion in Carthage, the affluent seaside resort next to Tunis.

But that is because *fusha* requires good education, and access to that is not any more equally spread across society in the Arab world than anywhere else. It's not a particular class accent. Nobody, apart from a few eccentrics perhaps, speaks it at the breakfast table. You can't predict for someone's social class or even name by hearing them speak *fusha* in the same way as you can with different accents in English – Ranulph or Chuck being more likely with given patterns of diction, say, than Darren and Dwayne. The tens of millions of Arabs who speak and write *fusha* fluently do so in addition to, not instead of, their mother dialects. In that sense, *fusha* belongs to everyone and no one in equal measure and is more like a life skill or technology embedded in language. That is one reason why it was at the heart of ambitious education programmes at the start of the independence era across the Arab world which were going to expand massively the social mobility already achieved by a few – notably the leaderships of the newly independent countries, men from modest backgrounds who succeeded through education, largely in *fusha*.

Those education programmes failed. But the elites of the newly independent states refused to acknowledge that any more than the other failures of the Arab nationalist project. And so the divide between *fusha* and the various dialects of Arabic became entrenched as one of social exclusion, ironically, since the cherished place of *fusha* in political culture rested on egalitarian notions. The theory had been that public life should be in *fusha*, since it was the language commonly available to everyone.

In fact, my first contact with Tunisia had been through learning *fusha* at the Habib Bourguiba Languages School in the summer of 1986. The school was subsidised in order to promote the Tunisian government and we spent six happy weeks in the dorms of Tunis University grinding through its demanding grammar. Classes were taught by immersion for four hours a day, so you either spoke classical Arabic or went silent.

Revivalist Islam, the other main political project of the modern age in the Arab world, was *fusha*'s other major sponsor. Fundamentalists bolstered the Arabic literacy of untold thousands with private classes in mosques and madrasas, religious schools, not as some abstract goal of political identity, but to increase access to the Qur'an. In Islam it is the Qur'an that is

God's major injection of perfection direct into the course of Man, not the Prophet Muhammad. It is the Qur'an that more nearly resembles the role played by Jesus in Christianity, not Muhammad, whom Muslims avow to be mortal like all men, not divine, as Christians claim of Christ. The Qur'an not only defines the standard of classical Arabic to this day. It is referenced by God within the text as being essentially Arabic: 'We have sent down a clear, Arabic Qur'an to you.'

The white-hot faith of the Prophet and his Companions created a vast empire in the historical blink of an eye, just two generations, and then cooled into the Golden Age of Islam, the Abbasids in Baghdad, the Umayyads in Spain, the mathematicians and astronomers and philosophers all over. During these centuries classical Arabic developed a further role. It became the standard bearer for Arab and Islamic heritage and science, and a mark of civilisation. Just as the Greeks before them had referred to all non-Greek speakers as 'bar-bar speakers', or 'barbarians', so Arabs of the Golden Age referred to the non-Arabic-speaking peoples around them – Persians, Kurds, Berbers, Turks – literally as *ajaam*, 'dumb' or 'speechless'. It was not a question of faith. The *ajaam* were Muslims like the Arabs, in contrast to infidel Franks or animist Africans. They just could not articulate in the language of God, or be party to any of the growing achievements of Arab civilisation.

There are two small riders to add to this picture. The first is that many Arabists might baulk at the rendering of *fusha* as 'classical Arabic'. The more common term is 'modern standard Arabic'. But the term 'classical', as well as being less of a mouthful, emphasises continuity across time, which is the more striking feature of Arabic from a European perspective than the present-day continuity across the space of the Arab world's twenty nation states. If you know 'modern' standard Arabic you can not only read today's *al-Hayat*, or follow a chat show on Al Jazeera. You can get the gist of Ibn Batuta or Ibn Khaldun, writing in the fourteenth century, and even make a stab at al-Ghazali, writing in the eleventh. In English, that's closer to *Beowulf* than to Chaucer, and contemporaneous in French with the *Chanson de Roland*, nearly 500 years before Corneille and Racine.

It is true that *fusha* will not give you access to Qur'anic Arabic without at least a crib. But reading the Qur'an in the original you nevertheless recognise the justice of the claim that it is the quintessential Arabic text, that Qur'anic Arabic infuses *fusha*, which in turn acts as a chain of transmission for it into the modern world.

That's not just at the level of articulated thought and *idées reçues*, though an apposite quotation from the Qur'an or other sacred texts will still carry many an argument, among the secular as well as the religious, much as a debater who knew his Bible could hold sway in Europe well into the twentieth century. It's in the very construction of the language, the system of triliteral verb roots and their hundreds of derivations captured in the Qur'an and still the way you learn *fusha* today. *Fusha* feels like Qur'an Lite, or conversely, Qur'anic Arabic, once you have penetrated at least its outer perimeter, feels like *fusha* through a magnifying glass, the same language as today's newspaper but its detail crisper and its presence larger than life.

The second rider is that *fusha* and the Arabic dialects have never been discrete entities without overlap and permeation. Tutting schoolmasters often tell you otherwise, but this is a traditionalist rather than historically rooted view, just as indignant letter writers to the *Daily Telegraph* might lament the decline of spelling as a sign of the decadence of English as a whole, unaware that orthography was all but invented by Dr Johnson with his dictionary in the eighteenth century and that such pillars of the English canon as Shakespeare and Marlowe paid it no heed. Many of the most common verbs used in Arabic dialects instead of *fusha* are themselves perfectly correct *fusha*. They have come to be identified as dialect by usage rather than any scientific rule. One of the most famous works of Arabic literature internationally, the *Thousand and One Nights*, is a collection of folk tales told in vernacular which over the course of time was worked into literary form, much as Homer fashioned the literary epics of the *Iliad* and *Odyssey* out of the work of bards that went before him.

In the modern age, the great convener of the different gauges of Arabic has been satellite TV. If you flip between MBC, Arabiya, Al Jazeera or any of the other talk channels, especially late at night, you are likely to hear conversations that can't be neatly categorised as either *fusha* or dialect. Speakers will use *fusha* constructions but with regional dialect pronunciations and suffixes. This is largely due to the role of these stations in hosting and appealing to the Arab world's different subregions. Doctorates have been written on the role of the new channels in reviving pan-Arabism, given last rites in its first emanation after the Arabs' crushing defeat in the Six Day War of 1967. Modern media and Islam may yet combine to provide enough gravity to prevent centrifugal dialects of Arabic breaking into separate languages, as the Romance languages did from Latin in the Middle Ages, despite the then commanding power of the See of Rome.

But the bottom line is that *fusha* has been intrinsic to most attempts to project authority in all areas of public life: politics, religion, culture and science. That would make it authoritative if you agree with the underlying value sets of Arab nationalism or political Islam. And authoritarian if you don't.

Imad Ktata and Shams FM clearly don't.

'When we first put out the news in dialect we got hundreds of complaints,' he said. 'People think of the news bulletin as something sacred. But why should the ordinary person have to strain to understand the news?' For him it goes with an editorial view of news selection which is also dramatically populist by the norms of Arab media.

'I'm not interested in bombs in Iraq. I'd rather cover a blocked drain in any part of this city, even if it only affected 100 people, than Iraq or the Middle East peace process. We need to become a media of proximity.' News you can use, in other words. Shock jocks can't be far behind.

Across town, the satellite station Nessma TV is language-planning to capture the 70 million people of the Maghreb – Tunisia, Algeria and Morocco. At some expense, they hired experts to work through the dialects of Tunisia, Algeria and Morocco and created a lexicon of 600 words common to all, which presenters and news writers are using to create programming.

'We're not Middle Eastern,' said Moez Sinaoui, the marketing director. 'More southern Mediterranean. Using this new shared language we can create the Maghreb as a unified media market. The Gulf channels mean little to nothing here.'

Even Arabs often dispute which dialects are mutually intelligible, unlike *fusha*, which is common to all. My own experience has been that region is only one part of an equation that would determine whether any two Arabic speakers could understand each other, the more significant other part being degree of education. You can understand a college graduate from anywhere and a high-school graduate from most places and they can understand each other. Except Morocco, where they just don't believe in vowels and make do with as few of them as possible. It's trickier when it gets to nomads, peasant farmers or artisans and the urban underclass.

What Nessma is cleverly trying to do is to find a sweet spot, concentrating on dialect to address people in 'sit back' mode, but forging their own style which then maximises how many people one channel can reach in this way. 'And don't forget the fifteen million Maghrebis in Europe,' Sinaoui said. 'There is no media that is naturally theirs.'

Two outlets, two very different language policies. The stranglehold of *fusha* on media and public life is now broken – officially. But one model will be replaced not by another one, but by another many. That's why it's a cultural revolution.

The politics of the revolutions in Tunisia and Egypt have been about breaking a culture of supposed consensus that has been constructed through coercion, with no room for difference. We all love Ben Ali, we all hate Ben Ali. We don't need elections because everyone agrees, or conversely, let's have elections as a show of unity. This is an approach that extended also to opposition movements. 'Everyone' knows the ruler is corrupt, or a Mossad agent, or an infidel.

What we now begin to see is the cultural corollary to this.

Among the many voices is English, now the international language not just of computers and business but of protest. Blogger Youssef Gaigi wrote of how, the day before Ben Ali fled, he toured the working-class district of Hay Ettedhamen. One of the graffiti on the walls read A.C.A.B. – All Cops Are Bastards, an old prison knuckle tattoo and the title of a song by the London punk band the 4 Skins. Demonstrators rejoicing in the streets of Tunis held up placards saying 'Game Over'. That same week, NPR journalist Andy Carvin reported deciding to start a non-stop alert stream on the Arab Spring after one Tunisian activist twittered: 'OK, Arab world, tag you're it.' International English has always served as a language of aspiration. In Tunisia and elsewhere those aspirations are no longer clustered around the private ideal of elite education and a banner poster ad style life of beautiful people in designer brands and Ray-Ban sunglasses in their sports cars or yachts. They now include rights at home and full membership of the global community. I don't think I've ever heard so much Bob Marley all at once as in the cars and rooms of young Tunisians in the Arab Spring.

And French, rescued from its pompous, long-lunch, pale-skinned past in North Africa by vital new strains.

Lina ben Mhenni became something of a poster girl blogger for the Tunisian revolution, partly because she was outstand-ingly brave and effective in posting news about the protests as they hit Tunis, winning a game of cat and mouse in an online war with the Ben Ali regime, and partly because she just looks it. A wisp of a young woman with a nose ring, she gives the impression of being both shy and, at times, quietly angry at the state of the world. She could be a real-world incarnation of Lisbeth Salander. She was part of the same group of bloggers as Hamed, who had led me to the torture testimonies in Kairawan, and when I met her was busy trying to help the families of some of those killed to build their legal cases.

Lina studied English at university and speaks it well. But in her blog, A Tunisian Girl, she naturally expresses herself more in Arabic and French. One of the French entries is something called the Chkoupiste manifesto, reproduced in full from a novel called *The Archaeology of Lovers' Chaos* published in 2010 by a young Algerian journalist, Mustafa Ben Fodil. The manifesto declares itself to be 'anartist', committed to engaging art in revolution.

To quote selectively: 'The natural place of the intellectual is in opposition . . . the natural place of the anartist is in hiding . . . We must install a revolutionary atmosphere in the country . . . The real battle is in the street . . . The street is the urban maquis, the field of contestation for all . . . We must take back history. We need cultural guerrillas. We must take territory aesthetically. We must occupy the town topographically, visually. We must reactivate communism. Revive Islamism. Free Carlos and Mumia Abu Jamal.

'We must abolish television. Free sound, free the image, break their studios and transmitters, liberate the airwaves. We must assassinate their frequencies. We must create a network of free radios, a literary battlefield on the Internet, multiply subversive blogs. Bloggers of the world unite!

'We should tag every wall in the town, explode everywhere. Our works should flow like liquid into public spaces, irrigating, submerging, inundating. We must celebrate the people, free the energy of the unemployed, the marginals, the losers.

'Derrida made deconstruction a manner of reading. We make it a method of combat. We must undo our governments and dissolve our institutions ... We must destroy the official Discourse and build in its place a Tower of Babel that disturbs and confuses. And once we have done this, we must kill our own language before it becomes wooden, then petrified, then an official language, then a dead language, then fossilised thought.'

My first reaction, after I'd recovered from the seduction, was how Paris 1968. My second, when I came back to it a few weeks later, was, my God, how Paris 1968! This is what actually happened in Tunisia in the first few weeks of 2011. Tunisia and Egypt both lived *événements* that triumphed, as though De Gaulle had resigned to seclusion in Colombey and Danny Le Rouge became French Minister of Love instead of a German Green MEP. That's why it's intoxicating to be among these people. The Tunisian revolutionaries, from Anis al-Shoaibi in Sidi Bou Zid, to Abdallah al-Souissi in Kairawan, to Lina ben Mhenni in Tunis, had beaten overwhelming projections of force by courage, total moral superiority, and dancing wit. They were also all under thirty. Student politics, in our silvering societies, have become a byword for Monty Pythonesque angels-on-pinheads rows, late-night schisms in the bar. But in Tunisia that kind of idealism and verve brought down the dictator where decades of more 'grown up' opposition had failed.

The smart English twitters and slogans and eloquent French blogs are minority voices, of course. But so, quantitatively, is *fusha*, or classical Arabic. In a new era of cultural as well as political pluralism, a voice no longer needs to represent some notional quorum of society. These are all now subcultures, to clash, coexist and subsume. Some of them exert influence on society way beyond their numbers, as the blogosphere consistently has. But the larger point is that they also all mingle freely with *sha'abi*, street influences, to recombine and reproduce. We are into complex systems here, where emergent trends can come from nowhere. Memes propagate virally. So sure, there are subcultures that you can safely define as minority elite, and elitist. But that no longer means, as it once did, that they are out of touch with the mainstream. Because there's no such thing as out of touch any more. All the emerging subcultures of the Middle East connect to each other at some level, whether in alignment, dissonance, studied indifference or something else. There still is a mainstream, of course, but it has become super-porous. An idea, or image, or sound bite can hit it from anywhere and go viral.

With more tools, gauges and discourses, with more nuance and contestation building a culture that is exponentially richer, Tunisia could be freer to simply be itself. Which is the point of most revolutions, after all.

Soufiane Ben Farhat is a phenomenon. A reporter in his fifties, he became a national celebrity when he resigned from his TV station over its coverage of police brutality against demonstrators. In the two hours that we sat with him in a boulevard cafe, three groups of young people came up to shake his hand. Now he's trying to put together investors for a new media group including TV, radio and freebie newspaper. He talks non-stop about the revolution, his novels, Facebook, and the unique identity of the Tunisians.

'We don't need anyone to tell us what it is to be Arab, what it is to be Muslim. I don't want my daughter to marry someone who will make her wear a veil. If she wants to, that's another matter,' he said. 'Tunisians are quite capable of fasting all day during Ramadan – and we do fast, nearly all of us – and then breaking the fast with a good bottle of red wine.'

This accorded with my own experience. Spend enough time in cafes and you see women smoking, men wearing jasmine, or, once, a sprig of rosemary behind the ear. A demonstration organiser steps up to the mike to recite a long screed of poetry which is greeted with rapture. Tea is traditionally served with pine nuts and almonds. Tunisia is a country where women are not afraid to be sophisticated, nor men to be aesthetes.

'I'm not happy with this government,' Soufiane declared, of the transitional arrangement. 'Why don't they want us to celebrate? It seems like they want everything to return to normal. But this is a revolution! It is up to us to create a new normal!'

Perhaps the subculture that most came into its own during the revolution is rap. Tunisian rap. Thousands of young men and women went into the streets against ranks of police with riot shields and batons pumped up by stars such as El General, Dali DJ, Psyco M and Balti.

7

You Didn't Get Us

I was in a cafe eating lunch in Kairawan, two weeks after Ben Ali had fled, when I heard his voice blaring through a loud-speaker onto a crowded street. I went out to take a look.

'I got you. I got you,' he quavered in that weird register of gravitas and old age he had. 'The unemployed, the kids, I got you. Although I have left you and gone to Saudi, I wanted you to know. I've left you some snipers. More than a thousand snipers.'

It was coming from the CD shop next to the cafe. I looked up and down the street. Nobody seemed much bothered, even though Ben Ali's voice was quite loud.

'And more than a thousand . . . how many are they, Leila? Erm . . . Special forces. Greetings from Saudi Arabia. I just want to say I got you,' added the disgraced president. A beat starts to build in the background. 'Yeah. One two. This is Ben Ali at the mike. Uh-huh. Yeah, number one at the mike. Ben Ali. No doubt. I got you.' The beat crescendoes, and . . .

'You never got us!' shouts back a young and angry voice. 'You ignored us for twenty-three years. You did the talking and shut us up.' It's well produced, rhymes smoothly in Arabic and fits a meter. 'You never got us! You wanted to rule for life. You never got us! You stole our money and left the country in misery. You never got us! You got us now, though, huh?'

Welcome to the world of Tunisian rap. The Ben Ali voice, of course, was a take-off. The track, posted on YouTube by Mohammed Ali Ben Jamaa, was slamming the last speech before he fled the country.

Like most visitors to the country in those days, I had heard how rap had been part of the Culture, as they say, which brought the country's youth onto the streets and toppled the dictator. And now here it was, loud, in your face, witty and fast, just there on the street. The Ben Ali voice starts starched and proper and then, in the way of pastiche, slowly crumbles into absurdity so that you realise, if you were gullible enough like me to be taken in, how you've been had.

Down in Sidi Bou Zid, a bunch of youngsters set up huge speakers in the main square, now renamed, as hundreds of graffiti announced, Mohammed Bouazizi Square. And blasted out a track by El General, real name Hamada Ben Amor, a twenty-three-year-old who became a national hero overnight when he was arrested for rapping against the regime, a week before Ben Ali fell.

'Mr President, your people died,' the track goes. 'The people you imagine are in cloud-cuckoo land, in your dreams. But it's 2011 and people are hungry, their voice not heard.' I watched an official video later on YouTube. It looks professionally grunge, as though a skilled producer was working with a limited budget. It opens with a few seconds of archive, Ben Ali visibly scaring a boy on a school visit with some presidential small talk in the class room. Then moves to El General, baseball cap forward, baseball hoody with the legend 'Chesapeake 08', leaning against an urban decay wall somewhere. As the lead-in builds, he walks down a rain-soaked passageway, into a cramped studio, up to the mike and pumps his disdain of Ben Ali into it, through a thick blue filter effect. It's very samizdat.

Depending on who you talk to, rap arrived in Tunisia in about 2000, but made it big from 2007 on. Artists recorded first abroad, such as Ferid Extranjero in Spain, and were smuggled back in – because it was naturally illegal. But in 2005 a new radio station in the coastal town of Sousse, Jawhara FM, started to broadcast regular programmes on underground music, run by a DJ called Adonis. By the following year, the mainstream Tunisian media had picked up on the phenomenon of rap.

It was a double import, coming first from the Beurs, the French Arabs living in the *cités* around Paris, Lyon, Marseille and Lille. French rap in turn, dominated by artists of African origin, got going in the early to mid-1990s under direct influence of the spiritual home of rap, Black America. The American cultural influence, as elsewhere, made little difference to attitudes to America as political entity. No Tunisians I met were actively hostile to the United States but many expressed a deep scepticism, most of all the young and the rappers. You could read this two ways. Either the transplanting of rap was so successful that it had lost all traces of its provenance and become a truly global medium. Or Arab rappers, when they dealt with America the Superpower, were doing no more than continuing the animus of rap's black American pioneers towards the Power in Washington, its wars and social divisiveness and assumptions of superiority. Or perhaps a little bit of both.

And as with American rap, it has triggered a storm of liberal establishment criticism about what is valid artistic expression and fierce debate about who has sold out and gone commercial. As far as I could tell, Tunisia has no gangsta rap. Instead, the masters of controversy are those who rap about the deviation of women, with insinuation. I was to meet a group of self-declared Islamic rappers in a working-class cafe in Tunis.

I bought a couple of CDs of mixed artists and listened to them on the long drive back to Tunis. The lyrics mixed Arabic liberally with French, and occasional blasts of English. But the French often escapes typecasting, which in North Africa is of self-assured authority, to go ghetto angry. I wondered how much it was there because of the provenance of rap in Tunisia, the French *cités*, and how much because it really helps with the rhymes to have two languages to choose from, interchangeably, word by word.

A lot of the tracks and artists blend Oriental melodies with the beat. In mellow mode this starts to feel like something recognisable as another of the many kinds of fusion that have swept music in the Arab world. Twenty years ago, genres that displayed fusion stood out, like *rai* in Algeria or an artist like Lebanon's Ziad Rahbani, who blended jazz to classical Arabic. These days, just about every musical genre is represented in Arabic. Find an easy listening FM and you get jazz and reggae and R&B. Switch and you get soft rock, hard rock, heavy metal, an Islamic version of Christian rock.

In that vein, one artist on these CDs, called Mr Mustapha, had a track called 'l'Islam' which ends with a soft American voice-over saying how good it feels to pray, how proud he is to be Muslim. And you feel bathed with warmth. Other tracks are socially engaged, dealing with migration to Europe and forced marriage.

I was particularly taken by the opening track on one of the CDs, *Layam*, or the Days, by an artist called Dragon Balti. Something about its mournful, quiet piano and violin background haunted me. Maybe also, it was the fact that deciphering Tunisian rap was quite a challenge, and I had to listen to each song three or four times before I could start to get the drift. In any case, I concentrated on *Layam*, absorbing its lyrics and rhythms again and again until I reached Tunis.

I got that road trip car stereo thing. Balti was list-making, in rap, in Arabic, as I piled down a Tunisian highway, past contraband petrol stations which advertised their presence with artfully sculpted piles of oil drums, through a small town where two boys guided hoops along with sticks, as they have since time began, past olive groves and fields of berseem set against mountains blued by the distance, and half-finished approach roads and underpasses. This was it, Balti was telling me. Life, death. Hell, Paradise. Betrayal, sincerity. The war in Iraq, brothers fighting each other. The one who prays and the one who prays to the bottom of a glass. Life made me a rapper, another a doctor, a third a dropout. People will laugh and cry today, live and die. Oui, oui.

I've always been a sentimentalist sucker. My family gets embarrassed when I blub in crappy Hollywood films that leave small children unmoved. I put it down to metabolism, the way I'm wired. In any case, by the time I reached Tunis I didn't really know what the message of the song was. But I had a big warm feeling about finding a route to the soul of Tunisian rap.

DJ Danger, the musical director at Mosaïque FM, the city's largest radio station, and himself a rap producer, put me right. Before the revolution, he said, Balti was big, bigger than El General and Psyco M and others who had come up in the past few months. He was big because he was the only one who got airtime on radio and TV. He remembered seeing him stage a concert out at Carthage, where Tunis goes to play. Balti arrived in a minibus with his logo embossed on it.

To put this in perspective, this was at a time when any performer wanting to hold a concert had to submit their lyrics in advance to the authorities. They came back with a police stamp on them. DJ Danger remembered promoting a concert just outside Tunis where a member of the group Filosof – the Philosopher – ad-libbed beyond the 'official' lyrics and was detained as he came off stage by police who had been waiting, quite literally, in the wings.

'It was almost as though the regime had decided it was going to be into rap, and Balti was rap,' he said.

YouTube is a wonderful thing. Hannibal TV, one of the stations licensed under Ben Ali, posted a clip from 2010 in which Balti performs live for a talk show. It's Ben Ali rap. He gets up from his panel chair, takes the wireless mike and roams round the live audience set. He's a great performer. Late twenties, heavy-set to match a forty-a-day voice, heavy five o'clock shadow, rhythmic and poised. The pre-planned camera positions shift between him and a long line of babes – there's really no other word for them and they're all magically sitting next to each other. He singles out a fellow panel guest, an intellectual in his sixties, mostly bald, thick glasses, and gives him the rap equivalent of a lap-dance routine. He moves round him, throws his fingers at him, bends into his ear, moves round and sits on his part of the desk, rapping the whole while. The old man at first looks absorbed and then starts to smile nervously. Meanwhile the presenter sits, head on one hand, looking as if he wants to doodle.

I didn't really get what the song was about. But by now I was beginning to wonder whether that was part of the point, and that Balti is rap as patina. At some stage the regime decided it wanted, or needed, to integrate rap. Balti was the star they chose to embrace. Banal and well packaged was what they needed. This is also the regime that chose to plaster wall-to-wall soccer everywhere on TV and import wholesale the culture of soccer as soap, complete with star signings, intense derbies, charismatic managers and acidic commentary. It was a regime that understood soma. I guess it's a sign of my age that I hadn't put rap music in the category of things that could be made bland and directly appropriated by dictatorial regimes.

But the Ben Ali flirtation with rap, part co-option, part attempt to look cool, backfired badly. With Balti officially sanctioned, aficionados like DJ Danger tried to play other edgier artists. Social and love themes which had dominated in earlier years started to be replaced by harder messages of crisis and joblessness. The regime knew the difference between our rap and other rap and started formally banning other artists. But Internet use had rocketed and the banned took to Facebook, which in turn drove higher usage.

'We had sixty- or seventy-year-olds who stopped us in the street, or on family occasions, quoting rappers, and saying "Yes, they're right,"' said DJ Danger. 'That's how far it penetrated.'

The banning of Facebook, for two months in 2009, completed the cycle. Rap was now an official battleground for political forces in Tunisia.

In 2009 Balti went on a nationwide tour that hit most of Tunisia's twenty-three provinces within three months. He was invited to perform at private parties for the elite. He was also endorsed by one of the high priests of American rap.

In 2010 Dragon Balti recorded a track with Snoop Dogg in California. Interviewed about it on local radio, he was the very model of aw shucks self-effacing artist in response to a series of luvved-up questions, as though he'd already been inducted to Tunisia's Hall of Fame: What was it like working with Snoop Dogg? How many takes did they do? When will it be in the markets? During the revolution, another artist from Snoop Dogg's studio, called Mr Green, explained that they themselves had decided to record a song for the Tunisian revolution because Balti himself had been put under watch by the government, and warned not to rap about the protests. Balti, who he called their homie, had been arrested previously and tortured by having his hand crushed in a door, implying he wasn't free to join the revolution. It would be fascinating to know the full details of how that relationship, between a Tunisian unknown outside his own community and one of rap's global icons, was developed.

Meanwhile, a protest 'Islamist' rap was emerging. When I first heard of this, I imagined gangsta rap gone jihad. *The Wire*'s

Avon Barksdale or more likely one of the foot soldiers, Bird or Cheese, turned suicide bomber, the equivalent of big bad mofo coming to a bus stop near *you*. Strapping my belt on and it feels good, yeah yeah. But Tunisia's rap has been truly embedded in its society, so protest mode is *we* not *I*, and this shit is all fucked up not because we, the people, are rootless, but because we abandoned our roots and allowed others to diss them.

And by others we mean women.

Psyco M, real name Mohammed al-Jendoub, released a track towards the end of 2010 called *Manipulation*. It's all awful, he said, because of atheism, colonialism, decadence, nudity and immorality. He named and attacked two women in the liberal elite. The first, Sawssen al-Maalaj, was a nationwide celebrity, a TV presenter who had commented suggestively on the bulge in a man's undies on air. The second, Olfa Youssef, was a scholar who had written a psychoanalytical treatise of some Qur'anic verses, a book which uses original sacred texts to argue that the veil is optional, and maintains a prolific blog. 'Sawssen al-Maalaj can't treat herself,' Psyco M repeats. A fan posted a video on Facebook which set this segment of Psyco M's sound track to footage showing Maalaj on her TV show pouting, laughing, working the camera – being generally female, attractive, professional and on top of things.

It created a media storm in Tunis which played out in late December 2010, even as Mohammed Bouazizi was dying and Anis al-Shoaibi and his friends were already on the streets of Sidi Bou Zid, 200 miles to the south. A woman lawyer announced that a defence committee for the two women had filed a lawsuit for libel and intimidation. Some intellectuals criticised that in turn, saying the women themselves were trying to stifle Psyco M's right to free speech. Others, speaking to international media, talked of how the affair exemplified Tunisia's gaping cultural void. Wajdi Trabelsi, a fellow practitioner, said that rap was unregulated by the state so anyone can say anything they like. He meant that was a problem.

But the Psyco M case was just the biggest incident in a trend. El General talked of deviation, a YouTube video with valiant fighters waving flags with the Islamic statement of faith – us – juxtaposed to a close-up of a whisky decanter and cut glasses – them. Balti got in on the act with *Passe Partout*, a takedown of flirty girls around town who are always on their mobiles and post suggestively on Facebook. Each time the battle lines are the same, as though channelling discontent against liberated women perfectly hits a culture wars fault line. Liberals object, the artists counter with their right to free expression, some intellectuals back them. As a social class the elite is split. But the state is in the middle, and therefore stands above the fray, its role as guardian of the peace enforced. And many of the marginalised feel that someone is finally standing up for *them*.

'Do you know what the real problem of young men is here?' Hichem Abu Khamsa, a film producer recently returned from New York, asks me. We're both in our mid-forties, sitting in the Golden Tulip, a post hotel next to Parc du Belvédère, one of the prime locations of the city, so I don't really feel set up for a discussion about Angré Yout. 'It's not bread or money or jobs. It's low self-esteem.

'They're not good enough for a job. They see all this stuff

from their cousins in the *banlieue* in Paris, or America come to that, which shows them they're thugs and druggies and terrorists. Don't get me wrong,' he adds. 'I'm a fan of rap. East Coast not West Coast. But it's the whole package we're talking about. With the stuff that's played here, the role models are downers.

'They're stuck at home under their parents' feet. They go out to watch a soccer match, because the regime was all about soccer, and the policeman there casually slaps them on the back of the head, just to confirm to them they really are a piece of shit.'

It was persuasive, especially because he wasn't just talk. Hichem was Tunisian born and raised but had returned from many years in the States full of the best of American can-do to make his own contribution to an answer. He had started an annual local film festival which hooked up with the Sundance Foundation to nurture film making among youth in the poorer districts of the country's cities. I'd met him through a friend of a friend to hear about his plans to set up human rights self-documentation centres around the country.

But if this aspect of Tunisian rap was a downer for Hichem, for DJ Danger it represents a precious voice that needed to be heard. He had argued with his station boss, Noureddine Boutar, at Mosaïque FM, to play some of the Islamist rappers. I had also met Noureddine as part of a media assessment, and a couple of days later he had called me back to ask if I could join a discussion he was having with his musical staff about the limits of free expression. I couldn't go but he described it to me later.

Noureddine had spent the twenty-five years of his career as

a journalist and then publisher in Tunisia tiptoeing around the ridiculous restrictions of the Ben Ali regime on freedom of speech. The last thing he wanted now was to become, or be identified as, the new censor. At the same time, he had a developed sense of the responsibilities of free speech and didn't want to play rappers on his station who he felt were using incendiary language that bordered on hate speech. I was in Sidi Bou Zid at the time, so could not join the Mosaïque FM meeting. But the debate seemed very similar to those held across what we call the free world, DJ Danger arguing for the authenticity of the rappers and their right to free speech, Noureddine pushing back with the idea that free speech was its own ecosystem and sometimes needed protection.

DJ Danger was so keen to meet some of the Islamist rapping groups that he drove me to meet one of them, a group he had been producing with the day before, in a cafe on the western edge of town.

ArabClan is a large and loose group, up to eleven people rapping on one track. Excluded from broadcast, they don't make a living from it, recording with producers like DJ Danger and releasing onto the Net. Some of them are college graduates, others left high school in the sixth grades. DJ Danger said that when they rapped about prison and drugs, they had experienced both: 'It's real,' was his verdict.

The large cafe was crowded, strip-lit, blue with shisha smoke, and deafening. The Neverending Football Match played on a screen in the corner, half a dozen backgammon games raged – slam, shout, slam, shout – and eighty metal chairs scraped non-stop against a tile floor. Three of the group sat at the table,

Mohammed Ali, Mourad, and Abdik Moslem. Abdik, bearded, thirtyish, chain-smoking Marlboro, did most of the talking.

'I've written poetry since I was a kid,' he said. 'And I write in *fusha*, classical Arabic. I was the first to do that though there are others now. It's a part of my identity.'

What were the issues they dealt with? I asked. Poverty and joblessness, he said. And the lack of religious freedom, said Mourad. The biggest problem in society today, he adds. Not bread, freedom. What was the track they recorded the previous day with DJ Danger? I asked.

'It's about the so-called revolution,' Abdik said, tapping his cigarette, fiddling with the cellophane from the packet in the other hand. The gist of it? I asked. 'This is not revolution. It's chaos. You're telling me there's a revolution and we're free. But it's not true. There are a thousand Ben Alis, a thousand and one Leilas.' This last bit is a pun. Leila is both the name of Ben Ali's hated second wife and means 'Night' in Arabic, so a thousand and one Leilas also means a Thousand and One Nights. So were you part of the revolution? I ask the group. Yes, say Mohammed Ali and Mourad, no says Abdik, smiling, and the others tut tolerantly, because not joining in the revolution, even if you're sceptical about what it will deliver, well, it's going a little far. Clearly, Abdik's the guy who always pushes it to the limit.

Without my leading, he moves into a discussion of why there's culture clash around their lyrics. 'They say we're extreme. But we simply want to give advice to our sisters. We're interested in redemption.'

ArabClan had recorded a track called 'The Guard'. In it,

Abdik says, we explain to our sisters how one day they are going to be mothers. They should not be *moumis*, he said, harlots.

'But see, we use this word *moumis*, it's *fusha*, classical Arabic. It's not a *shateema*, an insult,' he said. What he meant was that while there were many words a man might use to sexually harass a woman, in the street or in an office, *moumis* was not one of them. Therefore it was harmless. 'We're trying to help our sisters. Because women wound us when they are not correct. We are all wounded.'

I didn't grill him. It was clear he meant that the hejab and what goes with it, traditionally, was correct. It was also clear what he meant by *moumis*. I reflected on the fact that all the women I know are certainly *moumis* according to Abdik's definition. The mother of my children with her dazzling dress sense, unashamed of her beauty, running a posse of boisterous geeks in her tech charity. My sister with her loud cackle and rambunctiousness. My mum too in her younger days, a woman who hitchhiked and was always starting conversations with strangers, although at eighty-two she probably gets a pass. But the gap was too large in that time and place. Besides, we were not in journalistic interview mode, and he was not a politician. And when he said he was wounded, he meant it and looked it, his eyes smarting a little as he pulled one Marlboro after another down into his guts.

Abdik was unusually candid about his own life. He told me how he had been unable to marry the woman he loved because he couldn't get a job. He'd been a street trader in a local market but the state took his papers and stopped him working – the very same position as Mohammed Bouazizi. He had been in jail for a time. The state, he said, wouldn't let him get married because they didn't want him to be stable. They wanted to degrade him, make him use a whorehouse to deal with his natural urges.

'But I will make a state in my own house,' he said, apparently slipping into some of his lyrics. 'I will be the emir.'

So intent on respect and self-respect, the honour of his identity. And yet how his identity depends on yours! He asked if I was Muslim. I said I believed in God and had great respect for Islam. Say the *shehadeh*, he said, *la illaha ila allah wa muhammad rasul allah* – there is no god but God and Muhammad is his Prophet. In orthodox belief, whoever says that fully understanding it and believing it to be true is a Muslim. It's the mark of conversion. I don't think this is the right time or place, I hedged, apologetically. Just say it, go on, say it! he insisted, half-joking, half deadly in earnest. In the end, his friends intervened. It was the first time in many years that somebody had been so intent on converting me. I respected his sincerity and resented his coerciveness at one and the same time.

They graciously refused to let me pay for my coffees and Abdik accompanied me outside. 'I hope you have got an idea about us,' he said. 'We are not terrorists or extremists. We wish peace and tolerance for everyone.'

PART TWO

Egypt

8

We Are All Khaled Said

Just as my instinct in Tunisia had been to make for Sidi Bou Zid, so in Egypt it was to head out of Cairo and away from Tahrir Square. Tahrir is and will remain totemic in the Arab Spring, whatever comes next, a sparkling moment when crowds of millions were beautiful. Its imagery may outlive and even replace Che Guevara as the iconography of right-on revolt, at least in this part of the world. It was already with all the rebels across the Middle East, on overhead TVs in a hundred thousand cafes, in millions of homes, in real time.

But that was just it. Tahrir was extraordinary, not ordinary. Defining, not defined. Central not peripheral, where most Egyptians are most of the time. And now, in any case, it was over, since I had been in Tunisia when Mubarak fell, and arrived in Cairo ten days later.

I did go to the square for my own tour, late one afternoon. As I dodged the traffic with the others in the crowd to reach the central island of the square that had become a tented city of continued protest I remembered that this is where I had learned to drive, right here in Tahrir Square, twenty years before. I had just arrived in Cairo as a young correspondent and finally had a car to drive and a need to go places, so I signed up with an instructor to get an Egyptian licence, and at some stage in each lesson he always brought me to Tahrir Square. I think he thought negotiating crowds was an essential part of Egyptian driving. I made him crazy by driving too slowly, nervously, faced with a solid wall of humans just twenty yards ahead who were taking no notice of us. 'They will part, they will part!' Fikri shouted, like Moses at the Red Sea, jamming his foot down on top of mine on the accelerator since there were no dual controls. Once we clipped someone's shopping bag, just as they leapt off the road onto the pavement, and gutted it, and I saw its entrails spilling across the road in the rear-view mirror and a man waving his fist in the air, slapstick style. 'Donkey!' Fikri shouted, to nobody in particular, after we had already lost him from view. I got my licence, which I still cherish, by driving forwards and backwards through a single set of bollards at least five yards apart, and paying a $10 bribe. I know, I know. My family and friends think that explains a lot.

There were no demonstrators in the middle island back then and Tahrir was all traffic, cars and people. Nobody spent time in Tahrir apart from the street vendors catching cars at the lights. You went through it to get to the Omar Makram mosque, the Mogamma, the main government administration building, the interior ministry, the American University, the downtown shopping district, the Egyptian Museum, wherever. It's not as though there was even anything on the central island to linger over, like the Arc de Triomphe in Paris or the arches at the top of Park Lane, by Hyde Park Corner, just a dirty patch of grass festooned with plastic wrappings.

Now the middle was Hyde Park as it should be and maybe

once was, maybe 100 revolutionaries in residence, sitting on portable chairs, drinking tea next to their home-made posters, visited by commuters on their way home for vigorous political debate. Should we reopen the stock market now, against the wishes of its senior management, to signal business as usual? Who should go on strike and why? Why can't you – commuters to revolutionaries – just stop now and let the country get back to work? We will – revolutionaries to commuters – when they put all those filthy criminals on trial, the corrupt ex-ministers and fat-cat friends of Mubarak's.

Although there was more heat than light, a lot of finger wagging and people shouting themselves hoarse, it was an engaging spectacle, the foundation of Egypt's democracy being built, you hoped, with every argument that ended with a hand-shake. But it wasn't where I needed to be. I headed for Ramses Station and boarded the train to Alexandria, Egypt's second city, where Khaled Said had lived and died to become the icon of Egypt's revolution, as Mohammed Bouazizi had been for Tunisia.

As the train bounded through the Nile Delta, rich green fields flashed past. It was perhaps the oldest continually culti-vated land on earth, peasant or *fellah* culture here being at least five thousand years old. Now, though, urban sprawl was encroaching year after year. Every last town, village and hamlet was bursting its seams. The towns of Damanhour and Tanta, now cities, had skyscraper tenements fifteen storeys high, open, uneven brickwork on the outside as though the buildings were owed a coat of plasterwork. Through the two-hour ride, across Egypt's prime farmland, there was never a moment you could look out of the window at a plain country view and not see people and buildings, and barely one without disfiguring quantities of rubbish.

I contemplated my self-appointed task, to get to know Khaled Said's street, and wondered what I would find. Maybe the neighbourhood would just be too atypical in some way to tell enough of Egypt's story. Too rich, too poor, too much happening, not enough.

Maybe nobody would talk to me. Egypt's famous hospitality to foreigners is actually often conditional on their behaving as *khawaga*, foreigners, should – visiting ancient monuments, taking taxi rides or boats down the Nile, asking for directions, looking pink and slightly boiled in the sun. It can be very different if you speak Arabic and have come to find out about local goings-on. In my three years as a reporter in Egypt, I'd never actually been arrested and thrown in the *box*, the English word imported into Egyptian colloquial to denote the police pickup trucks used to ferry the criminal masses to the nearest station. But several times I'd been asked on the street to come for questioning in a manner that hadn't brooked refusal.

I was thinking so much about Khaled Said's neighbourhood and his world that I hardly stopped to consider his death itself. But once I got to Alexandria, dumped my bags in the Cecil Hotel and found his street, it was clear that the manner of Khaled's death and what happened in the six months that led up to the start of the Egyptian revolution, on 25 January, was the story of how Hosni Mubarak's Egypt worked writ small. And of how it stopped working and was overwhelmed by popular uprising.

One question kept recurring. Of all the thousands of young men who have died at the hands of the police in Egypt over the years, how had this one counted? Why was it Khaled's face on the posters in Tahrir Square, not Sayyid Bilal's, not Ahmed Shaaban's, not any of the other known victims of the police state?

When Khaled died, in mid-June 2010, in the hallway of an apartment block on the street where he lived in Alexandria, all likelihood was that his would be just another case of police brutality in Egypt. His friends would mourn him if they dared. Local and international human rights groups might or might not gather enough evidence to pick up the case, but anyway the police would be exonerated, if there were any proceedings at all. There had been thousands before and there would be thousands after. Life in the thirtieth year of Hosni Mubarak's securitised rule of Egypt would go on as usual.

Instead, it became the rallying point for protests that escalated until Mubarak's rule was shattered. A series of protests in the weeks after his death drew national attention to the case. And when, a few months later, pro-democracy activists felt ready to emulate their Tunisian brothers and take to the streets, it was under his image. A young Internet executive called Wael Ghoneim helped organise a call for a demonstration for 25 January in Cairo's Tahrir Square through a Facebook page entitled *We Are All Khaled Said*. Fifty thousand people came, not just the dedicated hard core but fresh faces, old and young. They came back the next day, and the next and the next, swelling to millions, and the rest is history. Just eighteen days after the start of the protests, Hosni

Mubarak had retired in disgrace to a secluded villa on the Red Sea coast.

'It was about eleven o'clock in the evening,' said Hassan al-Misbah, sitting at the desk of his Internet cafe. 'Khaled came in and saw two of his friends. Two plain-clothes police came in after him, held him back with his arms to his head and started beating him.' He got up, walked round the desk, and took me down a short flight of stairs to the front door, the actual scene. 'They smashed his head down against this mantel-piece.

'Well I wasn't having that. We pushed them out, me and my son Hisham. By the time we'd calmed everyone down inside, we heard they'd gone into the apartment block next door. I went out, to carry on the argument, to be honest. Come on!' We went out onto the street, walked ten metres past a barber's shop and through a doorway.

'They were inside, here, with Khaled. But they had this door shut and wouldn't open to me. Then a police car turned up, a single officer and a driver. The two agents opened the door and carried him out. But he was dead already,' said Hassan. 'This is where Khaled died.'

The marbled lobby bore no trace of Khaled Said's last moments. A man shuffled by with some plastic shopping bags, past a lift that didn't work and up the stairs. The street gave off regular low-grade bustle.

'They took him out. And then eight minutes later – more than five, less than ten – they brought him back,' said Hassan. 'Not the one car that had left. Ten cars, fifteen, maybe more.

As if the world came down on our heads. I couldn't even count the uniforms. They closed the street down, brought Khaled back and put him in the lobby. Lifeless. What were they doing in those eight minutes?'

The cover-up had begun. It was just before midnight on a Sunday evening, but in June this part of the street is normally still full of life. Average weather would now be a clement 18 degrees centigrade, perhaps a pleasant salt breeze rising off the Mediterranean just 100 metres away, across the Corniche. Ten metres across the street, two cafes side by side were doing brisk business. A small crowd had already gathered when the two policemen took Khaled into the apartment block. Dozens of eyewitnesses saw them carry his inert body out to the car, then the police invasion that followed when they brought him back.

Khaled's elder brother Ahmed was nearby and got to the scene in time to follow the ambulance taking Khaled to the morgue. They refused him entry and told him to go to the police station. He did and the police gave him the runaround. By the time he left, it was three in the morning. But then he did something that changed history. He went back to the morgue to give it one more try. There was no longer anybody guarding it, and he got in.

'That was their biggest mistake,' he told me, sitting in the family apartment. 'They'd set the guard to begin at six in the morning.'

Ahmed used his mobile phone to take pictures of his brother, laid out in the mortuary, and posted them on the Internet.

Two pictures of Khaled Said lie side by side across the Internet. If you can, right now, I'd like to suggest you use Google Images

147

to search for 'Khaled Said'. Be warned. It could make you cry and it's not for kids. But it will show you why there was a revolution in Egypt.

One is a standard pic of a clean-cut young man, hoodie down, slightly slicked hair, just the tiniest quiff escaping what would have been a widow's peak come middle age. Fresh skin, level expression. Everything about him says regular guy. The other, taken by Ahmed four hours after he died, is gruesome. His whole jaw has been dislocated to another part of his face. He's missing at least three teeth. Blood trickled and has dried on his mouth, his nose and a cut near his eye. His open eyes stare at the ceiling. Worst of all is the rictus, his mouth gaping. It must have been a horrific death.

The pictures sparked an outrage that reached far beyond Khaled's family and the usual small groups of activists and human rights campaigners into middle-class, middle-of-the-road Egypt. Whatever the details of the affair, there was a certain incontrovertible truth to them. Before and After.

'There are two things that made the Khaled Said case different,' said Ismail Alexandrani, one of the leaders of the protests that followed. 'The first was the pictures. For the first time, we had an image of police brutality in Egypt. The second was the strong reaction of the family.'

The night after Khaled died, a small group of committed leftist activists held a demo outside the district police headquarters in Sporting district which was handling the case. A couple of dozen people turned up but were broken up without too much fuss by standard heavy-handed policing. On the following Saturday, though, protesters tried something new: a

Prayer for the Departed in the Sidi Gabr mosque, one of Alexandria's landmarks and a few hundred yards down the road from Khaled's street.

From the first hours the police had issued a counter-story. Incredibly, the two agents, Mahmoud Salah and Awad Ismail, denied attacking Khaled, and that they had brought back his body to the street, contradicting dozens of eyewitness accounts. The official version of events said Khaled Said had died from suffocation, not beating, when he tried to swallow a lump of marijuana as the policemen detained him. They had stopped him because he had been sentenced in absentia to a month in prison for a street fight. It was a tragic loss of life, but the police were just doing their job. An official coroner's inquest confirmed this story.

The Said family, Ahmed and his uncle Ali hired lawyers and spoke to the press. Khaled was targeted for assassination by the policemen, they said, because he had gained access to a video showing police implicated in a drugs haul, and intended to upload it to the Internet. They raised a civil case and demanded trial for premeditated murder rather than manslaughter.

In other countries, even a corrupt police force might start to weigh the case differently now. The locale, this slightly run-down street, the cramped apartment where Khaled lived and the *sha'abi* or popular Internet cafe where he was attacked, was deceptive. The fact was his family were well connected and well-off. I was told of three properties that they owned or used, two in Alexandria and another one in Cairo. Ahmed had lived in the States for the best part of twenty years and was actually visiting when Khaled was killed. Normally he runs an industrial cleaning business in Philadelphia. His uncle owns some agricultural land. Put it together and it is not inconceivable that Khaled's immediate family owns assets worth over a million dollars. His uncle Ali, briefing the press, had been active in the opposition Wafd Party, the preserve in Hosni Mubarak's Egypt of people with enough standing to brush off low-level police intimidation. A more distant relative had been a member of parliament's appointed upper chamber, the Shoura.

And Ahmed, particularly, was unshakeable. He would not take prisoners and he would never surrender, and he'd blown the case wide open. He had obtained American citizenship in his twenty years residence there and got the consul in Cairo involved within twenty-four hours. Lawyers from the embassy travelled up to Alexandria and visited the apartment in the first few days. Egypt's strategic relationship was in play, however marginally. It was impossible to just do Ahmed in down an alley, like his brother, and set up some low-grade criminal for a mugging gone wrong. Though it's hard to believe nobody in the seething anthill that was now Alexandria's police force thought of it.

So a more flexible police state might at that point have served up Mahmoud and Awad on a platter, vowed stern justice always and everywhere for bent cops, affirmed the unswerving core commitment of the police to the service of society, and moved on.

But Egypt's repression industry was nothing if not Pavlovian, treading the only wheel it knew. The ordinary folk of Kleopatra district lived the confusing experience of two official Egypts in those few days. There was the legal and judicial arm, which in response to public outcry had commissioned a review of the coroner's report and was making highly publicised attempts to gather more witnesses. And then there was the security apparatus, the only executive arm that really mattered in Egypt, deploying its uniformed officers, plain-clothes agents and *baltagiya*, hired thugs, to intimidate those same witnesses. Several of Khaled's friends were mysteriously beaten up down dark alleys, but nobody was ever caught. One particularly strong witness, a thirteen-year-old boy called Haitham, gave a powerful interview on Dream, one of Egypt's private TV stations, which convincingly damned the policemen. But then his father changed his mind about him giving testimony and he disappeared from public view. The same official newspapers and TV that carried earnest appeals from officers, spick and span in front of the mike, for anyone who knew anything to come forward, also carried – on deep background of course – a swirl of rumour and insinuation.

Khaled was already dead but now they were killing his character. He was a druggy with previous convictions, he was high on hash when he died, he was high on Tramadol, he and his brother were locked in a deadly battle over the family's inheritance. Amid the general cloudburst of defamation there was a very specific target. Ahmed's pictures, which had not been denied early enough to take out of the equation, were after the post-mortem, of course! That's what happens in a post-mortem, dozens of articles explained. The head is opened up from the back and, especially if there's any question of ingestion, you have to break the jaw to see what's down there. The package of marijuana was found in his lungs.

It's hard to convey how effective these kinds of campaigns can be. I met maybe a dozen people who, when they heard I was following the case of Khaled Said, gave me a nudge nudge wink wink and said: 'Let me tell you what he was really like.' What followed was nearly always about the drugs. And when you quizzed them, it turned out they didn't really know Khaled. They went to school with a guy who lived on his street. Their brother once played football with him. They would then, in their second breath, go on to say how that in no way justified. Etc etc. Mostly they would mean that, but sometimes it was grudging or even bilious, as with one of his neighbours who, after paying lip service to Khaled Said's right to stay alive, then went on to say he would start a petition against any official move to rename the street he lived on after him, since he was a no-good work-shy druggy. But even without malice, the yearning to be on the inside in a society awhirl with gossip runs deep.

The family held their own in that propaganda war. Khaled didn't have a job because he was an entrepreneur, they said, working with his brother on import–export. He didn't take drugs. In fact he was a martyr and the victim not of a savage police beating that went wrong but a targeted assassination. The agents hunted him down, they said, because of his intention to expose their commander, a young officer called Ahmed Osman, as complicit in a drugs deal. Osman is known in the district as young, late twenties, the same age as Khaled, and ambitious both in terms of his career and extra-curricular activities. In his short time at Smouha the word was that he had already muscled in for a percentage of some of the local illegal cable TV companies that flourish all across urban Egypt.

Independent witnesses who saw the video said it showed a drugs haul. A team of police, smiling and triumphant, are counting wads of cash at a table, holding packaged bags of drugs and forcing the suspects to lift their heads and show their faces to camera. Khaled might have acquired it by Bluetooth, simply through being in the same room as a policeman who kept it on his phone and hadn't password-protected his wireless data channel.

The video, like Ahmed's pictures, became something that could not be denied so had better be incorporated. The official response concentrated on the fact there was nothing incriminating. It was perhaps tasteless, against internal procedures, even. But nothing in the video showed any illegal action, so it would be illogical to target someone for uploading it. Arms stretched, palms of the hands turned out, gentle, be-reasonable smile. But that in turn ignores two other possibilities. First, the video might show nothing incriminating in and of itself, but what about in conjunction with other facts as we know them? Like if some of the drugs and cash you could see in it later went missing? Second, even with nothing incriminating, if you're someone like Ahmed Osman, it's true you might not want to kill someone like Khaled on the street simply for posting your trophy video to the Net. But you might want to beat the sorry little fucker – with apologies, Khaled – within an inch of his life to scare the shit out of him. In this scenario, the hapless Mahmoud and Awad could easily have had orders to go find him and to make sure they went in heavy when they picked him up. The knocking about in Hassan al-Misbah's

Internet cafe, in front of twenty civilians, would have been quite unembarrassed.

As these allegations and counter-allegations swirled, another thing was happening to lift Khaled's death out of private tragedy and make it part of Egyptian history. The protesters who mobilised around it were using imaginative tactics.

The Prayer for the Departed service that Saturday after his death at Sidi Gabr mosque was chaotic. Ismail Alexandrani at that time was Alexandria coordinator for the Public Campaign for Supporting El-Baradei and the Demands for Change, a vehicle to channel support for Mohammed El Baradei the Nobel Peace Laureate who had recently retired from his post as head of the International Atomic Energy Agency to return home and campaign against Hosni Mubarak's presidency. He described how the service succeeded in drawing more than a thousand people, way beyond hard-core support and including many people from the neighbourhood. They maximised attendance by staging a procession to the mosque which passed along Port Said Street, past the intersection with Midhat al-Yazel Street, where Khaled Said had lived and died.

It was clear from that day on that there was impetus and two more demonstrations followed, on Sunday, the following day, and on Tuesday. There was another Prayer for the Departed and demonstration on the following Friday. By the Friday after that, the case was attracting national level interest, and top opposition figures like El Baradei and Ayman Nour, leader of the Ghad party, who had contested the last presidential elections against Mubarak, made the three-hour trip from Cairo up to Alexandria. The plan was for all the activists to attend

Friday prayers at Sidi Gabr mosque, then, after a pause, move on to a symbolic silence at various strategic points along the seafront.

Of course as well as opposition leaders and the attendance of thousands, the embryonic protest movement was also now attracting serious consideration from the police state. That Friday proceedings descended into chaos as the protesters clashed, unwittingly, with an unrelated funeral procession that had turned up at the mosque at the same time. Despite the deadly stakes, some of what Ismail narrates falls frankly into the hilarious, and he is unable to resist a smile from time to time.

'The *khutba*, or sermon, is normally about twenty minutes or half an hour. But the police had told the mosque's imam to carry on until past two o'clock. For over an hour. He ran out of things to say and kept repeating himself. The crowd was getting bored and started muttering "Shame on you" under their breaths to the imam,' he said.

There were over a thousand people inside the mosque and in the compound outside. Beyond the crowd, thousands of police ringed them in. When the other cortege turned up, the press was so intense that scuffling broke out between the protesters for Khaled Said and the other mourners.

'I stood up to announce that there would be prayers for the deceased first, for the other person, and then the demonstration for Khaled,' he said. 'That was the way to resolve it. And also we declared that nobody would speak. There were a lot of factions and parties there. If one of them spoke, all the rest would want to.'

Some of the factions raised their own banners and slogans, against the common agreement they had all reached beforehand. The demonstration broke up in tumult, leaving the organisers wowed by the turnout but dismayed by their failure to produce a more solid event.

Then El Baradei and the others came to Midhat al-Yazel Street to pay their condolences to Khaled's family in their small apartment. El Baradei was under intense media scrutiny at the time, having returned to Egypt not long before, and was also being pressured by other opposition figures to visit Khaled Said's family and show what he was made of. Ismail says he had already planned to visit the family, but privately. Now, however, he had been forced into declaring a visit publicly, with the result that he dragged the other opposition figures and media circus along with him.

'We were there in the apartment and it was so crowded there were cameramen climbing over the furniture, trashing it, just to get the pictures. At one stage El Baradei went to the toilet and a cameraman followed him,' said Ismail. 'I had to stop him, otherwise I swear he would have followed him in.'

Later that day, though, was the first in a series of *waqfat*, periods of silence, where hundreds of demonstrators stood at chosen spots all along Alexandria's busy Corniche, the city's main thoroughfare. They all wore black, faced out to sea and wore pictures of Khaled on their backs so that thousands in the city's frantic traffic would have seen them and registered something about that nice-looking boy who'd died. It was dignified and effective.

Not that they were left to demonstrate in peace.

'Just as we got ourselves into position, about two hundred kids turned up on buses and started marching,' said Ismail. 'They were from one of Suzanne Mubarak's charities, an anti-tobacco campaign to make Alexandria a smoke-free city. We were there for a silence in mourning and there they were in their buses, honking, blasting messages and music through loud-speakers. We asked the kids why they were there, exactly, and they didn't know. I have to admit, it was a good move.'

But by the third such silence the protesters had drawn in perhaps five thousand people in Alexandria and probably thousands more in other towns across the country – more than for any other general cause or action since the main opposition Kefaya movement had collapsed in 2005.

After a few weeks, the protests lost a little impetus, but they picked up again with the holy fasting month of Ramadan, which began in 2010 in August. An old open-air theatre stood opposite Khaled's apartment on Midhat al-Yazel Street. Nobody played there any more, but special *iftars*, the early evening meal that breaks the day's fast, were staged there during Ramadan. Khaled's family and their activist supporters organised one such supper there on the tenth day of Ramadan, heavy with the symbolism of victory, the anniversary of the 1973 war against Israel in which Egypt recovered Sinai and the Suez Canal. Hundreds of people came to the supper, and once again phalanxes of police invaded, cordoning off the theatre from the rest of the street.

By this time Wael Ghoneim had launched his page on Facebook, *We Are All Khaled Said*, from his residence in Dubai, where he was Google's marketing director for the Middle East, and was quietly gathering followers. Ghoneim was to become a national figure overnight during the revolution a few months later when he disappeared and Google launched an international appeal. He was released after ten days a hero of Tahrir Square, and gave a couple of wrenching interviews on national TV which rallied support for the protests just as it was flagging. The Facebook page said it all. Ghoneim had never met Khaled Said and didn't belong to the world of organised opposition to the Mubarak regime, although he was later to meet Khaled's mother Leila in Tahrir Square, where the two embraced, Leila calling him her son. He just saw in Khaled and the pictures of before and after the story of Mubarak's Egypt.

Meanwhile, Ahmed was doggedly building media support wherever he could. In the family apartment, he showed me a fat pile of business cards from journalists all over the world. And local copies on his laptop of videos. A Swedish politician declaring solidarity. A punchy video from Amr Khaled, a superstar Muslim televangelist, on a beach somewhere, raising his arms and shouting to the skies for justice for Khaled.

There was another lag with no obvious moments or events to ride. Then the court case began. Because by this time the pressure had made so much impact that Mahmoud Salah and Awad Ismail, the two plain-clothes agents, were indeed put on trial. Not for murder or manslaughter, but for unlawful arrest and excessive use of force. The charges, in other words, did not challenge the police story that Khaled had died by suffocation as a result of trying to swallow a drugs stash.

Busloads of Mahmoud's and Awad's relatives magically turned up from their home towns in the Nile Delta and noisily protested their innocence outside the courthouse. While Ahmed was busy in court, Ismail and the protesters realised they were outflanked and looked for other channels. They ended up chalking slogans on the ground at Sidi Gabr railway station, the main terminal for the tens of thousands who arrive in Alexandria from Cairo every day.

'Most people by now did not believe the government propaganda,' said Ismail. 'We had won before the court of public opinion.'

That still didn't mean a whole lot in Hosni Mubarak's Egypt. But for the first time the nation had a face and a name to focus its anger at police brutality. Even the ageing and isolated president would have heard of the case himself by now. Given Ahmed's connections and campaigning, somewhere along the line it would have made it as an item onto an agenda of a meeting with the US ambassador, or visiting dignitary from the State Department. He, Mubarak, might even know Khaled Said's name. Although if he did he might feign vagueness, as he sometimes did, to emphasise the insignificance of others – 'that young lad from Alexandria'.

Then came Tunisia. And Tahrir Square. And it turned out the momentum was not lost, just paused. There were of course a mass of issues that led even the long-suffering Egyptian people to go down into the street. But it was Khaled's name that united them at first. His smiling face was everywhere you looked, occasionally the gruesome death mask too. His mother Leila went to Cairo and was greeted as a national hero by hundreds of thousands.

Meanwhile, the court case was adjourned and adjourned.

Mahmoud Salah and Awad Ismail were held indefinitely. And Ahmed was pressing for the criminal charges to be upgraded to murder.

I went to see the lawyer defending the policemen, in a well appointed office in Smouha district. Mustafa Ramadan's mind and suit are sharp. He is watchful – he monitors his law practice constantly via a web of security cameras from the screen of his PC. And proud of what he has achieved. I counted twelve separate framed certificates on the wall declaring success at various stages of his studies and career. He was at least the second lawyer to take on the defence of the two policemen. The previous one had withdrawn and wouldn't tell me why, simply giving me Mustafa's number. He seemed like a police lawyer. A couple of times he got the roles mixed up, referring to the other side, Khaled Said's attorneys, as the 'defence', forgetting that it was the two policemen in the dock.

I ask him what the defence position is and he is mock indignation and smiles: 'That they are not guilty of any of the charges. That despite the tragic death of this unfortunate young man, there is no evidence that proves the case of the prosecution, and a lot that contradicts it.'

He gives me Khaled Said's previous, from memory. He is smart enough to avoid obvious character assassination, interrupting himself frequently to remind me that none of this means he, Khaled, deserved to die. But the case file he has built leads you inexorably to the impression he will serve up to the court: no-good waster. Khaled Said was first arrested for possession of hashish while doing his national service in the police force, and sentenced to thirty days in prison. He fled national service and was sentenced to a year for that, serving some time before being released on 6 October, the anniversary of Egypt's 1973 war with Israel and traditional date of presidential amnesties of hundreds of prisoners. Since then he had been sentenced three more times for, respectively, drugs, possession of an offensive weapon, and public disorder. It was this last case that led Mahmoud and Awad to arrest him when they spotted him on the street. He was on a list of some 120 people kept at Alexandria's state security headquarters, in Smouha district. Not that they were seeking him out, you understand.

'None of this was serious stuff. Khaled Said was a normal young man, a regular guy, not the sort that the police would turn the street upside down for,' said Mustafa, who had a way of smiling after almost everything he said. 'The tragic fact is that if he hadn't resisted arrest, he would probably have gone to the police station, signed a statement appealing the rulings, and gone home that night.'

Khaled's brother Ahmed told me later that this charge sheet, submitted by Captain Osman, he of the trophy video, was false. A separate case was ongoing against him for fabricating evidence.

It is conceivable that Khaled had some brushes with the law, but the broader point here is not Khaled. It's what the nature of a brush with the law was in Hosni Mubarak's Egypt. Mustafa Ramadan's summary of his charge sheet, or rather Captain Osman's charge sheet, is that with five convictions on a range of charges and prison time attached to all of them, Khaled Said could be thought of as a normal young man. And what's weird about that is it's true. The repression industry, operating under emergency law, systematically and proactively criminalised millions of Egyptians through appallingly low standards of evidence and trials in absentia.

A friend of a friend, Dr Fawzi, lives in the posh Cairo district of Maadi. A few years ago, just after he retired from his practice, he started playing the stock market and got into debt. It all went bad and he ended up sentenced to a three-year jail term for some aspect of his financial dealings. Now he lives under self-imposed house arrest and shouts at visitors through his front door for them to identify themselves. But nobody has come to get him to serve his term and probably nobody will. We think of something as serious as a three-year jail term as being handed down face to face, perhaps delivered by a jury, certainly by a judge, to a man or woman standing in the dock who is then taken down by police to the cells beneath the court for transfer to jail to start their term. As far as I know Dr Fawzi wasn't in court when he was sentenced. Khaled was not in court for the charge that he was nominally being picked up for that night in Kleopatra. The system convicts you first, so mechanically fast that you may not even know it's happening, then allows you to appeal.

This approach provides a huge pool of suspects, informers and candidates for extortion as and when needed. When a huge bomb exploded in a Coptic church in Alexandria in January, killing twenty-one Christians, police simply hauled in Sayyed Bilal and made him the suspect, because he was a *salafi*, a confirmed Islamist with 'previous'. Nobody in Alexandria believes Sayyed had any connection to the outrage. A day later his family were told to come and collect his body from the morgue. I remembered from my days as a Reuters correspondent based in Cairo watching a police captain in a village station in upper Egypt, who had forgotten I was there, tell his men to go round up 'anyone with a record' from a particular family that it would be particularly convenient to blame for an attack that risked being labelled as sectarian, thus inflaming Muslim–Christian tensions in the village.

Mustafa Ramadan himself, when we progressed onto more general discussion of legal process and politics, described the emergency laws which have underpinned this guilty-till-proved-innocent approach as corrupting.

We moved on to the specifics of the case. There had been not one but two autopsies confirming that the wounds Khaled sustained were light and not life-threatening, Mustafa said. Only if you accepted that the major disfigurement of his face was caused by the first autopsy, not by the beating in the street, I countered. Mustafa shrugged as though this were obvious. But that would mean that the police claimed that a formal autopsy had been carried out between midnight, when Khaled's body first arrived at the morgue, and three o'clock in the morning, when his brother managed to sneak in to photograph it. He shrugged again.

Most of the details were similar. There's an innocent explanation for this, would be Mustafa's defence posture, in response to the reasons for Khaled's arrest, testimony of the beating, or forensic evidence. And the explanation would be reasonable for just as long as you accepted a logical argument at face value, or a new piece of supporting evidence, from the same impugned security forces, as unimpeachable. As soon as you didn't, it toppled over like the clever house of cards it was. Pre-revolution this approach could work, all the way from street to scaffold, nine times out of ten. But not now. Not with Khaled Said.

Why did you take this case? I asked Mustafa. First, they have a right to defence, he said. But despite his mastery of the brief, he had struggled to remember the full names of his clients and didn't know which provinces they came from. This clearly wasn't about Mahmoud Salah and Awad Ismail. Second, said Mustafa, sometimes you aim high to get halfway. Manslaughter, then. I wondered what that would mean for him, Mustafa, this smart lawyer, still young, well connected to the security apparatus, helping it now in its hour of existential crisis.

It was as if he read my mind. 'You know, I could have thought about aiming to be a minister. But not with Gamal there,' he said, referring to Mubarak's younger son, who had been groomed to succeed him. 'I can forgive Mubarak many things but not that. Gamal wasn't suited, he didn't surround himself with smart people. I decided to stay in private life.' *Then* hovered there, unspoken.

Your weakest point, I said, returning to the case, is that your guys deny bringing Khaled back to the apartment block. There are scores of witnesses to that. Ah, he drawled, in a long-drawn-out way, as though he'd got me. He was rehearsing for court. Even if that were deemed false it would do nothing to prove they killed him. Not directly, I conceded. But it destroys their credibility as witnesses. They'll have been caught out in a big lie. That's your opinion, he said, smiling back. The court may take a different view. The most important thing is the *aqida* of the court, its orientation. They could decide it doesn't matter.

Was this some arcane legal point about discarding questions of character? About the relative weight of evidence between police and others? I couldn't tell.

I left Mustafa Ramadan's office wondering if I would see his name in lights some day. He'd be a gifted representative of the thinking right, natural ministerial material. Smart enough, pragmatic enough, political enough. And also bold enough. It wasn't just anyone who would defend the policemen on trial for the death of Khaled Said after the revolution had succeeded. The forces of conservatism should reconstitute themselves in time, as the old left had in eastern Europe in the 1990s. A couple of elections later, when the normal wear and tear of a working democracy had expended all revolutionary credit and the playing field was more level again, who knew?

That night I went back to Khaled's apartment for the third time. There'd been no answer the first two times and the *bawab*, the concierge, had said Leila, Khaled's mother, was in Cairo. I was beginning to lose hope. But as I climbed the cramped stairs I heard loud TV and raucous laughter inside. I knocked on the door.

Ahmed opened it wearing a dressing gown. I explained who I was and he ushered me in. I half expected him to be weary of talking to journalists, but he turned off the TV and offered me tea. He had three friends with him and we sat on the strange arrangement of furniture near the front door. He explained that nobody lived in the apartment now. He was staying round the corner with his wife and children but just came to hang out here with his friends in the evenings. That accounted for the bachelor-pad feel, the bare lighting, the haphazard arrangement of pictures on the wall, a large one now of Khaled looking like your heart would break to think of what happened, another large one of the Kaaba at Mecca, for Leila, their mother, perhaps. And maybe also why it was chock-full of furniture, as though either the family shifted stuff they weren't using from other places to this one, or they'd brought in extra seats in the last few months when it had become a campaign headquarters.

Ahmed wasn't physically imposing. Late thirties, five foot eight maybe, nearly bald and a little overweight, sitting there in his dressing gown and T-shirt smoking. He looked like a hard liver. But he was also a born fighter. If in Tunisia it was Ali Bouazizi who had made his cousin Mohammed the icon of the revolution, in Egypt it was Ahmed who had transformed the death of his brother Khaled into a cause that could lead to Tahrir Square. You just knew his response to an anonymous death threat would be to scream fuck you back down the line and carry on. He gave the impression of being someone who had learned to manage a hot temper better as he got older. We spoke mostly in English.

'I wanted to get the bastards,' he said, simply. 'But from the beginning I had friends phoning me from the States, telling me to keep cool, to do everything right so I would take my rights.'

I asked a little bit about the family. Not with the expectation of finding out what kind of person Khaled was, really. His character had become a battleground in a deeply conservative society. But any bit of context would help.

Ahmed, Khaled and their sister had been brought up abroad. Their father, long dead, was a civil engineer who built airports and they had lived in Nigeria for several years while he worked on Abuja Airport, then South Africa. Ahmed had gone straight to the United States from Africa. He showed me a business card for his cleaning company with an Americanised name, Alexander Stefan. The family had been in the Kleopatra district for a long time and he remembered the street as a kid, a lot less built up, gaps between the houses, the people who lived here mostly well off. But it seemed like the place they came from. Not the place they grew up in. Khaled had an application for emigration to the States pending when he died. I wondered how much he had thought about his future life, in Philly, say, or somewhere else, in those days and weeks before his death, if a vision of it lifted him out of the dirt and stress of the street, the struggle to fill his days, the countless confrontations with petty bureaucracy that are the lot of the Egyptian citizen.

'I didn't really remember what it was like to deal with this place,' said Ahmed. 'We came here as visitors and brought our own money. It was only during this process I understood, oh this is how it is here.'

But he might have been born for this struggle. Ahmed went on the attack, filing civil suits, connecting to the activists ready to turn Khaled's case into a protest movement, building the profile with international media.

Once they understood they couldn't simply bury the case, or Khaled's family, 'they' – the police? the government? the presidency? Maybe just 'The Power', as the Algerians say – tried to buy them off. Ahmed said how various envoys, well connected but never quite revealing their official rank and role, visited this small apartment to offer a free pilgrimage to Mecca for Leila, their mother, or a lot more land for Ali, their uncle.

'They wouldn't talk about it by phone. They came here in person and sat where you are,' he said.

At one stage, he managed to turn one of the policemen guarding him, paying him to inform on the ongoing campaign by the police. He showed me a picture of him on his laptop. But then the police caught on to that and transferred him to Cairo.

'I think he's still alive,' he said, ruminatively, as though posing the question to himself.

He destroys Mustafa Ramadan's case. The package of marijuana that Khaled choked on? 'Yes, did he tell you they said it was 7.5 centimetres long by 2.5 centimetres wide? We made a mock-up of it. You can't possible swallow something that size. The only way you can is if you're already dead and someone sticks it down your throat. And even then it gets stuck in the gullet. There's no way it can get down to your lungs, as they said in the report.

'Did he also mention they've never produced it?' he said. *What?* I exclaim, feeling blind-sided. The defence claims Khaled died by swallowing a package of marijuana into his lungs, which they removed in autopsy but then lost? Yup, he nods. I wondered what else Mustafa left out of his careful presentation.

It's late now, and the conversation is drifting away from the specifics of Khaled's case. One of his friends, Mohammed, is twentyish and film-star handsome. A young Clooney. Not only that but he has a sling because he was shot in the arm during the revolution. How glam can you get? I'm not surprised when he mentions he's worked in the tourism industry and just got married to Jenny, from Liverpool. I introduce him to the word Scouser and we try it out, gently, in a text message to her as she's driving home from a business meeting in Manchester. That small-world thing.

'What do you think about the World Trade Center, 9/11?' Mohammed asks. Osama bin Laden's great, he says, a guy defending a cause. But he didn't do 9/11, that was the CIA. Do you know how many Jews . . . Here we go. Ahmed takes me aside and tells me not to listen to Mohammed. You know how ignorant people are here, he says. He's nervous about looking bad.

There's one question left to ask. What happens if you lose? I ask Ahmed. We appeal immediately, he replied. His 'best-case' scenario, by contrast, is that the court accepts his petition to upgrade the charges, from illegal arrest and excessive force, carrying a possible fifteen years, to murder by torture used to extract a confession. If found guilty, Mahmoud Salah and Awad Ismail could then be sentenced to death.

'Would you take it if you could get it?' I asked. What? he replies.

'The death penalty. Would you take the death penalty if you could get it?'

Everyone's silent for a few moments.

'Yes. Yes I would take the death penalty,' said Ahmed.

And I want to say to him don't. You don't need it. You've already won. You have achieved something extraordinary here. This revolution, Tahrir Square, this new hope for 85 million people, is some kind of justice for Khaled. And it wouldn't matter if he did smoke hash, it wouldn't matter if he was a dreamer, or didn't conform to some model of Calvinist or Islamist puritanism. He was a normal, harmless, innocent young man brutally murdered for no reason at all. That's all that matters. And you've already made it count.

But I don't. I bid him goodnight and dash down to the Corniche to catch a minibus back to the hotel before the midnight curfew.

Allah yarhamu Khaled Said. God rest the soul of Khaled Said.

9

Midhat al-Yazel Street

It's 2 March, three weeks after Hosni Mubarak has left power. I'm standing on Khaled Said's street, Midhat al-Yazel Street, at the end where it meets the sea, caught in a reverie, standing in front of a cafe looking up at its sign. *Qasr ash-Shawq*, it reads, the Palace of Desire. It's the title of a novel by Naguib Mahfouz, the only Arab to win the Nobel Prize for Literature, and I'm wondering if they named it expressly after it or if there are other resonances I'm missing. And then I'm thinking about Mahfouz and his style of making a location the main character of a novel. A technique adopted more recently by Alaa al-Aswany with his novel *The Yacoubian Building*. And wondering what a novel in that vein would look like for this street, Khaled Said's street, and if I could ever get the inside access to do that . . .

A polite 'Can I help you?' snaps me out of my reveries. I look back down to the street to see a man about my age, balding, moustache, looking at me with an amused smile. The thundering traffic of the Corniche and the flurry of passers-by whoosh back into my consciousness. Erm, I fumble, I'm a journalist and I just came to get a sense of life on the street. Khaled Said's street, he asks, smiling again, and I nod. Well I'd be glad to be of any assistance, he says. What exactly would you like to know? And so I tell him about my daydream, Naguib Mahfouz, the street as character, the cafe's sign.

'Well I can help you with the last bit,' he says. 'It's my cafe. The answer is yes. We named it after the Mahfouz book.'

And so I sat down with Mohammed Shawqi and he talked me along the street, as it were, from one end, where we sat in front of the Corniche, to the other, a quarter of a mile away, where the tram passed on its way to Sidi Gabr station. Just like that. As though I had rubbed a magic lamp and a genie appeared to take me to another world, the same physical space but seen through time, and the eyes of someone born and raised on it.

First there was the Corniche itself. When it was built by the Khedive Ismail in the late nineteenth century it was one lane one way, heading west towards the old fort at Qait Bey, the heart of the old city. Then it expanded to two lanes, one each way. Mohammed remembered how as a boy in the 1970s he would rush home from school in the summer months, dump his books and then bundle down to the sea just across the road to the sandy beach just the other side. I remembered driving up and down it myself in the 1990s, on weekends up from Cairo, when it had expanded to two lanes each way.

The killer expansion came in 2004. Governor Abdel Salaam Mahboub decided to widen it to ten lanes – five each way – from just past Sultan Ibrahim mosque for some three or four miles east to past the old Automobile Club, to relieve the chronic traffic jams that were crippling the city.

Alexandria is not just a city on the coast. The city itself lies along the coast, a strip twenty miles long and two or three miles deep, squeezed between the Mediterranean to the north and the marshlands to the south. When Ismail built the Corniche the city had perhaps a quarter of a million people. Now there are probably 5 million people within the municipal boundaries, but that's misleadingly low because those boundaries have bled into the hinterland in one continuous urban sprawl. Alexandria in reality lies at the centre of an unbroken conurbation that reaches forty miles from east to west, bleeds into the last towns and villages of the Nile Delta, which used to stand apart, and is home to some 10 million people or more. The Corniche is still the main arterial road connecting the strip. The city is so densely built it would be almost impossible to clear space to build a new highway from scratch. And yet it is also so built up along the Corniche, a facade of historic hotels, apartment blocks, mansions and administrative buildings stretching mile after mile, that the only way to expand the road was on the sea side.

The Corniche expansion ate up the beach.

'Families used to go down to the beach. You could hire parasols and buy tea from people who came round. Now we are forty metres away from it, but can you see or hear it?' asked Mohammed. I listened but could hear only the thunder of the ten lanes of traffic, as heavy as the highway from LAX airport into downtown Los Angeles. 'You have to go through an underground passageway. And then when you get to the other side there is no beach.'

A few people hang around on the artificial boulders dumped as a storm barrier. A few boys clambering about. The odd determined angler or two. As Mohammed and I talked in front of his cafe, there was even a man who emerged out of the underground walkway and walked right past us and down the street in a full, dripping wet suit and carrying a couple of spears, the last of a breed of professional fishermen who set nets in the sea and sold their produce to the local restaurants. But the street, which like Alexandria itself was built facing the sea, for the sea, has become cut off from it. Khaled Said lived less than 100 metres from the sea, but if he followed the pattern of others on the street, he might not have been down to it since he was a boy.

'If you want to go to the beach these days, you have to get on a bus and travel five kilometres up the road,' said Mohammed. 'Not many people do that.'

There's also an issue of subsidence with the storm barrier, which was apparently not designed to adapt to currents and even though normal tidal flows are almost non-existent on this part of the Mediterranean. Global warming has become a staple of Alexandrian small talk as the Nile Delta stands close after Bangladesh and the Maldives as a place where a sea-level rise of fifty centimetres could force millions to leave.

Many of the shops running right along the ground floor of Midhat al-Yazel Street complain that business isn't like it used to be in the old days. To the untrained eye the street seems to throng from the mid-afternoon on, and would do so more in summer. But maybe the tradesmen, so many of them like Mohammed second or third generation in the family business, are also talking about the type of customer.

'This used to be a street for pashas,' said Mohammed. 'It had the feel of a resort. Now it's just like any other street, and Alexandria like any other city, with its Carrefour supermarket and Fantasia Land fun park, and the international airport.'

Many of the original families have moved away. If they keep property here they rent it out and live themselves in Agami, Mamouriya, Smouha, other new elite neighbourhoods which haven't yet been overrun by the population boom. Or use their apartments here as a pied-à-terre, like Khaled's family.

The street itself is over a century old in its present configuration. Old for Egypt, which despite its millennial history has morphed rapidly in modern times – far faster than any European country. E.M. Forster used to travel up and down the tramline at the other end of the street during the First World War, infatuated with one of the tram conductors. He mentioned in his guide to Alexandria that at the sea end of the street that led off from Kleopatra station – this street – was a cliff with a Ptolemaic tomb with painted walls at the base of it. It must have been within yards of where Mohammed and I sat, buried now under the weight of modern development.

Just opposite the cafe is the old Kleopatra open-air theatre, the one used by Khaled Said's family and the protesters in 2010 to stage Ramadan prayers in his remembrance. The greats of Arab classical music performed there in its heyday – Farid al-Atrash and Abdel-Halim Hafez. Then it became an open-air cinema. Later on it was used for weddings. Finally it turned into a venue used mainly during Ramadan. The space inside is dirty and dilapidated, a couple of guards loafing at the gate. A sign over the door announces a special place for women to pray.

Next to it, where the Kleopatra Hotel now stands, used to be a traditional sauna that used herbs gathered from along the north coast, Marsa Matrouh.

As you walk south along the street from the Corniche, directly inland to Kleopatra Circle, you pass rows of shops selling clothes, food, pastries, plastic flowers, reproduction oil paintings and frames, cafes, a barber's shop and two Internet cafes, including the one where Khaled was arrested, just fifty metres from his apartment. A few shops have closed, and the middle of the patch is hogged by a huge building site where another apartment block is going up.

The street is late to wake by Eastern standards. Plenty of people get up early to go off to work somewhere else, but the shops and cafes generally don't get going until after nine. From that point on, activity increases all day long.

At Kleopatra Place, where Midhat al-Yazel meets Port Said Street running parallel to the sea, four curved twelve-storey blocks complete a neat circle. At ground level below the Khan cafe, which packs a hundred backgammon players on a Friday after prayers, Pizza Napoli offers some of the most mind-boggling toppings globalisation and a lurid imagination can concoct, drivers jostling for precious parking spots. And there's the customary rubbish dump.

There is an agreed spot, in the road section of the place, just by where the LNG-powered buses from downtown pause on their way westward, where residents and shopkeepers throw their rubbish. By the time the truck comes for its pickup, twice a day, the pile can reach five metres across and rise almost to the height of a man, a lot of it loose and organic, hundreds of orange skins and sticks of sugarcane pressed in the juice shop. In summer I imagine it could get pretty ripe. Even now it was smelly and slippery in early spring rains. Each pickup can easily top a tonne, the bags hurled into the back of a compressor that can mince thirteen tonnes. I tried to interview one of the team of orange suits as they hurled the bags in. He directed me to an overseer standing nearby with a clipboard who directed me to a boss, in plain clothes, leaning on the bonnet of a car. Three levels of management right there on the street. The city had privatised rubbish collection in the 1990s, the boss said, and the contract holder for the last decade was a local franchise operating with the French firm Veolia on a 51/49 split. Surely you've heard of Veolia, he said, shaking his head incredulously when I had to admit I hadn't.

This was one of five stops the truck made for a catchment area that included all Midhat al-Yazel Street and a strictly demarcated segment of Port Said Street fifty metres either side. Its thirteen-tonne capacity was usually but not always enough for the five stops. Some of the rubbish is sorted at the dump and goes into recycling programmes, he said. I told them about the anal effectiveness of our rubbish collections in Berlin: plastics, green glass, brown glass, paper, other, your block mates eagle-eyed for any casual infractions. The small group which had formed nodded dreamily, with professional lust.

This is the only rubbish collection the street has. So rubbish also accumulates in nooks closer to home – the foundation dig of a building site, a small patch of empty ground, the inside of a building's stairwell or on the stairs themselves. And on the roofs, which when they're not housing rural squatters fresh from the Nile Delta are strewn with old furniture and bits of pipe and electrical goods.

Heading south of the place, towards the tramline, the

buildings thin out. On the right another gaping hole, 100 metres long, 50 wide, and 6 deep, where more blocks are going up at a furious pace, box-like apartments for several thousand residents-to-be. Egypt's population grows by a million every six months, you can't go wrong with residential development. On the left, a girls' middle school set in spacious grounds which was a government guest house in the days of British colonial rule, creepers and trees from the garden billowing over the wrought-iron fencing down onto the street, just by the second-hand DVD stall selling dubbed versions of *Shaun the Sheep*, *Ice Age* and *Madagascar* next to Islamic televangelist sermons. Egypt's older districts are full of this kind of time and space discontinuum, skyscraper over villa, sports club hard by shanty. Fattypuffs and Thinifers.

Past the Tawhid mosque on the right, where we shall return for Friday prayers, just next to the government-sponsored bakery, front line of the state's constant fight against anarchy and blood on the streets, and the huge Baba Korollos Coptic church nestled behind it, where we shall return for Mass.

At the end of the street, the tramline that stretched Alexandria westward from the site of the Greco-Roman city by the two natural harbours, the engine of growth for miles of suburb in the early twentieth century. There stands Kleopatra station, where polite knots of men and women can be seen through most of the day and night, waiting to be taken downtown, or to the train station at Sidi Gabr, and then on to Cairo.

This was Khaled Said's street, his physical surround. Older residents can still remember when it was called Mubastis Street, but it was changed by the powers-that-be after a soldier who fell in Egypt's war against Israel in 1973, Midhat Saif al-Yazel. Now it could become Khaled Said Street.

Its basic geography is still recognisable from a 1959 map, the backbone of Kleopatra, wedged in between the district still known today as 'Sporting', from Alexandria's old Sporting Club, and Mustafa Basha, the main army encampment. The Suez crisis had come and gone by then, and Abdel Nasser was firmly in control of the United Arab Republic. But Brit names, pursuits and conceits still peppered the map, a distillery standing a block to the east of the street, and just beyond that the barracks with its stables for officers who rode on Highbury playground, and its carefully separated summer camps for single and married soldiers, the tennis clubs and riding track and St Anthony's church to the west.

But it has also embraced Egypt's accretions since then, starting with the population explosion.

Khaled's city block is a regular rectangle measuring about 150 metres north to south to 40 east to west – 6,000 square metres in all. The apartment blocks are rarely less than six storeys, sometimes as many as fourteen. Walking round the block I counted about 260 apartments facing outwards onto its four framing streets. Khaled's brother Ahmed said he remembered when there were gaps between buildings and kids played in the spaces inside the city blocks. But the world has grown darker since then, literally. New apartment buildings have been thrown up sometimes no more than five metres away from older ones, and rise higher. Now there could easily be another 100, 150 apartments in these buildings on the inside, making perhaps 400 apartments in the city block in total. Average occupancy is hard to tell here. Even cramped, this is a prime location, and families who can afford it are unlikely to be on the breadline. Then there is the question of seasonal occupancy. Even now, cut off from the sea lapping just a few metres away, this is a summer destination. But take account of Egypt's national averages for occupancy per apartment and you could average four to five people in each apartment, making 1,500 people in the city block. Which is only one of half a dozen. This one street, barely a quarter of a mile long, could easily pack 10,000 people into its alleyways and tenements.

This would still make it relatively sparse within Alexandria. Ahmed Soliman, a sociologist from the city, published a paper in 1996 in which he said total density was then about 11,000 people per square kilometre across the entire area of the municipality, including all parks, squares, mosques and other public spaces – slightly less than Tokyo, slightly more than Manhattan and over twice as high as metropolitan London. But that rocketed to 87,000 people per square kilometre in the district of Moharram Bey, or an astonishing 133,000 people per square kilometre in Gumruk, enough to rival the densest parts of Mumbai and Chennai. Once you factor in the empty space of the streets around it, it's clear that the density of Khaled's neighbourhood in Kleopatra is substantially less than this, perhaps only 30,000 to 40,000 people per square kilometre.

There is too much poverty and dislocation in Egypt today for Midhat al-Yazel Street with its century of authenticity, its oral historians like Mohammed Shawqi and old families like Khaled Said's, to be in any sense average. But if it is not the mean, it is perhaps the median. If it is not typical, it is representative. Most of Egypt is here.

The traffic passing down the street, for example, is an unremarkable sample of the global auto industry. A strong representation of battered pickup trucks, perhaps, loading and unloading to the shops and houses, but also including the occasional new four-by-four and, once, a golden Ford Capri with a farty exhaust, so lovingly maintained I half expected Starsky and Hutch to come bounding across the bonnet.

The born and bred Alexandrians are steeped in the refined accent of the city and its cosmopolitan pretensions – street vendors shouting *tomatim* not *oota* for tomatoes, *falafil* not *taamiya*. The migrants, mostly from the Delta, bring the rest of Egypt with them, and the few from the south wear gelabiyas and stretch their vowels.

The vast majority of women cover their hair with hejab. Here and there some don't, some dour Coptic matrons, others apparently Muslim both old and young. Women mostly seem to be in motion, mostly on the street only to pass from A to B, unlike many of the men who are stationary, just hanging out. Although there is one exception to this: some chairs and tables laid out down an alley next to Marzouq Pastry Shop appear to be a women-only open-air cafe. Inside the apartment blocks, especially during the day, you hear lots of women's voices, chatty, laughing, or sometimes vexed and hassled, seeping under the doors into the stairwells. But they remain largely out of sight to the foreign man.

Anyone who made money probably moved out to more secluded neighbourhoods. Anyone who made serious money probably moved to a gated community, which has become in Egypt, as in parts of the USA and white South Africa, the archetype of a successful lifestyle in the past twenty years. But the original properties on the street retain a lot of the old middle class, like Khaled's family, while poorer and less august families populate the newer blocks, or the more run-down apartments in the older ones. There's a remarkable assortment. One block can house an army major returning home in full uniform, professionals such as a dentist and a professional translator, in suits, as well as others in loose synthetic clothes and plastic flip-flops. Property prices have rocketed in recent years. A freshly appointed apartment near the seafront can sell for a million Egyptian pounds, or $170,000, when it might have sold for a tenth of that just a decade ago. But many longer-term residents live at peppercorn rents.

Soliman's paper chronicles the various stages of progression of new arrivals. First there are the squatters who come right into the heart of the city and camp on its roofs, in its stairwells, anywhere they can place their belongings and a bed under cover from the sky and not be moved on. After the initial influx, the trade-off is location for security of tenure. Out to old public housing which is decrepit and lacks services but tantalises with entitlement to future public projects. Or to semi-formal settlements where you can own the land but never get building permission, but this is Egypt so who cares? The general rule in Alexandria, he says, is that the further you move south, away from the sea, the more informal is the housing sector. Midhat al-Yazel certainly reflects this. The few hundred metres in from the seafront take you from the Corniche, an Alexandria whose lines and function recall an ambition to be the Gateway to Egypt, to Egypt itself, all warmth and chaos.

Sometimes the process of gentle decay is multi-generational. Halfway up the street, surrounded by tall apartment blocks, a fully grown tree has sprouted out of the middle of an abandoned villa. Its seed must have germinated at least twenty years back in what was once, likely more than twenty years before that, a salon, or perhaps a study with gilded Oriental baroque furniture in the style known as Louis Farouk. A sign tells passers-by that the property is *not* for rent or sale. Water, at least we hope it's water, frequently drizzles from pipes on upper-floor balconies for whatever reason. A pillbox at the entrance to the street from the Corniche seems to be crumbling into the pavement, weathered by decades of Mediterranean storms.

At Space Net, the Internet cafe where Khaled spent his last moments, most of the clientele late morning are teenage boys in multi-player video games connected online. You fight and leap and fly across a lunar cum desert landscape that seems like a more exciting version of Egypt's northern coast, and in one of the bottom corners there is a text chat going, Arabic language, Latin fonts. The boys wear loose, synthetic tracksuit bottoms for the most part and plastic flip-flops and pay by the half-hour, one Egyptian pound at a time, ragged-trousered Internauts.

On the sofa near the front door two boys pick up games consoles and hack away at each other in a game called *Silk Road*, one under the moniker of love_allah, the other H_E_R_06000. This is the sofa that Khaled saw his friends sitting on that night, when he came in to greet them and was then dragged away. Up the half-flight of stairs to the back part of the cafe, another lad sits watching a video on YouTube telling him how to survive at the level of the same game he's just reached.

Hassan al-Misbah, owner of the cafe and confronter of the police the night they killed Khaled, is very comfortable with this. 'This is uncensored space, alongside the censorship that more normally prevails,' he says. 'Most of the people who live around here, there's a limit to what they can learn from the people they meet in real life. You go to work or to school, you meet someone on the street, it's always the same. But here there is new thinking.'

He is that type almost lost to the decadent West, the social progressive who is also a stern disciplinarian. He upbraids one teenager for talking too loudly, evicting several others the minute their half-hour runs out. Hassan has something of the teacher manqué to him, telling me that he abandoned his safe civil service job as a clerk at the Inspectorate General in the 1980s to take on the training of his three sons in the martial arts. His youngest, Hisham, was Egypt's only medallist in the Beijing Olympics, winning the bronze for judo, and was with him the night Khaled died. They pushed the agents out of the cafe together.

Hassan, who is in his mid-sixties, decided in 2005 to convert the old cafe he had inherited from his father into an Internet cafe. This involved going down to Cairo more than once to get the requisite licences, from the ministries of Culture, Interior and Information, and, for a time at start-up, recording the names and ID numbers of every patron.

You could spend weeks immersing yourself in the world of video games and barely scratch the surface. There is the generic name of a game and then the name of its latest version. *Call of Duty*'s last edition, for example, was called *Black Ops*. The last version of *Generals* was called *Zero Hour* – these names are all in English. The emphasis is on Middle Eastern type shoot-em-ups, no science fiction, only larger and cleaner than real life. The *Silk Road* team in the cafe take a small mountain next to the sea against a desert backdrop. A loner chain-smokes while doing battle in *Counterstrike*, joining forces with players somewhere else in cyberspace to assault a desert fort in a Muslim land – the architecture could be from nowhere else, sandish yellow sand sandily strewn across the walkways, drawbridges and battlements. It's an aesthetically enhanced version of fighting which even as I watch is raging a thousand miles to the west as Libyan rebels and Gaddafi forces charge backwards and forwards between towns on the coastal road between Benghazi and Tripoli at Brega and Ras Lanuf and Misrata. With *Medal of Honor* you can actually configure at start-up whether you're going to be an insurgent against Saddam Hussein's vicious regime, or the US occupation of Iraq.

Mahmoud, an old hand, says expert gamers earn money on some of the more popular games, spending days and weeks building credits, a profile, the number of kills you need to get to Level 5, say, and then selling the online ID, sometimes for hundreds of Egyptian pounds.

But it's not all boys and games. A couple of young men are looking through an online test. A couple more print out what looks to be an architectural plan. A young woman unobtrusively checks email and text-chats in the corner. And a man comes in to get Hassan's help in writing a letter of protest.

Samir Kanil worked at a family planning clinic that used to be supported by USAID, the American aid agency. But since the grant came to an end, the local organisation has been unable to meet the payroll. After nearly a year the proprietor of the apartment which the charity rented is reclaiming his property and Samir is writing to the military governor of Alexandria to petition for back payment of wages. From who is not clear, and he can't tell me. It's a classic case of overblown expectations. Hassan types a letter at his dictation groaning with bureaucratic entitlement: 'We, the undersigned, have not hitherto received due compensation'. Samir confides that the salaries were nominal anyway, 200 Egyptian pounds a month, or $30. I wondered how much genuine family planning the organisation delivered in its short aid-dependent life, and how many other boondoggle charities and social entrepreneurs were out there, in the business of selling hope that Egypt would turn out like 'we' in the West normatively wanted it to in return for small chunks of hard currency. While I mused, Hassan and Samir fell out because Samir was unwilling to pay for Hassan's time and expertise in framing and writing the letter. Hassan dismissed him brusquely and he wandered out to try his luck somewhere else.

Two of Hassan's sons turned up – Hisham the Olympian, looking suitably built, and Haitham, somewhat older, who had just returned from Libya, where he'd been working for a multinational. He asked me keenly about various Western companies he'd applied to here in Alex. The political question of the day came up: whether Ahmed Shafik, Mubarak's last prime minister, who had survived him, should resign as the Tahrir protesters wanted. The two brothers disagreed, adopting the classic positions of the two sides in the debate, but amicably. Haitham said Shafik was tainted. Hisham said what Egypt needed now was stability and expertise. It only occurred to me later that as the country's only medal winner, he would have gone to the Palace, photo-opped with Mubarak, maybe rubbed shoulders with his ministers and the businessocracy.

I asked Hassan if he was happy at the revolution. 'Of course,' he replied. 'There was such a lack of respect from the police. We need police of course, but to serve the people not oppress them.'

Just down the road I meet a man who's baked 100 million loaves. Mohammed Abdelillah runs the bakery next to the Tawhid mosque which every day takes in a tonne and a half of government-subsidised wheat, yanked off a pickup truck by lean workers in raggedy loose clothes and scarves wrapped tight around their foreheads to stop the sweat dripping down into their eyes. Inside the bakery is one large bare room whose only daylight comes in slices through the small grille where customers crowd, thrusting change through the bars to be the next served. A team of eight slashes open the sacks one by one with box cutters, and folds the flour into machines that mix measured quantities of water, some soda, maybe one or two other simple additives. A relay of two young men stand at the other end of the dough machine, grabbing, spinning and stretching it into the small rounds that are Egypt's staple food and slamming them onto trays. When an industrial trolley with a dozen tray slots is full with maybe 100 rounds of bread it's wheeled over to the oven. Another man slaps the loaves down onto a conveyor belt passing through the oven at the rate of one a second at peak. The other side, another two men grab the bread, now piping hot. They shovel some directly through the grille to customers and store the excess on pallets. On a normal day outside the fasting month of Ramadan this process starts just after the dawn prayer and continues until about one in the afternoon. A notice on the grille outside carefully explains the bakery's opening hours and other policies.

Each loaf costs five piastres, a little less than one US cent, or half a UK penny. Outside customers in separate queues for men and women form a non-stop press. Most of them have shopping bags with them. Few buy less than ten loaves at a time and if you ask, as I did, for a single loaf, you get a look of faint disdain as if to say *That's not what this place is about.*

Mohammed says he can make 500 loaves out of a 50 kg sack, meaning the daily input is around 15,000 or 16,000 loaves. That's over 5 million loaves a year. Although it uses government-subsidised wheat – the 50 kg sacks cost him just $2.50 – it's a private business which a plaque on the wall proudly announces he inherited from his uncle, of the same name, some twenty-five years ago. So he and his team really have baked 100 million loaves.

Egypt's government spends hundreds of millions of dollars a year subsidising staple foods, a hangover from the early days of Nasser's republic, when socialist thinking willed the state to meet all basic needs of the people. And of all the subsidies, bread is the most sacrosanct. The formal word for bread in

Arabic, *khobz*, is often replaced by the more colloquial *aish* – literally 'life'. In some traditional families, if bread falls to the floor you must kiss it when you pick it up, so sacred is its role in daily life. Every few years, urged by the World Bank, the government tries half-heartedly to cut the subsidies and raise prices 'in line with international markets'. They nearly always cave in after a few days as it is political suicide. The biggest civil unrest before the 25 January revolution was the bread riots of 1977, when several hundred people died. A staple of newspapers is stories about how consignments of flour have gone missing or rotten, how this man broke a tooth or that child suffocated on stones still left in the coarse brown loaf.

Mohammed is not insensible to his role on the front line of the war against poverty and anarchy combined. 'I tell my boys the most important thing is to keep working. You see these people' – he gesticulates to the arms poking in through the bars. 'They keep coming from morning until we shut. If we weren't here, producing, every day, they'd be on the streets within twenty-four hours. If one of my team doesn't show up, and I don't know why, ahead of time, he's out of a job.'

It's a loose business. Many people try their luck queue-jumping, just poking their head round the door to come inside the bakery. Some are shouted out, others are accommodated, with no rhyme or reason I could see. You could see all kinds of special arrangements with the popular restaurant trade, enabling the bakery to up its margins. A significant segment of Egypt's informal economy is reselling – the stand selling fava bean sandwiches outside, the concierges of fifty apartment blocks up and down the street, some enterprising boys standing with bread repackaged on a street corner in the early evening, when the bakery itself has shut.

Egypt eats plenty of other kinds of bread. A large queue outside Abu Shanab's every evening to collect *fatayir*, savoury pastries, and European-style bread bears testament to that. It also has other staple foods, such as macaroni, used in *koshri*, rice, and super-high-sugar tea to boost calory consumption. But it's *aish baladi*, local bread, at five piastres a round, which underpins what's left of the social contract.

At Mohammed's neighbour bakery, halfway down the street at eight in the morning, a photo tops the grille where customers are queuing. A man in a suit and dark glasses, surrounded by a crowd, holding up a round for them to see, a mouthful ripped off and in his other hand. Adel Labib, secret policeman and much-hated governor of the city up until the revolution, is communing with his subjects. I too eat *aish baladi*, the photo says. Its very staginess provokes an automatic reply: *Not often*. And not if you can help it. I look round at the queue to see how many of them might be thinking the same thing. But most of them still seem asleep, many in flip-flops and the shellsuits that ordinary Egyptians often use as casual indoors wear. As though the bakery is an extension of their homes and they haven't woken up yet.

Just round the corner, Salah sits out front of his corner shop. Overhearing a conversation between him and a woman customer about the latest corruption scandal, I linger and get invited to a cup of tea.

'What to believe?' says Salah. 'We're told what a man of integrity, this prime minister. Then this website says he's earning two million pounds a day.' He's referring to documents starting to appear on Egypt's own version of Wikileaks, a Facebook page publishing documents purporting to come from the archives of the political police, whose offices have been overrun in the past few days. 'I have no idea what to believe any more.'

One cup of tea turns into another and another. Salah and his nephew Hani, helping me out, treat me to a front-row view of the street.

It's a corner shop like a dozen others up and down this street alone, but Salah carries a lot more sweets and toys – he aims for the kids' market. They turn up in gaggles, fiddling with the toys at the front, peering over the counter at this or that, hopefully. Occasionally Salah drops a chewy gum or two into their hands. As we sit discussing the state of Egypt, the world and life, one boy, no more than eight, keeps coming to whisper in his ear. What does he want? I ask. Fireworks, Salah says. He wants fireworks but his mother is against it so I told him to come back later.

And there's something very cute about the whole set-up. It's a time when Egyptians are worrying even more than usual about insecurity and if you watch TV you'll barely get through a report from a serious foreign correspondent that doesn't talk of the barricades, the disappearance of police from the streets, the gnawing concerns about what comes next. And yet there is more social fabric taken for granted in these anxious prognostications than we in the West can easily imagine. A dozen five- and six-year-olds scampering to Salah's shop, along this crowded street, alone. Some of them pay now, some of them have family accounts held inside his head. A car stops by us as we chat and a man hops out of the passenger seat and berates his two children, one of them seven perhaps, the other no more than four. Where do you think you're going? he asks. But he's not so concerned he has to see them home himself. He gets back in the car which moves off, leaving the kids to go home by themselves.

And Hani, Salah's nephew. Hani, it turns out, is one of the policemen who've been off work for three weeks now because of the revolution. As the hours pass and I hang on in there, Salah frequently disappears to unload new stock, consult with a supplier in the street, or just go somewhere else. But Hani is just there to help his uncle out – or maybe it's the other way round – and doesn't know the price of anything. Most of the time he tells the hapless customer to wait, but sometimes they seem too impatient so he just makes it up. On one occasion he seriously undersold a plastic car, but all Salah does is tut him, indulgently.

So tell us all about the police stuff, I say to Hani. What can I tell you? he asks. I'm just *amn al-'aam*, normal constabulary. He'd started out in criminal investigations but asked for a transfer.

'I saw the convoys going out and bringing back truckloads of prisoners and I thought: "What is this? Is all of Egypt criminals?" And then I saw how they treated the prisoners and asked for a desk job. The street stuff just wasn't for me, to be honest,' he says.

Hani is married with two kids. He's on Salah's case because he's not married. 'It's not because of money. He has an apartment of six rooms where he lives by himself, just round the back. He could easily get married but he doesn't want to. Sometimes he cooks for himself, sometimes he just gets take-away.

'He has these moods when he gets low. He'll just lock himself away for a couple of days and read the Qur'an. Sometimes his sister comes up from Cairo with her children, and then they all live as a family together for a few days. But that's it. That's his family life. Why don't you tell him to get married?'

Salah has a smile which says he's heard it all a hundred times. Why don't you want to get married? I ask him. 'The Prophet said women are *heila wa makar*, a crooked rib. But you must accept her as she is,' he adds. 'Maybe I'd marry a foreigner but Egyptian women love control too much. My brother lives in Chicago. He was in Iraq for eight years, then Saudi, then he won the Green Card lottery. He's been in America fifteen years now. Maybe he can find me a wife,' says Salah phlegmatically. This talk may not be politically correct but it's gentle grousing – You'll never guess what the missus did, down the pub.

Like Hassan, he inherited the shop from his father. His sweep takes in half the street: pretty much all these guys inherited shops from their fathers. We all know each other.

We get some *foul, fava bean,* and *tamiya, falafil* sandwiches and munch them in our row of chairs in front of the shop. A young man comes up bursting for a soft drink but only has a 20-pound note. Salah helpfully suggests he goes change it some-where else and I laugh to be on the other end of this trans-action. Why do Middle Eastern shopkeepers never have change? The answer has been staring me in the face all these years, hidden because unacceptable to the Protestant work ethic I didn't know I had. Because they don't give a toss. Because they're not profit maximisers.

Hani meanwhile wants to ask me about Hollywood. Excuse me for asking, he says, but how can women appear in those pornographic films? I mean, you know, with all due respect, what happens if their mother sees them in the film? Well, I reply, you have to understand that the kind of film an actress's mother would normally see is not considered pornographic. A kiss or something like that is normal. Oh, he says. While we're on the subject, I say, I've always been curious about why parents here are happy to let their kids see huge amounts of violence on TV, orgies of killing, but a simple kiss, an act of love, freaks them out. What's that about? Hmm, says Hani, and I gather this particular cultural interchange has run aground.

Two young men have turned up and start ribbing Hani about the police's very contentious role in the revolution. They were both strong protesters, from day one in Alexandria, so he's kind of in the hot seat, as the representative of the other side. We all stand now and sip fizzy drinks provided courtesy of Salah. Mahmoud, one of the young men, is *salafi*, his big, long beard denoting deep commitment to some version of fundamentalist Islam. But Hani's very haplessness would defuse the most rigid ideologue.

'Look, you know, I was in my post and the order came down from state security to abandon it. And so we did,' he said. State security are seen as the real villains, the politicised police force who did Mubarak's bidding, spied on, arrested and incriminated millions of their fellow Egyptians. It was the state security branch of the police that killed Khaled Said. Hani is just your regular cop by contrast.

He tells us how, as a non-commissioned officer – the police follows army ranks in Egypt – he had had to run errands for an officer from state security. The major, from a different part of Egypt, lived in a tied house next to the police station. But his hot water didn't work and he would frequently send round to the station to get Hani to boil some up for him. His duties also included shopping for the major, who would send him out with token amounts of money and a shopping list five times more expensive. But everyone in the district would know he was coming from the major, hand over the goods required at the price offered, and bid Hani greet the major on their behalf. Micro-extortion.

'OK, well,' said Mahmoud, listening to this. 'Maybe the police can come back on the streets if they dress up in Bambi costumes.' Or go out on rounds with the army, suggested the other guy. How about both? I suggested. We laughed and clinked our bottles of fizz. Then *ishaa*, the last call of the prayer, goes out and Mahmoud says he's off to pray. Handshakes all round.

I leave myself shortly after. It's been a long day and I've spent most of it with Hani and Salah.

I spent a long time on the street because I couldn't easily get off it. Apart from Khaled Said's family, who have their campaign to run, I have no pretext to be barging into anyone's house. And although people are very generous with their time, money and hospitality, invitations inside apartments are complicated because of the crowding. And the one significant encounter I did manage in a living space was not that of a family. Ramadan, who is fifty-one, is the *bawab* or concierge of the apartment block that Khaled lived in. He lives in one room under the stairs, maybe four square metres, his roll-up bedding tucked into the corner, a portable gas stove in the middle of the carpet where he makes tea and cooks simple man-alone food. He's been living like this since he came to the city fourteen years ago from Buheira province in the Nile Delta. His home there is two hours away. He stays here, in his cubbyhole under the stairs, for ten, eleven days at a time, then goes home to Buheira every other weekend. His wife died two years before so he married again quickly 'so there was someone to look after me', his second wife, as is common, being considerably younger than him.

'So can I ask a question?' he says. 'Why is everyone so inter-ested in the case of Khaled? I've seen so many people turn up here, Egyptians and foreigners, asking after his family. What is it that attracts people to his story, exactly? I mean, there have been so many stories. Why his?'

I explain about how Khaled became a symbol, first for the hard-core activists and then at the heart of the revolution. What did he think about the revolution? I asked.

'It's just hard to believe it's happened,' he said. 'I mean for thirty years, Mubarak was like this nail in the wall' – he fingered a picture hook just above him. 'And then suddenly, from one day to the next, he's gone.'

But life was hard for the young, he said. Ramadan has three grown children, a married daughter, a son of twenty-four and a seventeen-year-old daughter just finishing school. But his son, back in Buheira, can't get a job.

'He works in a restaurant serving *foul* and *tamiya*,' said Ramadan. 'But that's just to make pocket money. You know, for cigarettes, the Internet, clothes and food and so on. I mean it's not right that I should pay for that, he has to make himself a life.'

Why would people risk their lives in boats to get to Italy and Austria if they could stay at home? he asked.

One of the residents stops in to ask for some bread. Ramadan has half a basketful that he got from Mohammed's bakery earlier in the morning and holds on order for the twelve apartments he manages. I can't see in the exchange of coins round the corner how much he is charging but it's safe to think there's a reasonable mark-up involved. How much does he earn? I ask him. His basic salary was about 300 Egyptian pounds a month, he replied, or $50. 'But, you know, people are kind, and there are services,' he says, patting the bread basket with his hand.

If he didn't mind, how did he find a husband for his daughter? I asked. Well, he replied, we knew each other already.

'He bought the apartment. He brought some of the furniture and I brought the rest of it. And he has money to spend on her,' he said, summarising the transaction. We discuss marriage. 'Men and women need each other. We complete each other,' he said.

So what did he think should happen now that the revolution had won, and Hosni Mubarak had retired to Sharm al-Sheikh? I asked. Well, he said, so much money has been stolen, if they could just get it back and then put it to work on land reclamation everything would work out.

Now numbering 85 million people, Egypt has been thinking

about how to deal with its population explosion since the days of Anwar Sadat, Mubarak's predecessor, when its population topped 35 million. The favoured solution of that generation was land reclamation, expanding agricultural land beyond the 1 per cent of the country's land surface along the banks of the Nile, into stretches of desert parallel to the river, to nurture new generations of peasant farmers using advanced irrigation techniques. It was a tarnished dream. No large scheme had ever succeeded, but that didn't dent the enthusiasm of Ramadan, and many from his background and generation, who grew up in *fellah* families that had been dispossessed by the population boom.

'If they gave us acres, not just the ministers, we could grow anything. This land can grow anything,' he exclaimed. What about the Cairenes or the Alexandrians, I asked, these boys don't know anything about agriculture. They can work in factories, he said.

After an hour or so, I took my leave. Ramadan stood up in his cramped cubbyhole to shake my hand. 'May God be generous to you, and to all of us,' he said. 'Is there anything I can do for you?' And I realised that while I thought I was cultivating a potential source, Ramadan thought he was building a potential client. I saw him on the street several times after that, and he would always hurry over to ask if there was anything he could do for me.

10

Of Mosque and Church

It's easy to get excited when it comes to Muslim fundamentalism in Egypt. The stakes are so high. I was hanging around outside the Tawhid mosque in a manner I hoped was inconspicuous when someone thrust a leaflet into my hand and slipped away into the night. What was it – a new campaign by Muslim fundamentalists to take on the secular constitution? Surely even the fact they felt free to leaflet like this openly in the street heralded a new era. I unfolded the bill in my hand and read ... new, takeaway pizza from Abu Hashim's. Free delivery if you spend more than 15 pounds. Try our new chicken flavour!

Nevertheless, I was keen to go to Friday prayers at the mosque. Like many of the mosques in Egypt, Tawhid, whose minaret peaked just higher than the Coptic church next to it, had been built by subscription from the local community. The voluntary association that managed the mosque was in full swing, announcing in notices on the door that the path was now open to new subscriptions, and advertising a range of medical services – heart specialists, A&E, dentistry – now available 24/7 to members of the community, posting the mobile phone numbers of its practitioners.

A bulletin on the door also announced a campaign on clause 2 of the Egyptian constitution, which decrees that *shari'a*, Islamic law, be the source of inspiration of the legal system. This looked like being an early battleground between Islamists and secularists and risked dispelling the sense of national unity that the revolution had created. Secularists and some in Egypt's Coptic Christian minority were demanding the annulment of the clause, while others, including the association of the Tawhid mosque on Midhat al-Yazel Street, maintained that the clause had effectively lain dormant in recent years and were demanding its fuller application.

The mosque itself was already full by the time the preacher began his sermon and men began laying plastic mats across the street. There was no question of traffic passing down the street once the *azan* had called for Friday prayers. By the time he reached his crescendo the worshippers in the street stretched back as far as Marzouq Bakeries, practically back to Kleopatra Square. I felt self-conscious. The *khutba* was being broadcast at 90 decibels all over the neighbourhood and should therefore, by any reasonable measure, count as public discourse. Nevertheless, as I leaned against a car staring intently down at the ground to avoid being looked at, I was acutely aware that I was doing what thousands of government informers had done week in week out at mosques across the country for years, eavesdropping on the sermon for political cues. And in the minds of many here, I was an unbeliever to boot.

It was a far cry from the mosque in Amman's posh neighbourhood of Abdoun where, invited by a friend, I had taken my two-year-old son for Friday prayers. No one had batted an eyelid as a lemon-headed toddler clambered in and out of the ranks of the faithful, prostrating himself as best he knew how, weaving in and out of the rows of adults as they stood in lines. Here, though, you could feel people's eyes.

There was nothing in the *khutba*, the sermon, you could label as direct incitement. But the undertone was lugubrious. Suspicious. Dark. It started off with a general injunction about the need to bear witness in these turbulent times. That meant personal experience, the preacher maintained, not falling prey to images controlled by others – the media in other words. The bearing witness should extend to the slightest encroachment on Islam. There is a group in the United States of America, he said, building momentum, the so-called Association of Progressive Islam, that has announced that group prayer could be led by a woman. Yes, that's right, a woman! Now many sages have warned against simply swallowing the precepts of a book. Books hold secrets and you need the guidance of an expert to unlock them. Best to hold to the wisdom of the elders. And since the time of the Prophet, blessings and peace of God be upon him, the community of believers has agreed: women cannot lead the prayer. It is a simple technical matter. Prayers led by a woman can no more be valid than if *wudu'*, ritual ablutions, had not been performed.

Then we were onto Moshe Dayan, the eye-patched former Israeli defence minister, 'that malicious Jew' as the preacher described him. 'Moshe Dayan said that Arabs don't read. If they read, they don't understand. If they understand they don't act.' I missed the link but it seemed to be something to do with Al

Azhar University, which during the Revolution had been prevented from issuing a statement in support of the protests.

And then community. 'I'm sure some of you here today don't know each other. Yet you don't ask "Who are you?" or "Where do you come from?"' said the preacher. I stared even harder at the ground in front of me. Again, it wasn't clear what the point was. Just a general sense that we should all be watchful.

Finally, we were onto a theological question. '"Who are the people who hope to die?", Abdel-Malik ibn Marwan asked Abu Hazem,' said the preacher. A story from the Abbasids, a thousand years ago, part of Islamic lore of prophets and warriors and a certainty in the power of the Unseen which is balm to the troubled modern soul. Abu Hazem replied there are two kinds. The first are those who simply don't realise the import of the Day of Judgement, he said: that there is first an examination of good deeds and bad, and then a weighing of the one against the other, and then a path. And only the truly righteous can follow that path. So the first category, said the preacher, paraphrasing Abu Hazem, is those heedless of all this. The second category is the truly virtuous, who pine for God as you pine for your family after you have been away for months or years.

Although *khutbas* have been parsed since time immemorial for their coded commentary on the politics of the day, I am in no way fit to do that here. It was one speech in one mosque and the first time I was there. Like Kremlinology, reading a Friday sermon is an intricate art, requiring close knowledge of the latest events and a mosque's own particular history. It helps also to be well versed in the various religious disciplines of

Islam, *fiqh*, jurisprudence, and the sacred texts, not just the Qur'an but the major collections of *hadith* and *sunna*, the sayings and actions of the Prophet Muhammad, and the rites and rhythms of observance, with all of which I can claim no more than a passing acquaintance. There must have been dozens of references that escaped me, as well as a few basic links that might have given the sermon more coherence than it seemed to have.

There was a general aura to it, though, which induced claustrophobia. Not just in the cadence, the tone of alarm to which it seems many *khutbas* need to build, but also in its configuration of thought, which was all about the need to guard. To be watchful. To be wary of outsiders, especially false friends who claim to embrace the faith and then distort it. To not forget we have enemies and that they could be here among us. Not that any of this is in any way unique or essential to the Islamic faith. My extended family includes Low Church Ulster Protestants, and I well remember the shock on trips to Belfast as a schoolboy in the 1970s of being catapulted into a different world, one that was in some ways perhaps deeper and richer than our sunny suburban London lives, less vapid, but darker and full of foreboding. A world turned in on itself and deeply suspicious of outsiders.

But it's those childhood memories that lead me to this next question, which I put despite the fact that it is unanswerable here and possibly anywhere, because it seems to me to be key: How seriously is all this to be taken? Because there's an easy working assumption, induced not uncommonly by the unconscious interest of journalists in selling their story against a dozen others in their newspaper or TV channel, that grim is deep, and religious is profound, that to tune in on fire and brimstone is to touch the heart and soul of a community. But is it? Are the archetypes in this half-hour on a Friday any more potent than the soccer game down the road that afternoon, the Facebook messaging in Hassan al-Misbah's Space Net cafe that evening, the sneaked cigarette or the flirtatious text, at any time during the rest of the week?

A couple of days later I went round the corner to the Baba Korollis church. Two young men manned a security barrier at the gate, rolling it back to let the cars of the community through. There was a large hall on the ground floor, a ten-year-old girl in pigtails was having a birthday party, and a Mass was taking place in the consecrated church above it. I walked up the stairs past a series of framed inscriptions of the psalms written out in Arabic, and into the chamber.

Despite having lived in Egypt for three years, I had never attended a Coptic Mass and was taken aback to see its rites. It wasn't so much the similarities with my native Catholicism. We'd gone to church in a Lebanese village on Palm Sunday the year before, where I was stunned to realise halfway through that the translation of the service wasn't coming from the grown-up part of my brain that had slaved over classical Arabic, but my ten-year-old altar boy memory, the Maronite Church having embraced the liturgy of the Catholic church I was raised in. Nothing could top the cognitive dissonance of that, though the altar boys, incense and snippets from the Bible here in the Coptic church were eerily familiar. No, it was the resemblance to Islam. The priest and altar boys bowed and prostrated themselves in close proximity to *salaat*, the main act of Muslim worship. The congregation was strictly separated, men on one side of the church, women on the other.

The prayer book was a dog-eared photocopy printed in three columns: Coptic, an Arabic translation, and an Arabic transliteration of the Coptic so that regular churchgoers could mouth the rites without understanding the sacred language.

When I hovered outside, watching the congregation disperse, one of the church wardens recognised me as a stranger and hailed me. Camille Fayez offered me tea in the garden of what appeared to be the priest's house, apparently untroubled by the priest himself flustering up acolytes for the next service.

What did I really think of the revolution? he asked. I gave him my best burst of enthusiasm, all for one and one for all, no extremism in Tahrir Square, the Qur'an and the crucifix. The works. The Coptic community had been rocked particularly in Alexandria by a huge bomb at a church down the road in Sidi Beshr which had killed some twenty-one worshippers on New Year's Day. Camille looked doubtful.

But, he said, I'm not an educated man. I never had the chance to go to college. There were circumstances. But I like to read. And I've read that there are bad bits in the Qur'an. War and bloodshed. What about the Old Testament? I said to him, Christian to Christian. There's all kinds of bloodcurdling in that. But that's different, he replied. I think it's that when the people of God did something good, then God rewarded them. And when they did something bad, He punished them, like when Nebuchadnezzar enslaved the Israelites. But it wasn't an incitement. That's just what happened according to God's will.

Well I don't know, I said, all I can tell you is that my own family background, Catholics and Protestants in Ireland, tells me anyone can exploit any religion, it's not a Muslim thing. He nodded, unconvinced, but I was being politically correct and it was hard to argue.

You know there were plenty of Copts in the revolution, don't you? I asked. He nodded again. But it didn't seem to count much with him. Maybe it was a generational thing. Most of the protesters were young and Camille was maybe forty and had grown up in a Coptic community conditioned by its spiritual leader Pope Shenouda to get close to the Mubarak regime. Shenouda, once put under house arrest by Mubarak's predecessor, Anwar Sadat, had bought the Mubarak sell that extremism was so rife in Egypt, that so many Muslim Egyptians were mad fanatics just waiting to stick a knife in their Christian neighbours, that the Copts needed to hug the regime as protectors. It had apparently never troubled Mubarak that this paradigm was deeply insulting to the faith of his fellow Muslims.

In taking this path, Shenouda cast Egypt's Copts in the role of nervous reactionaries, a tragic betrayal of their proud legacy at the forefront of every progressive and nationalist movement in modern Egyptian history. And here I was, debating comparative theology with Camille in the garden of the priest, just twenty metres away from where Tawhid's preacher had barked his sermon the previous Friday.

He perked up a lot more when I tried the theory of the new pluralism on him. That it didn't matter, big picture, what the Muslim Brothers or the factional extremist Islamic groups said or did. The Internet and Facebook had given access to a bigger, broader world and there was no going back from that, ever. The imams could say whatever they liked on a Friday morning but they would never be the sole authority again. Facebook rules! Yes, he said, pondering, that could be so. I hadn't thought of that.

The next day I arranged to meet a friend at the Alexandria Library, on the Corniche. He was fashionably late and so I had a chance to witness an astounding new phenomenon for Egypt: a political demonstration by Coptic Christians, right there on the Corniche. About five hundred of them were gathered, complete with megaphones and slogans – 'Civil! Civil! Not sectarian or segregated!' There had been a nasty sectarian clash in the province of Helwan, near Cairo, in which several Christians in a majority Muslim village had been killed, and a church demolished. The demonstration erupted into cheers when an army officer took the megaphone to announce that the military High Council had decreed a new church would be built to replace it. This was definitely a new era. Many of the passers-by stopped to stare in bemusement. Copts might be 10 per cent of Egypt's population, but they didn't draw attention to themselves or muster in public places. Shenouda had encouraged them to strive to be inoffensive, invisible. Watching these neat young men and women, no headscarves, chanting slogans led by a priest carried shoulder-high, must have been like walking down your road to find an impassioned sit-in of librarians, or trainspotters, or anglers.

It's clear the future of sectarian relations in Egypt will not run altogether smooth. But it's equally clear there will be no going back to the slightly forced and painful claims of unity of the past. On balance, that's likely to be a good thing.

Whatever the nature of communal relations – and there is a lively ongoing debate about that among both Egyptians and foreign observers – at least the revolution itself is not a complicating factor in Egypt as in other countries. The Mubarak regime reflected the country's religious mix reasonably well – a Sunni Muslim majority of about 90 per cent with a Coptic Christian minority of about 10 per cent – and that is unlikely to change in any new dispensation. The minority has never aspired to hold power over the majority, as in Syria with the Alawis or Bahrain with the Sunni royal family and ruling elite. Nor is there a complex multi-communal dynamic, as again with Syria and Iraq, between Sunnis, Shia, Christians, ethnic Kurds and a range of smaller minorities like Druze and Turkomen, or Yemen where a local version of a Sunni and Shia divide is overlaid on divisions between former North and South Yemen and complex tribal alliances.

11

The Muslim Brothers Are Just So Twentieth-Century

We have already met Ismail Alexandrani as one of the organisers of the protests around the death of Khaled Said. But I discovered that by accident. There were two reasons I'd gone to see him. The first was because he'd written a long and detailed account of the storming of the state security headquarters in Alexandria, which Colonel Mohsin had described that night in Smouha. The second was that he'd described himself in his Facebook profile as 'Muslim and post-islamist' and I wanted to know what he meant. Not Islamist. Not secularist or anti-Islamist – 'post-islamist'.

First we met in the lobby of the IT company where he works, in a different part of Alexandria, while in the next room a team of young men and women, none of them over thirty, worked on websites and graphic design, joshing and chatting as work colleagues will. All the women I saw wore hejab. The following day he came down to Midhat al-Yazel Street, which he knew well from the protests last year, although he lives in a different part of town, and we spent the morning in the cafe opposite Space Net. He explained why he thought the Muslim Brothers were about to be eclipsed, not by liberal secularism as we know it in the West, but by post-Islamism, a vision of pluralist democracy infused with the traditional values of the Islamic faith.

'There is no institution or party that currently embodies post-Islamism in Egypt,' he said. 'But I think if a party was founded with a clear vision, on this basis, it would absorb a lot of other political currents. It would become the basis of stable government in Egypt in a very short space of time. Three years perhaps.'

From the very first days, political Islam was the skeleton in the cupboard of the Arab revolutions as far as the world at large was concerned. *That's all very well*, the refrain seemed to come, from liberal intellectuals and policy wonks in the commentariat, defence establishments and especially Israel in response to the demonstrable triumph of people power in the streets of Egypt and Tunisia, *but what about the men with beards?*

On the pessimist side, there were lots of dark warnings about how Iran had turned out after such a promising start to its revolution in 1979, how Islamists might make nice for a while but were cunning as well as brutal and only ever followed their own agenda. One vote, one man, one time. On the liberal side, an American friend sent me a summary of a meeting he had attended inside the Beltway in Washington, where the Indonesian ambassador had explained how the world's most populous Muslim country had steered the path to democracy within the best part of a decade. In a post-9/11 world everyone, it seemed, wanted to know what this would mean for 'our' relationship – the West's? All right-thinking people's? – with political Islam. To define, contain, endorse or oppose it almost in real time, before anything could happen.

From the ground that seemed plain neurotic. Religious faith is everywhere in this part of the world, that's just a fact. God is on the tip of everyone's tongues all the time, woven into the fabric of dozens of everyday transactions perhaps at the rate of once a minute. We'll meet at four this afternoon, *inshallah*, God willing. I hope she doesn't come down with a fever, *rabbina yustur*, May Our Lord Protect. And then he didn't turn up at all! *Allah yusaamihu*, God forgive him. You took the last piece of pizza? *Yakhrab baitak*, May God destroy your house (a joke). Not infrequently you get shown in to see someone while he, or I imagine she, is still performing prayers. He just carries on, you sit down, maybe someone asks you if you want tea. Drive down a highway and there's a burly truck-driver spreading his prayer mat on the hard shoulder. Prayer is considered as normal and basic and unembarrassing as eating, and the lack of self-consciousness can be charming. So what are we to make of protests in Tahrir Square where demonstrators stop their revolution five times a day to line up, in their tens of thousands, and perform their prayers? Not a whole lot. The simplest and most far-reaching conclusion is that they include the main-stream of Egyptian society.

There seems little doubt, though, that one of the factors that governed the Obama administration's see-saw act on the Egyptian revolution was worry about the Ikhwan al-Muslimun, the Muslim Brothers, the country's oldest and biggest funda-mentalist movement. Particular flip-flops in the nuance of US comment fell in news cycles directly after the first pictures were transmitted of protesters praying en masse, news that indi-vidual Muslim Brothers were indeed taking part in the protests, and apparently when some bright young thing at the State Department finally read the Egyptian constitution and worked out that a constitutional scenario for Mubarak's immediate resignation would require a presidential election within sixty days and, with the Brotherhood so strong, anything could happen.

Founded in 1928 by a schoolteacher, Hassan al-Banna, the Muslim Brotherhood inspired and is still connected to similar movements across the Middle East, including Hamas in the Gaza Strip. In Egypt alone, by the 1940s it had gathered something over a million followers, challenging both the liberal establishment in the last days of Egypt's monarchy and Nasser's Arab nationalist revolution in its early days. Then Nasser banned it, executed some of its figureheads, and drove it underground for a generation.

The response of the Islamist movement to this repression was complex. Some of its younger cadres, whiling away their years in Nasser's prisons, formulated new interpretations of the holy Islamic texts which justified and even compelled violence. The most famous of these was Sayyid Qutb who, after a study tour to the United States, became one of the earliest thinkers in the Muslim world to articulate well the idea of the cultural imperialism of the West, and the need to oppose its decadence by all means. He and others were executed for their positions and their thinking became the basis of splinter groups such as *Gama'a Islamiya*, the Islamic Group, which led campaigns through the 1980s and 1990s targeting not just the regime and police but Egypt's Coptic minority and tourists.

Meanwhile the leadership of the Brotherhood resolved to

abandon political violence, formally declaring a ceasefire in the early 1970s which has held ever since. The Mubarak propaganda machine mixed the stories both of the Muslim Brothers, with their decades-long abandonment of violence, and splinter and unrelated groups, to project all Islamists in Egypt as steeped in blood, the equivalent of FIS in Algeria, or the Taliban, or later al-Qaeda and Zarqawi. This conveniently ignored the fact that splinter groups, and later Osama bin Laden, condemned the Muslim Brothers as sell-outs because they expressly refused to join a global jihad. At the same time, the Mubarak regime allowed the movement to re-emerge partially, while remaining illegal, opening some of its social networks and services. In the 2005 parliamentary elections the Muslim Brotherhood became the nearest thing Mubarak's Egypt was ever going to have to an official opposition when its candidates, standing as independents, won eighty-eight seats, the only significant group outside the ruling NDP.

If they were not violent, the Muslim Brothers' programme nevertheless represented what might be called Islamic Fundamentalism Classic. Their avowed goals were the imposition of *shari'a*, Islamic law, and adoption of hejab by women, formal restrictions on women's role in public life, the banning of alcohol, and curtailment of the freedoms of minorities. In foreign policy, if they steered clear of the pan-Islamist idea of global jihad against Western culture, they were strongly opposed to US foreign policy in the Middle East and to the existence of Israel, in solidarity with Hamas, their Palestinian branch. They had adopted civil and democratic tactics, but their fundamental goal was an Islamic state, a clear alternate vision to the nominally secular state they were struggling against.

And they were often just plain grumpy. I remember as a Reuters correspondent trundling along to their office in Cairo in the 1990s for comments and reaction to the news flow. It was an ordinary second- or third-floor apartment in one of the old downtown blocks which looked nondescript – darkened stairwell, lift that worked spasmodically – but was, of course, under intense surveillance. On the wall was a framed list of Hassan al-Banna's ten recommendations for correct living in the modern age. One of them read: Don't laugh too much. Curbing the famous Egyptian sense of humour was a formal part of the Brotherhood's programme! When you got to see anyone it was usually some curmudgeonly old man who told you you were wasting your time, beat down the premise of every question, and then refused to be quoted.

The Mubarak regime had a scapegoat opposition exactly where it wanted them – visible but marginalised, illegal, and ideologically extreme.

Not only that, but the various Islamic groups were rancorously split among themselves. The Brothers were fundamentalist but modernist, after a mid-twentieth-century fashion. The dress code of senior leaders, for example, was mainly jacket and tie. They were doctors and engineers, schoolteachers and merchants, and businessmen both small and large. *Salafis* on the other hand in Egypt sought a more literal return to the early days of Islam and often wore traditional dress. They are the men with the beards you see in the protests but, the revolution apart, they could adopt political positions that might range all the way from quietism to espousing political violence. Even the tiny splinter groups who advocated violence were split. *Jihadis* believed in fighting a war against the forces of the oppressive state, while *takfiris* went further, declaring the whole of society to be godless and a legitimate target.

The state security apparatus was up to its neck in all of this, infiltrating groups, opening rifts. Many extraordinary tales will doubtless come to light in the months and years ahead, as more documents are exposed, of the gruesome intelligence war fought in Egypt's noisy tenements and dusty streets these last thirty years.

So all eyes were on the Ikhwan, the Brothers, in the aftermath of the revolution. But as I travelled across North Africa and spent time with ordinary people, something seemed misplaced in this concentration on the possibility of extremist takeover and power dynamics – groupings, parties, leaders, and bids for power. And it was that which had led me to seek out Ismail and others who could articulate political Islam in a new way.

Part of it was my root scepticism about how many Egyptians really supported the Brothers and why, or Tunisians the Nahda party, their equivalents. For sure, the classical Islamist parties in both countries enjoy a solid core support which means in any genuinely representative landscape their leaders will always be national figures, could never be ignored, and might often be crucial coalition partners. But nobody knows how big that core support is, nor if they could reach even a simple majority in a genuinely open system. Personally, I doubt it. Anything can happen in early-stage and fragile democracies, of course, and I have no evidence to offer other than a hunch built from several thousand cups of tea over a couple of decades, during which three long-term impressions have formed in my head.

The first is that it has been almost impossible in the various autocracies and occupations of the Arab world up until now to disentangle protest vote from core ideological support. Take Hamas in the Gaza Strip, where I once lived for the best part of a year, or Hizbollah in Lebanon – unless we think the sizeable numbers of Lebanese Christians who rallied in support of Hizbollah during the 2006 war with Israel really would welcome an Iran-style theocracy. In Egypt in the 1990s I saw defendants caged together by the score in military trials of fringe Islamic groups shout *Allahu Akbar* and anti-Mubarak slogans when they were sentenced, some of them to death. What you might expect. Except that an informed view of Egypt's military courts would also lead you to guess that in that cage there are men convicted who are not only innocent of the charges but who were also not even Islamist when they were picked up. So why would they identify with the two or three hard-core *jihadis*, or guerrillas, in there with them, swear vengeance by God, punch their fists in the air, tears streaming down their cheeks? Because they're screwed anyway. The natural urge for dignity and self-respect says in that situation, better hanged for a sheep than a lamb.

A Franco-Algerian friend of mine found himself in a bar in Algiers late one night in the mid-1990s, as the civil war between the Islamists and the military-backed government raged. A journalist, Suleiman made what he thought was an innocuous joke at the expense of the Front Islamique de Salut, the FIS, the main Islamist group opposing the government. The man sitting next to him at the bar angrily challenged him. But, Suleiman said, I'm sorry but I thought nobody in here would be for FIS. It's a bar after all. I am FIS, the man said, so's he, and him, and him – he swept virtually the whole bar with his hand. Nobody felt obliged to explain how they reconciled backing an Islamist party with knocking back copious quantities of beer.

The second impression, which has grown steadily in the decade I have lived in Muslim countries, is that what 'Islam' can mean is as much about form as substance. Which means the Islamisation of Egypt and many other Arab countries over the last thirty years, which is undeniable, doesn't necessarily mean the one thing that Western fears fixate on – rage, barbarism, oppression of women, and 9/11-type atrocities. It *could* mean that, as it did in Afghanistan under the Taliban. But it could mean many other things. Or nothing at all.

If that's too vague, let's take consumerism. Islam may have been borrowed as a vehicle for social protest, anti-Americanism and anti-globalisation in the Eighties and Nineties. But the more striking appropriation in the Noughties has been as marketing brand, as consumerism took root across the Arab world. Mecca Cola, Islamic luxury holiday resorts, Islamic banking. The rampant surge of marketing has applied not least to political Islam itself. Hizbollah's Manar TV sells jihad as effectively as other channels sell shampoo. Islamic tele-vangelism diversified into different market segments. There's Youssef Qardawi if you're devout but with radical leftist urges, Amr Khaled if you're young and aspirational, Ahmed al-Shugairy if you were once drawn to a Western lifestyle, and so on.

Finally, there is the explosion of popular culture and the Internet, which has created a marketplace of ideas in the Muslim world like never before. And that means that whatever level of support the Muslim Brothers or other classical Islamist parties do have, they now have to keep on earning it over and over again, just like everyone else. Because the Internet is quite simply the end of the era in which one idea can prevail. Everywhere. Faith is, always, culture as well as faith. And culture is now mash-up. In 1979, Ayatollah Khomeini fomented revolution in Iran from Paris using cutting-edge technology – the cassette tape. He recorded masterly invective at Neauphle-le-Château, acolytes copied his tapes 'en masse' – by the dozen – in banks of machines and undertook perilous journeys to smuggle them into Iran, where they were played out in mosques, at Friday prayers, and other gatherings. Whereas in 2011, by some estimates, 80 per cent of households in Egypt have access to either satellite or cable TV. It just feels like, other things being equal, single-party takeover should be a whole lot harder in the channel-zapping age.

All of which meant the existing explanations and categories of the policy wonks, Islamist or secular, 'modern' or fundamentalist, didn't feel right but I could not articulate exactly why. Which is where I'd got to when, surfing in the Space Net cafe on Midhat al-Yazel Street for local bloggers in Alexandria who could give me background to the protests around Khaled Said, I came upon Ismail Alexandrani and his Facebook status of post-Islamist.

So what is post-Islamism? I asked him, sitting in the cafe

opposite Space Net, at just the spot where we might have seen Khaled Said dragged out by Mahmoud and Awad and into the apartment block next door.

'Post-Islamism is the adoption of a discourse which is not religious, and support for civil and democratic institutions, at the same time as being concerned to grow piety in society,' he said. 'Classical Islamism is concerned with form as much as substance. Post-Islamism privileges substance over form.'

What is the substance? I asked him. Core Islamic values, he said. Honesty, love, forgiveness, social justice, freedoms, equal and balanced rights, and a certain social conservatism. And the form? Dress codes, rites and regulations.

For instance, he said, implementing *shari'a* law and banning alcohol would not be part of a post-Islamist programme in Egypt now, whereas they might be for the Brothers or another classical Islamist party. It's not so much holding different positions about the issues at core. Alcohol remains morally reprehensible for post-Islamists. The *shari'a* remains God's Law. But there is a pragmatism at work which is intense. It says we are just emerging from generations of dictatorship, 40 per cent of the population lives on the breadline, more than a quarter can't read. A *real* Muslim society, one oriented towards the worship of God, needs real human development, as measured by education, health, stability and a decent standard of living, which in turn need pluralism and freedom in order to flourish. Now is not the time to focus on symbols, labels, and what in the United States would be called wedge issues.

'In the case of alcohol, it's not really a problem. It's not served in restaurants, and even Coptic Christians who drink recognise that it is a social taboo, and would only do so in their homes. So the question of a legal ban is not a priority,' he said.

In some respects, post-Islamism is a recognition of the excesses of the original Islamist movements, who often appeared hungrier for power than for serving a constituency. The tiny liberal elites across the Arab world had long stressed this element and have sometimes been quick to impute venality to Islamist movements and leaders. But post-Islamism means this recognition of Islamist excess has spread to the mainstream of society, including segments who might formerly have been members in these movements.

The ramifications of the idea have been best expounded by Asef Bayat, an Iranian-born sociologist who began to formulate his thinking while in Cairo, later moving to the University of Illinois. To paraphrase him, the classic emphasis on taking over the state and imposing *shari'a* forged a paradigm in which the state was righteous, and therefore ordinary Muslims were duty-bound to conform to it, and other top-down power structures. But the post-Islamist emphasis on building a religious society brick by brick triggers bottom-up paradigms of rights by contrast. That society itself, like William Blake's New Jerusalem shining on the hill, cannot be mandated by a legal code, a constitution, or a fatwa, but must come from the work and initiatives of its citizens, empowered by their freedoms and rights. Hence post-Islamists embrace democracy and civil society not as a tactical play but as an integral part of the strategic vision. For real.

As Islamism aged and became a part of the scene in the Middle East, it lost its sheen for many middle-of-the-road

Muslims, especially for Ismail's generation. I had noticed this in my travels over many years.

When I first arrived in the region in the mid-1980s, Iran's Islamic revolution was only just cooling down and political Islam seemed free of the muck that attached itself to other ideologies, partly or wholly failed. Those were the days when the classic Islamist rallying cry 'Islam is the solution' rang loud and ordinary people would often try to engage you as a Westerner in theological discussion. Once, surrounded at a wedding in an Egyptian village by a bunch of keen proselytisers, I was only saved by my friend Ahmed wading in and asking each of them in turn who the third caliph after the Prophet Muhammed was. When none of them could answer, he asked me, and being a history nerd I was able to say that it was Uthman ibn Affan. Then he rounded on my would-be recruiters and told them to get to know Islam themselves before they sought to persuade others.

But by the 1990s, armed groups were known for committing atrocities in conflicts such as Algeria's civil war, and Egypt's own low-grade Islamist conflict. Then came 9/11 and al-Qaeda. Western media largely clocked the first two stages of evolution of Muslim public opinion, first some degree of solidarity with the United States in the immediate aftermath of 2001, and second, the violent revulsion at the invasion of Iraq in 2003.

But a third stage went largely unnoticed because it didn't make good TV. There was no good picture and it didn't engage the emotions. From about 2005 on it became clear that al-Qaeda had overplayed their hand. Public opinion polls across the Muslim world started to show large swings away from support for political violence because of the grisly, almost orgiastic nature of al-Qaeda operations in Iraq. The vast majority of Muslims found these actions not only horrific but also offensive to their faith. They were also not insensitive to the fact that, for all its anti-American rhetoric, al-Qaeda was mostly about Muslim-on-Muslim violence. Many stayed wary of the political West and hostile to its now multiple armed interventions across the Muslim world. But not disposed to violence against civilians. The barbarity of al-Qaeda had pushed mainstream Muslim opinion to become non-aligned, to borrow a term from the Cold War.

The way Ismail explains it, post-Islamist is the new middle of the road for the Muslim world. 'I'm talking about the realities of today. For now we can have no liberalism, no Marxism and no classic Islamism. Classical Islamism might be the most suitable political ideology in some future period. But not now.'

Being a liberal myself, with a small l, I was struck by the way he put secular liberalism into the same category as the all-embracing ideologies of Islamism and Marxism. But it's not hard to see why.

Secular liberalism was imported into Egypt over a hundred years ago by the large foreign communities that lived in Cairo and Alexandria. But it has never taken root in the mainstream although, like Marxism and Islamism, it thrives in a particular subculture. In the early independence phase, a certain form of secularism was married to political power in Egypt, as in Syria, Iraq and other exemplars of the national security state. This was literally exemplified in the First Lady phenomenon – Anwar Sadat's wife, Jihan, Suzanne Mubarak, Leila Ben Ali, Bashar

Assad's wife Asma, Queen Rania of Jordan – and why, incidentally, elsewhere in the Middle East the accession of Abdullah Gul to the post of president in Turkey in 2007 when his wife wears hejab was such a hot political issue. What post-Islamism suggests is that many, perhaps most first ladies in Egypt in the future will also wear hejab. But, unlike classical Islamism, or indeed power structures in traditional Muslim societies, it does not then predict they will be hidden from public view.

As time went on, Arab nationalism failed to fulfil its promise, politically, socially and culturally, and Islamism and Islamisation started to fill the void. Political elites responded by embracing public piety and private hypocrisy. If secularism was not formally discarded, it was increasingly marginalised. It became more of a mistress to be visited in the pied-à-terre than a wife to be embraced in public. But just at the time when that was happening to the social aspects of secularism, in the 1980s and 1990s, economic liberalism appeared in the Arab world. Communism collapsed, the ultra-liberal Washington Consensus established global ascendancy, and Egypt and Tunisia both adopted IMF and World Bank austerity programmes and privatisation. Seen from the street, this was when the elites proclaimed laissez-faire liberalism to be the new answer, without admitting that the old answer of socialist economic planning had failed, and just imposed it. With meagre results for the poor, and rich pickings for the crony capitalists. Against that background, many ordinary Egyptians, if they were inclined to acknowledge liberalism at all, would see it not as a set of ideas but as empty rhetoric concealing more tricks to keep them poor and marginalised, cooked up by elites conniving with foreigners.

We talked of Turkey, often cited as the example of things to come, how Islamism can 'go Christian Democrat'. Ismail said that the leaders of Turkey's AKP, men like Recip Erdogan and Abdullah Gul, Turkey's current prime minister and president, had come to Egypt around the turn of the millennium to seek the intercession of the Muslim Brotherhood in a rift they were having with Necmettin Erbakan, then the acknowledged leader of political Islam in Turkey. As the founder branch, the Egyptian Muslim Brothers held great authority over what had become a worldwide movement. But the Brothers' then General Guide Mustafa Mashoor had refused even to meet them, perhaps considering that he needed to support Erbakan's authority. It was that rebuttal which led the Turks to decide to start their own party, which would be Islamic in values but not in agenda, even while they were in Cairo.

Now the boot is on the other foot, and within the Brotherhood there are various tendencies to split and form new parties on the AKP model, religiously inspired but with a political programme expressed purely in civil terms. But while op-eds in international broadsheets frame 'the Turkish model' in terms of its appearance on the scene in the form of political parties, with Necmettin Erbakan's Islamic Welfare Party in the 1980s, Ismail, as a scholar of the movement, goes back another couple of decades.

Fathullah Gulen is a Turkish Muslim scholar in his seventies who now has a movement named after him, the Gulen Movement, with schools and intercultural institutions of one kind or another in over 100 countries. Perhaps indicative of his brand of Islam is that he left Turkey in the late 1990s, when he was just about to undergo trial for comments that could be interpreted as being in favour of an Islamic state, to take up residence in Pennsylvania, where he has been ever since. There is an interfaith institute named after him attached to the University of Houston.

Gulen, who has written extensively about his life, was born and raised in a traditional Muslim environment and became a preacher. But he deviated early from the career path of conventional Muslim cleric, and from the mid-1960s began to build a network of schools and training institutes. It flourished and spread quickly and is today a worldwide movement.

'In my opinion, it is Fathullah Gulen and his movement more than anyone else who prepared the ground for post-islamist politics within the secular Turkish republic,' said Ismail.

The movement has several institutions in Egypt, including the International Salahuddin High School in Cairo, which is very exclusive and sought after. Salahuddin is the Arabic pronunciation of Saladdin, the Kurdish general who duelled with Richard the Lionheart of England and retook Jerusalem from the Crusaders in the twelfth century. The school is designed to combine traditional Islamic values and strong academics. But it is not a madrasa, a school that specialises in specifically Islamic learning such as those in Pakistan, which have become infamous for being hotbeds of jihadism. Religious classes are taught but the school follows the American high-school curriculum, in English. Its aim is to produce a future leadership class in Egypt who are both competent and devout.

'That right there shows you the essence of this thinking,' said Ismail. 'These institutes are backed by Turkish businessmen and foundations as part of their charitable donations. And when they set up institutions abroad, they always adapt to the environment they are in.'

Gulen might be considered as the modern equivalent of Jamal ad-Din al-Afghani, an Afghan scholar who wandered the Islamic and European worlds in the nineteenth century, advising potentates and founding schools, attempting to help the Muslim world adapt to the onslaught of European civilisation, then at the height of its imperial expansionist ambitions.

Gulen, in turn, followed the teachings of an earlier Turkish scholar, Said Nursi. Nursi wrote a seven-volume commentary on the Qur'an, designed to make it accessible to Muslims not steeped in the traditional religious sciences, which have a formidable learning curve.

So by the time Erbakan's Islamic Welfare Party began to attain electoral success in the early 1990s it had a ready-built constituency waiting for it.

Gulen's story shows how different the trajectories of modern Egypt and Turkey have been. He could build his movement because of the way Turkey dealt with the vast web of traditional Islamic charitable endowments, called the *wakf*.

The iron-hand secularism of modern Turkey's founding father Kemal Ataturk is well known. And yet, while he imposed strict regulation on the traditional Islamic endowments, he did not absorb them into the state, unlike the government of Gamal Abdel Nasser in Egypt, which effectively nationalised them. This is of huge importance. The endowments represented something pretty close to what we now call civil society, a web of institutions and funds devoted to promoting religious learning, but also to societal and personal development, such as in schools, hospitals, and cultural associations, sanctioned by the Prophet himself and built into the fabric of all traditional Muslim societies. In Turkey the religious classes were excluded from all functions of the state but, once marginalised politically, allowed to keep their internal autonomy. In Egypt they were absorbed into the state to be better controlled by it. The Grand Mufti of Al Azhar is an Egyptian government employee. The state also appropriated all the land that the endowments system in Egypt used to own or administer, including, Ismail said, large stretches along the Northern Coastal road to Libya that subsequently ended up in the hands of private property developers and were turned into luxury tourist resorts and gated communities. Fathullah Gulen and the builders of the movement in Turkey therefore had a huge resource base to work from and an unbroken tradition of religiously inspired civil society.

The Muslim Brothers and other Islamists in Egypt have not been idle in this regard. Much ink has been spilled over the last twenty years about their parallel welfare networks, clinics and hospitals, such as the ones advertised on the door of the Tawhid mosque on Midhat al-Yazel Street. But the difference is many of the Gulen institutions are elite by any standard, and aspire to be globally competitive. Not free, or subsidised, and basic. The best you can get. Compare this approach to learning, the desire to be globally competitive using English-language curricula, with that of the Taliban, who banned education for girls and used to round up people on the streets of the Afghan capital Kabul simply for speaking Persian rather than their own Pashto.

A second major difference between the two countries, and one that may paradoxically have smoothed the way for Turkey's Islamists, is that the Turkish constitution is aggressively secular and off-bounds for political debate. This is not the case in Egypt, particularly now after the revolution, where there is already a conflict over clause 2 of the constitution, which states that 'the principles of Islamic *shari'a*' are the main inspiration for the source of the laws. A small minority of strident secularists want it removed. A larger body of Islamic fundamentalists demand its 'enactment', claiming it has not actually been in force.

So it seems every country is different, and that comparisons – such as between Egypt and Turkey, which are often supposed to be similar, largely because they operate in the same foreign policy space for the Western powers – can be dangerous if they are simplistic. I put this to Ismail.

'Part of this thinking, post-Islamism, more generally is the need to escape comparison,' he said. 'In this sense also, classical Islamism is sometimes presented as an anti-Western programme. But what about who we are, in ourselves?'

This chimed with the experience I was having talking to all the young protesters in Egypt and Tunisia. Democracy and an open public life were no longer ideological debating points but inalienable givens, unconsciously assumed as part of one's identity and rights. The idea that these values represented some kind of contradiction to the Islamic faith would leave anyone under forty bemused, whether it came from patronising Western Orientalists or their fundy neighbour living down the road.

I also wondered, from the Arab and Muslim perspective,

how taxing it might be to be constantly monitored and analysed for whether you liked or hated 'the West', and in particular the United States. For all my great affection for America, my two years studying there, my sister and her family in California, several close friendships and an undying addiction to *The West Wing*, it felt like there was something a little neurotic in a foreign policy, shared across the administrations, which insists on dividing the world into those who like you and those who don't, often identifying it straightforwardly with consumerism. The idea that a major political movement in the Middle East might claim the right simply to be indifferent, or take it case by case, was refreshing.

'The Gulf countries, for instance,' Ismail continued, 'certainly don't deny their Muslim identity at one level. But they are drunk on consumerism. In Dubai they have to have the highest skyscrapers, the best hotel in the world, all the artificial islands. But it's like they're saying "In our gelabiyas and skullcaps we are just as good as you. Look, we have iPods and Rolexes." In other words, even as they differentiate themselves from the West, it is still their pole of attraction.

'And yet that model is driven by oil. All the people who make the engine work are foreigners, from the Asian construction workers to Western consultants and managers. And when it all collapses, as it did in Dubai with the financial crisis, they just drive to the airport, leave their cars there, and go home. I'm convinced the Gulf will be the last region in the Arab world to change.'

But the difference in the constitutional positions of Turkey and Egypt also pointed to a key issue. What happens in Egypt,

I asked Ismail, where there isn't the same constraining hand, not just of the constitution but the unquestionable devotion of both the judiciary and the armed forces to keeping it intact, as is the case with Turkey? If those parameters don't exist or are as of now unknown in Egypt, what is the guarantee that things like *hodoud* punishments wouldn't be introduced – amputation for theft, stoning for adultery? There are no agreed ground rules.

We went back and forth on this a little. He pointed out how unlikely that seemed in the current climate in the country, and it does. I countered with the observation that that didn't mean it couldn't happen at some stage. In the end he said: 'Well, in the end, if the majority of people want these things, and they are part of the faith, what are the grounds to oppose them?'

So here's the nub of it, the point where a clash of civilisations could happen if it wanted to. *Would you denounce please, categorically, without a waiver, not here and now and under these present circumstances, but once and for all time*, is a basic tool of political activists. It works on the assumption that maximum clarity is always good, and a necessary part of the political process, which is by and large true in democratic politics. Anything short of black and white counts as a fudge, which, in the dogma, is bad.

But there are times when there's another phrase for fudge – constructive ambiguity. From a liberal perspective, the effect of post-Islamism's intense pragmatism is to appear to arrive at constructive ambiguity by re-ordering priorities. It posits a picture in which the new thinking says: 'I'm not abandoning my controversial demands, I'm putting them at 173 on the list.

If you ask me whether I no longer believe in them but can't say so to my own constituency, I won't tell you. If you ask me whether I still do believe in them but feel that the way to achieve them is step by step, including getting you to like me, I won't tell you. The position itself is clear. I'm just not going to discuss the reasons for it.'

I should add that Ismail himself rejects the idea that this thinking involves any ambiguity, constructive or otherwise, saying that there are no necessary contradictions between a 'partial secularism' that reinforces democracy, citizenship and human rights, and encouraging and promoting piety in Egypt and other Muslim countries.

Some secularists or outsiders might disagree with that, and therefore see post-Islamism as no more than an attempt to fudge what remains an irreconcilable gap between two points of view, Islamism and secularism.

'Can we trust them?' asked Suha, a marketing executive, as we sat at the top of a skyscraper in Cairo. She was power-dressed, smart and successful. We'd just been discussing duty-free in European airports, Dolce & Gabbana and Chanel, not some crude or competitive label recital, but droll and self-aware, how crazy Arab elites get for labels that Europeans have stopped noticing. Then we somehow moved on to my experiences on Khaled Said's street, the state bakery, Friday prayers, the migrants from the Delta, and Ismail's theories of post-Islamism in the cafe opposite Space Net. Which seemed half a world away, as Cairo lay so far beneath us we could barely hear the honking traffic through the open window.

'I mean I agree with everything you say about how being

religious isn't the same as being fanatical,' she said. 'But being *Islamist* is something different again. They will say they want democracy just as long as they think it will help them get power.'

It's true that Ismail's subtle, considered arguments are more refined than the reality of the Arab street. The Tunisian taxi driver who shouts at Moufida the lawyer that women can't be heroes, she should be at home, and that the *shari'a* is the only constitution worth having. The cafe on Midhat al-Yazel Street with the framed aphorism: 'Whenever a wife dies and her husband was satisfied with her she will enter Paradise.' The Libyan men I was to meet in a barber's shop in Benghazi who were incensed that anyone would take government-backed personal loans, because they contained interest and were therefore *haram*, forbidden under Holy Law.

But the larger point is that this new mood, of piety joined at the hip to political freedom, is emerging strongly and credibly enough in Egypt and elsewhere that discussions about whether *they* really mean it begin to feel like conspiracy theory, or at the very least an impulse to arrive at ultimate intent which is so dogmatic it induces claustrophobia. Surely an agreed democratic and development project for the foreseeable future is enough common ground to work with?

Part of the answer to Suha's question comes down to trust, which in turn partly comes down to getting out and about. Nobody I met who had been on the streets during the protests in either Tunisia or Egypt, or in Libya come to that, believed that the revolution could or would be hijacked by classical-style Islamists who could use it to seize the state. In large measure because they saw the kind of people who were there. They

themselves *were* the kind of people there. That kind of sentiment is just harder to grasp when you're on the twenty-fifth
floor, or in a different country.

Another part of the answer is a question back: Who's the
we and who's the *them* in the trust question? Because if Egypt's
democratic process is to succeed, Suha needs to consider not
only whether she trusts Ismail, or the Muslim Brothers come
to that, but also whether Ismail or the Muslim Brothers trust
her. The only alternative, theoretically, would be to attempt to
rule by force. But in Egypt today that seems unthinkable. True
secularists, those prepared to go down fighting for it as a political system as opposed to those who like the odd fling with
Johnny Walker, are a tiny minority and no longer have any
power base.

Perhaps a third part of the answer is to rethink a little the
relationship between religious faith, politics and secularism in
the West, inventor of the idea. Secularism gradually evolved in
Europe over the last two and half centuries, from the
Enlightenment, but it is only since the Sixties that practising a
faith has actually become a minority pursuit. In the United
States religion is still very much to the fore in public life, but
in both Europe and North America the politics of religion has
often come to be seen as of the right, crystallised in culture-
war issues such as abortion and gay marriage. Of course we're
talking about hundreds of millions of people, so these gener-
alisations have exceptions. Big picture, though: there is no
Christian Left to match the Christian Right. This affects the
liberal and secular perspective on the relationship between politics and religion in the Middle East.

But this positioning of religion in politics is only since the Sixties revolt against all forms of vested authority. The previous century and a half of politics had seen deeply religious leaders, rank and file and institutions at the forefront of major social advances, from Wilberforce and slavery to the Reverend Martin Luther King on civil rights, with prison reform, education and hospitals in between. One of the achievements of candidate Barack Obama in the 2008 presidential race was some slight revival of the concept of progressive politics connected to faith.

Is it possible, then, that the Egyptian Revolution could be a milestone in the defusing of political Islam not despite but because of the fact that so many of its protagonists are deeply religious? That prayer time at Tahrir Square, where the Copts in the crowd guarded their Muslim comrades in arms and helped them perform their ablutions, was the first public manifestation of post-Islamism? That it could herald the beginning of an era in which a faith-based social justice is integrated into competing visions in an open political system, instead of being the central ideological conflict?

Ismail had one last observation on this.

'You know the days of total secularism are pretty much over in the Arab world. One thing I noticed during the protests was that even our colleagues in the leftist and liberal parties are personally observant. They all fast, for example. A friend of mine from the liberal Ghad Party fell to his knees to thank God on January 25, when the crowds of protesters turned out larger than anyone had dreamed. Our friend Youssef Shabaan is from the Revolutionary Socialist Movement, virtually communist in ideology. When he was jailed last year he asked for two things from his cell. One of them was a new pair of glasses to replace the ones broken during his arrest. The other was the Qur'an.'

12

Counter-revolution!

As the weeks passed after the stunning fall of the Pharaoh there was talk that a counter-revolution was growing. Lots of people wondered about why there were quite so many strikes all of a sudden and the police, who had withdrawn three weeks earlier after an outcry at their tactics with the protesters, were still off the streets, heightening fears about law and order, which was clearly the intention. Down on Midhat al-Yazel Street, there were two classes of people who were against the 25 January revolution as it had quickly come to be known. The quietists and the reactionaries.

Ali the Shoeshine doesn't live on Midhat al-Yazel Street, or even in Alexandria. He leaves home in Buheira, the Nile Delta, at 6 every morning to be here by 8.30 a.m. He's thirty, has two toddlers, and has to fight to keep his family going. He charges one Egyptian pound for a spit and polish and hopes for more. He might get twenty-five customers a day and he takes Fridays off. His take-home, once he's paid for travel and other work expenses, varies between 500 and 800 Egyptian pounds – $90 to $130. That's what he has to feed four mouths for a month.

I asked him how he ended up on Midhat al-Yazel Street and he tells me how, one day twelve years ago, he pitched up in

Alexandria, the big city. He just came wandering, without a clear idea of what he was going to do or where, until he ended up in the next street along, where a guy said, Come and help me in my shoeshine business. The next day he came back and decided to strike out on his own. He moved a street along, pitched to the cafe I found him in, and twelve years later here we are.

Did you join the revolution? I asked. His answer is just a tut, the jerk of the head up, Middle Eastern body language for no. Why not, I asked.

Ana mish bita al-hagaat dee, he said, roughly translatable as 'I don't go in for that sort of thing', or 'It's not for me'. Why? I persisted.

'God created us and gave us what we have. We should be satisfied with it,' he said. But what about all the corruption and police brutality? I say. 'We should be satisfied,' he repeats. 'Those ministers, they shouldn't have been stealing the country blind. And the lads, the protesters, they shouldn't be turning the world upside down.' Quietism. The other rural migrant I had met on the street, Ramadan the concierge, had also shown traces of it.

Ali's world view – provide, trust in the Almighty, and do not aspire – is certainly shared by millions of his fellow countrymen and women. They may not be a majority but they are certainly silent, not so much counter-revolutionary as the backdrop to a counter-revolution, and one of its justifications.

Hussein, a factory manager, is a different story. Middle-aged, tweedy and paunchy, with an ill-advised starched yellow shirt and sunglasses, he overhears my conversation about local history with Mohammed Shawqi, the cafe owner, on the corner of the Corniche, and stops to grace us with his incensed views on the world. He's not impressed with our literary flights of fancy.

'Don't write about Naguib Mahfouz. Write the real story,' he says, having taken my pen up from the table, unbidden, to stab the air with it. 'The army are dying every day. We can't have democracy here in Egypt. Not now. Every time we concede a demand the protesters make a new one!'

Hussein runs a factory in the industrial belt behind the city which makes up a third of Egypt's manufacturing. But he professes worry about those on the breadline. 'There are nine or ten million people in this country living hand to mouth, from day to day. We have to get the "wheel of production" running,' he says, parroting a phrase bandied about by the state newspapers which have curiously become the opposition. 'And don't talk to me about Khaled Said,' as he realised why I was hanging around on this street in particular. 'If they try and change the name of this street I will be the first one to stand up and oppose it. Midhat al-Yazel was a hero who gave his life for the country. What did Khaled Said do? Smoke hashish and who knows what else.'

Mohammed sat, deeply sad, repeating 'No comment', 'No comment' while Hussein fulminated about Khaled. Among people with traditional manners in the Arab world, 'No comment' can be more an expression of disgust than neutrality. What Mohammed meant was more like 'That's so low, let's not even go there.' After Hussein had gone, he said: 'Whether Khaled Said was a martyr, that is between him and his God. But we should remember the words of Abu Bakr, who said he would not be sure of entering Paradise even if he had already had one foot inside it.'

Abu Bakr was the first caliph to succeed the Prophet as leader of the early Muslim community. It was a cultured way to say Hussein should be more humble, we all live in glass houses and shouldn't throw stones.

Two things happened which ensured that civil opposition to Egypt's revolution was muted. First, the revolution happened so fast it was over before there was much concerted reaction to it. Second, those who supported Hosni Mubarak and the regime expected the police state to take care of things as it always had. But the army stayed neutral and the police, after having tried and failed at intimidation, stayed at home in a kind of calculated sulk.

This left it to emerge piecemeal after Mubarak had gone. First there was the issue of whether his last appointee as prime minister, Ahmed Shafik, should stay on. A huge banner hanging from the girls' school opposite Tawhid mosque read: 'Ahmed Shafik man of experience, needed by the country'.

You couldn't calibrate counter-revolution by social class. Many in the establishment were disaffected with the Mubarak regime by the end, whether it was someone like Mustafa Ramadan, the clever lawyer who resented the attempt to allow Gamal Mubarak to inherit the presidency, or even businessmen and army officers. One Friday I attended Alexandria's Automobile Club, a social club frequented by the city's old elite. The clubhouse sits on the Corniche, dating back to the time when its traffic load would have been mostly horses and traps with the occasional stylish Bentley. Ten lanes of traffic came crashing past it now, and colonial villas had been replaced by twenty-storey skyscrapers along the seafront. But inside old buffers still sat by a swimming pool, looking out to sea. One conversation was between a retired admiral and a successful businessman, whose name I didn't catch, about the New Year's bombing of al-Qiddisin church. Both were convinced that rumours suggesting the interior ministry had itself staged the attack, which killed twenty-one people, were true. No starry-eyed idealism about the regime there. Another thread came from a retired businessman who asked me if I thought the revolution was just against Hosni Mubarak's thirty-year reign, or rather the whole sixty years of the republic since the Free Officers' coup d'état led by Gamal Abdel Nasser. His own view was the latter, on balance, and rightly so, he felt, since it was the deprivation of civil liberties and the atmosphere of nationalist emergency installed by Nasser which started the rot in the first place.

That afternoon at the club was an object lesson in how autocracies can appear to be monolithic when stable and yet conceal a multitude of resentments, equivocations and plain free thinking among people you would figure for its most committed supporters.

Or industrial-strength cynicism among its strongest supporters. In the Nineties, when I lived in Cairo, I used to go to the Gezira Sporting Club on Fridays to run round its horse track, under the 6 October overpass built across the grounds of this exclusive club in the heart of the city, or play squash. Once we were hanging out after a game when General X, recently retired and with a clutch of directorships, as was becoming the fashion, approached me and my squash partner, whom he knew. The general came to berate us for our coverage of Islamic group violence, which was just appearing on the radar then. Why do you make such a fuss about it? he asked. They tried to kill the prime minister last week, I replied. You think we're exaggerating? The prime minister, the general repeated, snorting with derision, Who's he? He's the man nobody notices when he gets out of the car.

And Mubarak, he went on, even if they got Mubarak, you think that would make any difference? Suddenly my antennae were buzzing. I was a twenty-something European whose job as a wire hack encouraged me to be politically naïve, to take Egypt's public processes seriously and write about them every day, many times if possible. According to that view, President Mohammed Hosni Mubarak was the man. The game was whether you supported him or not. Conspiracy theorists to me were UFO nutters who probably lived in the middle of nowhere, which was just as well considering they might have questionable personal hygiene. They weren't urbane ex-generals, clearly moneyed and influential, chatting over lemonade at an elite social club.

'Mubarak, not-Mubarak,' said the general, flipping his hands methodically as if weighing up the two worlds. 'If Mubarak disappeared, we'd just find another one.' His casual tone opened my eyes to a whole new strain of thinking that was clearly all around me but hidden, just beneath the surface, in the penthouses and soirées along the Nile where foreign correspondents are often invited. I left Egypt shortly afterwards to be the Reuters correspondent in soon-to-be-independent Palestine following the Oslo accords of 1993, as we then thought. But I often thought about who the general's *we* was, and whether I, or anyone else who wasn't actually them, could ever access them more fully. The Algerian civil war was raging at the time between the military regime and Islamic extremists, and ordinary folk there, caught in the middle, had developed a moniker for the president, the army, the police, the government, the guy at the end of your street watching you – collectively, they were just *Le Pouvoir*, 'The Power'. Clearly, if the general's insinuations were to be trusted, something analogous existed in Egypt, though possibly more muted.

But the army had stayed neutral during the revolution. Was it buoyed by the daily phone calls that were reported between US Defence Secretary Robert Gates and Field Marshal Mohammed Hussein Tantawi, the man leading the High Military Council? Maybe, but we won't find that out for years.

It was the police who formed the heart of the counter-revolution, both during the protests and in the days and weeks after Mubarak had fallen.

A friend of mine lived in the district of Smouha, a mile down the road from Midhat al-Yazel Street, and while I was hanging out on the street, in early March, I went to visit him. The street was built just a few years ago and everything still works, as yet relatively unexposed to entropy: eight-storey apartment blocks with clean lobbies, liveried staff and new cars outside. Straight opposite the blocks was an old house with gardens, a tied police house dedicated to a career officer. During the revolution, the men of the neighbourhood had manned a barricade here, outside his house, and a spirit of camaraderie was thrown up, tea round the fire. We went to see him, one thing led to another, and we ended up sitting outside again, chewing the fat.

When Colonel Mohsin found out I was interested in the case of Khaled Said, he wanted to brief me, explain how autopsies create disfigurements similar to the one we saw in the photo on the Internet, give me the phone number of the lawyer, tell me the effects of hashish in the blood. *Maybe*, he said, *maybe*, the two agents had lied about bringing the body back. But that was just their inexperience.

Since he seemed up for it, I said, with all due respect, hadn't the case caught everyone's imaginations because it hit a raw nerve? People in this country think that police brutality is systematic – isn't that the power behind the Khaled Said case, whatever the specifics of the case before the law?

'I blame the media over the last four to five years,' said the colonel. 'They have the legal right to lie and they boast about it. As the government I need the power to stop them lying, and to have my own media which tells only the truth.' Hmm, I thought. Isn't that pretty much what the last regime tried?

A couple of the men of the street came to join us as we sat out. The talk expanded. I was in favour of the revolution, Islam said, until they got rid of Mubarak. But now it's enough. And I'll tell you another thing. They talk about work. But people don't want to work. We have jobs posted for 500 or 600 Egyptian pounds a month – about $100. But nobody applies for them. It's the 25th of Losses, not the 25th of January, Mohammed said, a play on words in Arabic since Losses, *khasayir*, rhymes with January, *yanayir*. My company's losing half a million dollars

243

a day, that's just in production, Islam said. It won't be long before their entire investment is at risk.

Usama, who had lived in New Jersey, spoke archetypal American – 'Hey buddy how are ya?' He said crime was spiralling out of control now. Well, wouldn't the police staying off the streets be something to do with that? I asked Colonel Mohsin. He smiled at me as though I was naïve.

'We can't go back until it is clear we have the authority to do what we need to do,' he said. 'We need a law.' It wasn't clear what he meant, I said. Egypt was full of laws. But people aren't aware of what they are, he said. It was confusing. He seemed to be suggesting that the solution to a crisis of confidence in the Egyptian police was to give them more authority and power. He was all scare stories, about how an officer had been attacked by a nutter with a sword in Cairo and then attacked again by a crowd when he fired into the air in self-defence, how lots of police and army had been murdered during the revolution but it had all been hushed up.

What you don't realise, he said, is how the Muslim Brothers are all influenced by Iran. The way they divide themselves up and slip into a crowd, each encouraging those around them to shout slogans? That's pure Iran. Islam, Usama and Mohammed listened in silent respect. The Mubarak regime peddled the Iranian thesis for years. When I was a correspondent based in Cairo in the early Nineties Iran was held to be behind every last incident that happened. But it was surprising this particular meme could have lasted into the second decade of the twenty-first century. Hadn't the last few years seen the sharpening of a Sunni–Shia division across the Arab world?

As we sat talking he kept getting calls and texts on his two phones. What's going on? we asked. They are raiding state security headquarters, he said. We all knew who 'they' were. Where, we all asked, Cairo? No, here, he said. Alexandria? Let's go there, I said. The colonel shook his head. It's very bad. There's an exchange of fire. My friend didn't look keen so I sat back down.

You see, he said, turning to me. You see how organised they are? This is the Muslim Brothers who've gone to the police station to find their own records and expunge them. Because in the future they're going to be in high office and they don't want anyone to know what they were up to. And yet the newspapers tomorrow will be full of stories about how they opened fire from inside the buildings, as though the officers were responsible.

It was fascinating to be taken into the mind of a master conspirator. Mohsin could already spin all possible fallout from what was happening in real time, in a way that kept his world view intact. The newspapers were indeed full the next day of reports that police inside the building had opened fire on demonstrators. Because they had. I spoke to three people separately who were there, who all said the same thing, none of them Muslim Brothers. This was, in fact, a new stage of the revolution. For some days, there had been reports of document bonfires inside police stations, particularly the hated state security, the political police. That day demonstrators in Alexandria decided to go to the buildings, supposedly abandoned because the police weren't at work, to check it out. And police inside opened fire on them. It was the political police, not the protesters, who were shredding and burning documents.

Didn't the police store files in a central database? I asked. Well yes, he mumbled, the important stuff. But there were a lot of low-grade files at local level. It sounded like he didn't really know what he was talking about but I let that pass.

Colonel Mohsin's version was a kind of tailored anti-matter of the truth. It reminded me of the 1990s when as a wire agency reporter you got wind of a new attack by the Islamists from your stringer network only to have an official statement arrive from the interior ministry confirming its details by denial. We deny there was a bomb in the second Pyramid. A white Toyota Corolla did not then pull up and three men get out . . . Cross out the negatives and there was your story.

With every call and text from police headquarters, under attack from determined fanatics, the group was getting edgier. Do you remember, Islam was asking Mohammed, the night we caught the thief and had to hold him down? Tales of carjackings and handbag snatches. Oh and look at those buildings over there, Usama said. I swear they've built three storeys in the last three weeks. The building in question did seem to lean out precariously, with some impromptu scaffolding applied to its upper floors. The group explained how since the revolution – sigh, tut – nobody even pretended to respect building regulations any more. Everyone was building floor extensions just as fast as they could, to be finished by the time law and order were re-established.

Other street residents were passing, with increasing haste as curfew drew near. Several mothers with children, all greeting us fulsomely, like we were fine, strong, decent men they could count on. Heady stuff.

Then there was a car passing with something on a mega-phone that we couldn't catch. Colonel Mohsin sent off one of his bodyguards to check what the story was. He came back saying a small girl was missing and her family were distraught. We stood up, ready to break into groups and head off into the night to rescue her. But before we could, the bodyguard came back to say she'd been found.

I probed with the colonel what a solution to the security impasse might be. But it was hard to pick up from his answers and reactions anything other than a professional sulk. How about full powers back to the police, together with the undisputed right to citizens to film? I asked. Citizen media was a massive part of the revolution and everyone had mobile phones. If the right to film was explicit and acknowledged it would be widely practised. That won't work in current circumstances, he said, because there will be excesses and when they are filmed they will get blown out of proportion. Almost as if he were demanding a police right to abuse power. What about if police all wear unique IDs on their shoulders, as they do in most of Europe? I asked. We don't need that here because everyone knows who the police are, he replied. I was stumped.

Well come on, I said to Colonel Mohsin, there's got to be something you think went wrong and needs to be done better next time. He went silent for a moment. And then came back with a chilling response. The old minister and spin, in effect. We didn't spin well enough.

Habib al-Adly, he said, the now disgraced minister of the interior, was too close to Suzanne Mubarak, the president's wife. Because she liked him too much, the other ministers didn't like him and left the door open for him, and the ministry, to be attacked. Plus, he was old school and arrogant. He would never issue denials, which meant the media was fed with the opposition version of events and that went unchallenged. We need a proper media department.

That's it. After twenty years on the force, Colonel Mohsin's analysis of what went wrong with policing in Egypt is a fragment of palace scuttlebutt and bad public relations. Oh by the way, he said, as we parted, if you're interested in finding out about Khaled Said's neighbourhood, there's a cafe on the corner of the Corniche you might want to go to. What's it called? He pretends to rack his brains for a moment. Ah, yes. *Qasr as-Shawq*, the Palace of Desire. Yes, you could find out a lot there.

He was telling me he knew where I had been. I had told my friend who presumably, quite innocently, had told him. Now he was telling me. The *We know where you live* gambit. Old habits die hard.

A key part of the philosophy of counter-revolution is faith in the School of Hard Knocks. A businessman, Mahmoud, largely self-made through links to the regime, has spent an afternoon telling me how everything is going to pot, how the high-profile businessmen now being questioned over sweet land deals, some of them his sponsors, are misunderstood – who else would have got land development going along the northern coast? But then he suddenly lapses into reminiscences about national service and the time he was sentenced to thirty days in jail for desertion because he'd been a week late back from leave. He'd already started a successful career when he was called for service, and, after a week of farcical exercises in the desert, almost absconded altogether in horror at the thought of two more years of hunger, discomfort, excruciating boredom, and sitting in the middle of nowhere in a uniform that never fitted.

So I was up in front of the court, said Mahmoud. We have a distant cousin who I'd never met with the same family name, a general. The colonel barked at me, why were you late? At that time he could have sentenced me to six months, a year even, I was really sweating. I told them I was ill. I had food poisoning, I said. My mother took me to the hospital. Why didn't you go to the military hospital? the colonel shouted. Because I didn't. Because I was ill and my mother just took me to the nearest hospital. Then he went silent, Mahmoud said. He was thinking what to do. Did you ask the general, I asked him, General Metwalli? Silence, he shouted, but I could see what I'd said weighed with him, he was thinking it over. Finally, he said, I'm going to send you to the doctor to find traces of this food poisoning. If you're lying, I'll put you away for six months. But when I got to the doctor, I treated him as a conscript, like I was, and appealed to him, like we're all in this together. He said he couldn't find anything but I said, well, you can take my word for it that it hurts, can't you? So I got the paper from him and only had to serve thirty days – and half of those were in the military hospital.

Then, when I got out, I managed to pull strings to get to a desk job in Cairo. I only had to turn up half the time and they offered me a week on, a week off. But I said, how about ten days on, ten days off? I wanted to create a schedule they wouldn't follow so they didn't come to rely on me, to know when I would be there or not. The officer agreed. And then I found a conscript

I could bribe to let me sign the attendance book whenever I wished. I didn't bribe him outright. That would have been too dangerous. I just asked him to buy stuff, sugar, coffee etc., and always made sure to give him three times what it cost and never ask for the change. It was over soon enough.

Just as I was thinking what a nightmare, to have that hanging over your head from the time you reach college age – how are you going to get through it, how are you going to get over it? – Mahmoud said contemplatively: 'It was a great experience. I learned so much. How to work with people, project what you need to, work the system.'

I began to see why he might hate the revolution. He'd spent all those years learning, working and yes, suffering here and there. And they, these kids, were going to render that all worthless. He'd been clever. But they were going to best him, effortlessly, just like that. A friend of Mahmoud's, the same age but of a more liberal persuasion, turned to me and said: 'You know, if we'd only known the regime would collapse if you just blew' – he breathed out like a child blowing out candles on a cake – 'we'd have done it ourselves twenty years ago.'

I was back on Khaled's street a couple of days after the evening with Colonel Mohsin, when Hisham and Ahmed turned up. They were bloggers and revolutionaries and had come to talk about the documents they had found in the state security headquarters that night I had been over at Smouha.

'We're calling it Revolution 2.1,' said Ahmed, grinning at his own *bon mot*, the phrase Revolution 2.1 in English. He told me the story of a friend of his who had had a run-in with a state security agent in college who had forced him to change his studies, and on the night of the storming of the head-quarters had come face to face with his tormentor.

How could an agent make you change your major? I asked. Long story. Basically state security police were also on the campuses of all colleges and universities, the friend had got into an argument with the agent and he had simply decided to demote him. Like many countries, you need particular grades in your high-school exams in Egypt to be allowed to study particular subjects. The friend had scored high and was in the engineering faculty. Afterwards, he was forced to switch to commerce, a middling catchment subject.

'And that's it right there. You've got to understand there's a big element of envy in the story between the police and the activists,' said Ahmed. 'For example, I scored ninety-nine per cent in my high-school exams and the average state security agent got between fifty per cent and sixty per cent. If he sees me on campus, he wants to show me I'm not so special.' The example wasn't theoretical, I sensed. Ahmed really had scored 99 per cent in his *tawgihi*, the high-school exams.

It would be easy to label Ahmed as arrogant as he talked about how awful the prime minister Ahmed Shafik was with his $500 pullover, as though that made him a worthy statesman, and how he'd said just that to a cabbie who'd taken him some-where the day before who was full of common-man praise for him. Hisham too, as he recounted how he'd told off a friend who supported Shafik because the friend had said he was afraid to voice his opinion. '"You're afraid? And you think we weren't when we went up against the bullets of the police?" I said to him!'

Both of them were lightning-fast, funny, rapier-sharp, unafraid of anybody and could be bruisingly direct. Ahmed, who was dark, also had this retro Black Panther look going on, huge, heavy glasses, white T-shirt on sticky ribcage, Afro haircut, and perfect grunge jeans. He was a hero of the revolution at twenty. Forget your average police conscript, *I* was a little jealous of him.

But he wasn't arrogant, he was twenty. He had no experience of power and didn't expect deference. He simply expected others to be as smart and principled as him and was impatient when they weren't. He had no concept he could be intimidating.

'This is the first revolution that wasn't about bread,' said Ahmed. 'It was about freedom, not bread. You know what they say: revolutions begin with risk takers, are completed by the brave, and then ridden by cowards'. So, all right, maybe he was a bit cocky.

I told them an experience I'd had in a cab the day before. The radio was on, the news had come at the top of the hour and the presenter read: 'The new prime minister Essam Sharif greeted and congratulated the noble leaders of the January 25 revolution . . .', monotonously, without conviction, just as she had, presumably, one month earlier, for the comings and goings of Mr President Mohammed Hosni Mubarak. The cabbie was one of those unsettled by the police absence from the streets, worried everything was about to go belly-up. Surely they, Hisham and Ahmed, could understand that many people thought they were simply a new National Democratic Party, a new clique that was going to appropriate the Egyptian state?

'But the last thing we would do is be one party,' said Hisham. 'That's what we fought the revolution about.' Though he added: 'Now that you mention it, I remember the day Mubarak left there were a couple of us who quite unexpectedly became unhappy. They wanted to stop. We do need to protect the revolution. But we also need to build, now, in society.'

So what about those on the breadline? I asked. The *fellah*, the petty official, all those struggling to make ends meet?

'There's a simple solution to the economy,' said Ahmed. 'Some time ago lawyers representing the unions put forward a proposal for a minimum wage in the public sector of twelve hundred Egyptian pounds. I think that would be a simple way to let everyone understand the revolution is for them too.'

Twelve hundred pounds, or about $200, was about six times the current effective minimum in the public sector. Ahmed's 'simple' solution was to raise salaries sixfold. It also didn't address the tens of millions who worked in the informal sector, prey to both poverty and insecurity. Like Ali the Shoeshine. We were sitting at one of his cafes. I looked up and down but he wasn't there just then. In my mind's eye I saw him, though, giving his latest pair of shoes some elbow.

College boys, he said, tutting. He didn't bother to look up.

13

Read All About It

Here, look at this, a friend said. *Al Ahram* is doing exactly what you are – a takeout on the world of Khaled Said. Sure enough, there was an inside spread, with a large picture of Khaled set against a wide shot of Manshiet Nasser, one of Alexandria's famous tourist spots, and the legend 'The key to the revolution'. I was interested to see how a feature like this would turn out in the Arab world's oldest newspaper, in its 136th year now since the Takla brothers, themselves Lebanese, had launched it.

Al Ahram had seen the British Protectorate, King Farouk and Abdel Nasser come and go, had reported on everything from the *Titanic* to the Tea Party – the two world wars, Palestine, Suez, the Six Day War, the Iranian Revolution, Sadat's assassination, the implosions of Lebanon and Iraq, 9/11. T.E. Lawrence had pored over it as an obscure subaltern, looking for clues in its pages as to where, in the great tectonic shifts of empire in the First World War, a chink might lie for a man to go and forge his legend. Fifty years later, spooks and analysts across the region parsed every word of its editor Mohammed Hassanein Heikal, seeking to know the mind of Gamal Abdel Nasser and the future of the Arab nation. If it had in more recent years descended into a mere cheap propaganda organ for the regime, maybe the revolution could change its fortunes, restore its greatness.

But it would be hard to be more disappointed in the end result. There's a paragraph at the start that somehow succeeds in trivialising the death of Khaled Said by its penny-shocker tone, a reference to his face as captured by Ahmed's photo at the morgue and its features 'disfigured by the brutality of Habib Adly's schooled torturers that sad, melancholic day'. And then he, Khaled, disappears along with his world. No reference to the street or even the neighbourhood. The rest is a soup of tired clichés about Alexandria the city that could have been pulled out of a guidebook. A list without purpose. The poet Cafavy and his friend Lawrence Durrell. Nasser's speeches at Manshia. The tram built 'by the Italian architect Antonio'. The world-famous singer Demis Roussos. Anfoushi district, next to the port, shelled by British gunboats in the Orabi revolt. The old fort at Qait Bey. Sultan Ibrahim Mosque. Saad Zaghloul Square with its gardens 'distinguished by their simplicity and beauty'. I was staying on that square, as it happened, at the Cecil Hotel, and as I'd crossed the gardens that morning, had noticed how threadbare the grass was and how the gutter reeked of piss.

A 5,000-word feature untarnished by a single piece of original reporting, even its imagery as old and shabby as an organ grinder with a monkey.

I went down to Cairo from Alex for the day, to a conference convened by Internews on the future of the media in Egypt. What to do about *Al Ahram* and the other newspapers, and most of all the state TV, was the burning question. State media had long been the propaganda arm of the regime, but it took the revolution for them to distinguish themselves with a level of incitement and disinformation that was simply without moral compass. Day Four of the protests brought the Battle of the Camel, when the *baltagiya*, hired thugs supporting the government, broke into Tahrir Square riding horses and a camel, all captured on camera. It was supposed to play as noble Arab manhood, the knight on his steed, the Bedouin with their camels, against a base rabble, and was covered at face value by the state media that day. A narrative of mind-boggling poverty. This was Cairo, a groaning concrete jungle of 15 million people. The animals had been rounded up from tourist rides near the Pyramids. All of the 'uncouth rabble' were peaceful, and a huge number were college graduates, the cream of their generation, autodidactically steeped in the writings of Gandhi and Martin Luther King, baring their chests to live ammunition and chanting witty slogans.

'I have a lot of sympathy with the idea that you can't really reform these media,' said Hafez al-Marazi, former Al Jazeera correspondent to Washington and now dean of a faculty of journalism. 'You'd go in as the reforming director and face a bunch of old faces. And they'd say "I covered the protests on the third day", "Well, I did on the second day", "I never joined the NDP". That's what you'd have to manage while meanwhile there's a whole new world to cover. Seniority. Self-justification. It would be better to scrap them all and start again.'

As if in unconscious confirmation, various journalists from *Al Ahram* and state TV stood up to declare their own, clean, personal pasts, the essential role of the 'national' sector as they called state-subsidised media, and the need for balance, not to throw the baby out with the bath water. Groups of young bloggers who had reported the protests to social networks sat looking on, a little ill at ease in the ballroom of the Semiramis Hotel. In a matter of weeks, they had first circumvented, then exposed, and finally forced a change in editorial direction of Egypt's huge media organs, but without a game plan, all just as spontaneous reaction to what they saw was needed. Now this arcane debate left them befuddled.

It was the sheer scale of Egypt's state propaganda effort that was hard to grasp.

'The only part of the government budget, apart from defence, that has remained secret, is the information budget,' said Hisham Qassem, publisher of the independent daily *al-Misry al-Yawm*, which has gained a strong reputation since hitting the newsstands in 2003. 'I believe that when those accounts are opened up, they will show the regime spent more on media than on health and education combined.'

He estimated the Egyptian state could have been spending 25 billion pounds, or $4 billion a year, on telling the people how great Hosni Mubarak was. State media employed 80,000 people. The Al Ahram group alone employed 17,000 people.

Egypt was not North Korea. The police state's preferred methods of controlling information were not to ban but to proliferate, banalise and financially control media, creating a system where 99 per cent of all censorship, statistically speaking, was self-censorship, from the reporter on up. That way you got to demoralise the journalists as well as simply controlling them. There were over 500 print publications under the Mubarak regime but the government was the biggest owner. When it didn't own publications, it often dominated their advertising and distribution networks. There were prosecutions of individual journalists for supposed defamation of Egypt, or impinging on national security in ways that were left deliberately ambiguous by catch-all laws. But actual shutdowns of entire publications were rare.

In broadcasting, the undeniable fact of Al Jazeera and mass ownership of satellite dishes had created a more complex reality. State control had had to yield some ground in the face of this new information order just to stay in the game. The government responded to the satellite TV phenomenon by launching its own state-sponsored satellite networks and allowing a couple of private Egyptian channels to operate, as long as they weren't political. Similarly, with radio, private broadcasting was sanctioned as long as it was in banal, commercial format. Jukebox FM.

Chief architect of this empire for a long time was Safwat el-Sherif, founder member of Mubarak's NDP. Safwat had worked for military intelligence. Despite a year's jail term in 1968, when he was convicted of extortion and blackmail for his own benefit, one of Mubarak's first acts on becoming president in 1981 was to appoint him as minister of information. There he stayed for many years, eventually graduating to become speaker of the upper house of parliament.

The 180-degree volte-face by the state media was reminiscent of a story of Mullah Nasruddin, a fictional comic figure across much of the Middle East. Nasruddin, often portrayed as the village idiot, was appointed judge and had to hear a complicated case. The prosecutor stood up and denounced the man in the dock as a dangerous criminal guilty of a heinous crime. 'You're right!' exclaimed Nasruddin and prepared to sentence the condemned man. 'But, mullah,' said the clerk of the court, 'you have to hear the defence yet.' The defence got up and delivered a scathing attack on the prosecution for impugning this poor, innocent, upright citizen. 'You're right!' exclaimed Nasruddin again. 'But, mullah,' the clerk of the court intervened again, 'they can't both be right.' 'You're right!' exclaimed Nasruddin once again.

Headlines in the government newspapers referred to 'the uprooted president', a phrase used by the revolutionaries in Tahrir Square. Footage appeared, apparently shot on mobile, showing one of the highest-profile Mubarak-era businessmen, Ahmed Ezz, being pushed around in a prison courtyard and insulted by his jailers, like some bizarre tribute to the execution video of Saddam Hussein by supporters of Moqtada al-Sadr, the same mobile vérité shakes, the same feeling, perhaps real, perhaps part of the production, of footage shot by stealth. Virtually every item talked of the 25 January revolution, or the youth of 25 January.

'I insist on media respecting values,' said Marazi. 'Mubarak is not "the dictator" or "the deposed president". He is "former president Hosni Mubarak". And Ahmed Ezz is innocent until proven guilty.'

Funnily enough, the basis for independent media began to operate in Egypt several years ago. Perhaps prodded by the satellite TV revolution to think of a media opening as inevitable, some say under the liberalising influence of the now reviled

Gamal Mubarak, seeking the role of great moderniser, the regime began to grant licences to newspapers and magazines that edged towards independence, story by story, taboo by taboo. They covered the Kefaya protest movement in 2004–5, began to carry stories of individual abuse of power by the police and others, and formed a tactical alliance with the blogosphere, in which each broke stories carried by the other.

Khaled Salah is editor of al-Yawm as-Sabia', the Seventh Day, a news website established in 2007 which is now backing into print. The operation is jammed into about five apartments at the top of a skyscraper in Cairo's Mohandisin district, some 250 journalists in total, buzzing with that newsroom feel. His own office is invaded non-stop as any managing editor's should be. At one stage he is discussing wording with one of his lead reporters – 'Not *the* cause of the revolution, Hala, we can't say that. *A* cause of the revolution perhaps!' – negotiating with a Jordanian colleague come to enquire about plans to expand investigative reporting, and chatting to me.

A reporter, Mirette Ibrahim, takes me round the operation. It's heaving. They take sports seriously. They have translation services into and out of not just English, French and Spanish but German, Dutch and Farsi. I never thought I would pass the time of day with someone in Farsi in Cairo.

The site got a licence as a weekly print publication and now, after the revolution, as a daily. But their roots lie in the web. When I ask Mirette how they rate themselves, she says number of unique visits. They get five million a month. They're the sixth-highest traffic site in Egypt, but once you take out the generics – Google, Yahoo, YouTube – they're the top Egyptian content provider, she says.

But if the future belongs to Hisham Qassem's *al-Misry al-Yawm*, and Khaled Salah's al-Yawm as-Sabia', there is one genuine and deep aspect of Egyptian life the old state media have always known how to serve up – the crime pages. When I was a Reuters correspondent in Cairo, twenty years ago, whoever was on the morning shift had to 'read in'. This meant getting through three newspapers and filing any 'pickups', stories of note that it was worth paraphrasing to the world, that there might be on . . . the Middle East peace process, the IMF reform programme, what the Islamists had been up to . . . before you could get on with the business of your own reporting, what was going on out there through the window. And I remember memorising their formats, isolating the pages and writers that might need to be picked up, and speed-reading the headlines so I could scour those three newspapers in forty minutes. So I could get onto the crime pages.

Because they were fascinating. You had a hard time, as a foreign correspondent, converting these stories into material you could use, since they neither affected Egypt's place in the world nor its ruler's place on his seat, and they rarely mapped onto the other story lines that tickled the things readers already knew – Egyptology, flailing bureaucracy, faded grandeur. But I loved them because, if you lived in Cairo, you were constantly passing through this huge city along preset vectors that barely touched the throbbing humanity you saw out of the window. I was a foreign correspondent, I loved the culture and spoke the language, but I rarely felt like I knew what drove most people's lives. And these pages yielded just a glimpse of what you passed by several times a day.

So I spent a couple of train journeys trawling through the crime pages of the state newspapers, and discovered that, revolution or no revolution, this Egypt had not changed in the least.

One day, two newspapers.

A man in the Alexandrian neighbourhood of Montaza kills his friend for not paying back 20 Egyptian pounds, or $3.

A girl gets pregnant at fifteen. She flees her family and, walking the street, finds a man who takes her to the middle-class Cairo neighbourhood of Madinat Nasr to work as a maid for an elderly lady. But the lady keeps her under lock and key. Eventually she escapes and is walking the street again. A man of thirty takes her back to his flat and rapes her so violently she loses the baby.

Safa, from the Cairo slum of Imbaba, waits until her family are asleep and then, at midnight, buys acid from a local petrol station. She waits for her neighbour Emad, aged fifteen, who comes back in the early hours from his job delivering pizzas on his moped. And throws the acid in his face for verbally harassing her. He denies that, and says the two families are in a land dispute.

Ahmed A, twenty, came from Upper Egypt to Alexandria, jobless and sleeping in the street. He befriends Chico, the driver of a tuk-tuk and when he discovers Chico earns 30 Egyptian pounds a day, decides he's going to kill him to take the tuk-tuk. He invents an excuse for them to drive out of the city along the coastal road, persuades Chico to get out of the tuk-tuk, and stabs him to death. Chico is thirteen years old.

A man gets a phone call from his friend that his wife is having an affair. He puts the phone down and kills her.

A 32-year-old divorcee from the Nile Delta has been caught distributing self-made porn videos.

A young husband kills his wife because he's impotent.

A son kills his father because he won't give him the money to buy an apartment.

A married man with two kids stabs his lover to death on a bridge in Imbaba, late at night, and then fakes an attack on himself. The investigating policeman gets him to confess by telling him she survived the attack and has testified against him.

A hairdresser kills his wife, a former employee, when she asks for a divorce.

A father drowns his son, seven years old, in the lake at Fayyum after taking him for a visit from his estranged wife. He is sentenced to ten years in jail.

A brother kills his sister at the command of her husband because he's convinced she's had an affair.

A team of eight people are caught digging for antiquities in the old Alexandria neighbourhood of Gumruk.

A gang are caught in Giza counterfeiting $100 bills. One of them is an accountant, the other a driver who works in the tourist industry, both in their early thirties.

A 28-year-old man kills his father when he taunts him that he is illegitimate. But meanwhile he is living a fantasy life that he is an undercover policeman, already at the rank of colonel, about to depart on a secret mission to southern Egypt, hotbed of extremism. He'll be disguised as a fruitseller. 'Satan whispered to me,' he says. 'Obviously I'm upset because I have ruined my glittering future.'

A man of sixty-three goes to call on a young colleague in a village near Damietta. Only his wife is there but the man says he has brought supper and asks to come in. She goes to the kitchen to make tea and when she comes back he is stark naked. She screams for help. Her husband and a friend rush to the house, beat the old man to death and dump his naked corpse outside, making no attempt to hide it.

Maryam is woken by her father, brother and uncle to be strangled in her bed for going out too often and staying out too late. They dump her body in a different part of Cairo but the police trace her by her T-shirt, one of a limited number given out by an Italian charity as part of a project.

A gang are caught at Marsa Matrouh with 250 kilograms of hashish.

The head of a petroleum distribution company is reported missing after two months. Police trace his mobile phone down to a shop in Ismailia, then his car. Two men and a woman lured him into a honey trap, killed him, then wrapped his body in a carpet and dumped it on the desert road at kilometre 75 between Cairo and Ismailia. The body isn't discovered until after the murderers confess. The woman, seventeen, is married to one of the men, who is thirty-two.

Maybe it's not so surprising there should be so much violence – these are the crime pages after all. It's the instability and hyper-anonymity of life that throws the rest of what we know about Egypt into relief, particularly what we might be tempted to describe glibly as its religiosity or moral conservatism. It's chaos out there, especially if you're poor, and many Egyptians are gut-wrenchingly poor. You don't have to be crazy or feeble-minded to look for something to hold on to.

14

This Revolution Will Be Televised

'I'm grateful to OnTV for staging this programme, and I'm grateful to you for coming here,' Alaa al-Aswany says, leaning forward to address Egypt's prime minister, Ahmed Shafik, who nods back. 'At the same time I'm telling you that on Friday I will go down into the street to join the demonstrations that call on you to resign.'

Public life was changing in Egypt alright. Just three weeks before, this combination of guests, let alone the nature of the dialogue, would have been unthinkable.

Aswany and Shafik were appearing on a late-night chat show called *Baladna*, Our Country, on the satellite channel, perhaps the most successful and widely watched of the plethora that have come on the air in the last few years. Hosting the discussion were Yosri Foda, formerly of Al Jazeera, and Reem Maged, and there were two other guests: Hamdi Qandeel, a veteran journalist, and Naguib Sawiris, the billionaire businessman who owns OnTV.

It was 3 March. Mubarak had been gone for nearly three weeks now but the protesters were still in Tahrir Square insisting that the goals of the revolution had not been met. The economy had ground almost to a halt, as dozens of wage strikes broke out and the police were still off the streets. Foremost among the demands of the protesters was the fall of the current government, appointed on 29 January by Mubarak, before he fell. The premiership of Ahmed Shafik had become the latest battleground.

Aswany has become a world-famous writer since his international bestseller *The Yacoubian Building*, published in 2002. But he is just as well known inside Egypt as a political activist. He was one of the founder members of *Kefaya*, 'Enough!', the reform movement that gathered momentum for a while a few years back and then sputtered out after the 2005 presidential election. He writes a well-known column in the *al-Misry al-Yawm* newspaper which for years now he has been signing off with 'Democracy is the Answer', a play on the slogan of the Muslim Brotherhood, who for a time would summarise their discussion of absolutely anything at all with the slogan 'Islam is the answer'.

He sits there, slightly ursine, in the kind of jacket and stripy tie you might expect from a successful mid-career dentist – exactly what he was before his literary career took off. He is, in fact, the only one of the panel of guests wearing a tie.

Shafik, opposite him, is an ex-military man, a former commander of the air force, but has adopted the power-dressing style of smart casual popularised in Egypt by Gamal Mubarak in the Noughties, the button-down shirt unbuttoned down, open at the neck, shirt a discreet light blue, tasteful cufflinks. The word was that he, Gamal, had imported advice from the same image consultants who advised Tony Blair and New Labour in the UK. The 2005 presidential election featured Mubarak senior, who was by then in his mid-seventies and had spent his whole life in rigid institutions and uniforms, sporting casual jackets at rallies, shirt open, as though he'd just dropped in from Kennebunkport, or a Silicon Valley boardroom, or as though this was a real election, in fact, and he was Bill Clinton or George Bush Senior on the stump. Shafik's navy jacket, with gold buttons, likewise declared him to be a successful man of the world but prepared, generously, not to stand on the ceremony of his office or rank, as betokened by his open collar. Only his comb-over revealed him to be from an earlier political generation.

In those three weeks the prime minister, the leading civilian figure in transition Egypt, had not given any kind of extended interview. Yosri Foda opened the door a crack, apologetically almost. Let's be direct from the start, Mr Prime Minister, he said. I've been reading the comments on the Facebook page of the new cabinet and I have to tell you the responses veer more towards disappointment. What's your comment?

Judge me on my record, said Shafik. Sweet words are not enough. Just judge me on what I've done and what I can do, not on words where maybe we would have different understandings. He senses it coming. Just after his appointment and with Mubarak still in power, he had joked that he would send some chocolates to the protesters just to show there were no hard feelings. Dozens had already been killed by that time, by savage beating or snipers that everyone believed were hired by the interior ministry. The remarks made him look inane at best.

But Aswany doesn't start there. He starts with an unimpeachable point of principle. With great respect for your person, Mr Air Marshal, and for what is said about your achievements as a technocrat, you were part of the old regime. After this revolution against that regime, there is no way that you can fulfil its demands. I would have expected you to have resigned.

Foda asks: 'I want to hear from the prime minister. Does he really want what the revolution wants?'

Shafik struggles for words. 'The revolution represents the development of Egypt. I am for development. So I am revolution.' Literal translation.

Aswany tries to engage him in a discussion of the idea that being a minister is political. 'As a minister for Hosni Mubarak you either endorsed his political thought, or you regarded it as of no importance.'

But Shafik will have none of it. I am a technocrat, he exclaims, tech-no-crat! I didn't meet Hosni Mubarak until I was a colonel. But since I'd been a lieutenant people had been predicting I would be head of the air force one day. 'Was Hosni Mubarak with me on the two, three, four successful missions I flew in the war?' he asks. 'I want to ask Alaa al-Aswany something. Hosni Mubarak appointed me as he appointed everyone else. Why does he choose to home in on me?'

Erm, because you're the prime minister, is the gist of Aswany's response. That's a political position.

'You don't understand,' Shafik says again. 'I'm a technocrat. I built an airport and an airline to world class. We became a country respected worldwide aviationally, OK?'

It's clear that Shafik really does embrace the technocrat world view. One of his main arguments for retaining a state security apparatus, now the subject of much debate, is because 'advanced countries and great powers' have them. When Foda asks him to specify, step by step, how he plans to disentangle the internal political security functions of the police from its other more everyday tasks, he says: Well, if we can't figure it out right now, let's take a successful country as a model and bring in experts to advise us how to do it. For him, and those who support him, politics is a dirty word and people like Aswany who are using it don't understand that there is politics and then, above it, there is technocracy and statesmanship. Like a lot of people who are patronising, he doesn't realise that actually, he's the one who's lagging behind.

It was past one in the morning by this time, but Egyptians were up watching, mesmerised. I witnessed a fierce debate about it at Friday breakfast a few days later.

'He was a bitch. I hated him,' Mahmoud said of Aswany. But his friend Abdel Hamid replied: 'You just didn't like his tone. That wasn't a problem for me.'

By this time in the discussion, Shafik is also losing on body language. The armchairs are too deep and you kind of get muffled if you lean right back in one. On the other hand, he's leaning forward, waving a small notebook and a pen around. He looks a little desperate. Aswany is also perched on the front of his seat, but he's looking straight into camera, so it doesn't project as much.

The contrast with how it used to be is indescribable. Mubarak rarely gave interviews to Egyptian TV. State TV would carry his happenings daily, at great length, and his speeches on state occasions in full. CNN, ABC, CBS, Charlie Rose, Christiane

Amanpour, sure, timed for every trip to the White House or other piece of foreign policy grandstanding, Iraq, the Middle East peace process. The US channels held the keys to constituencies that, however much he might dissemble as a proud nationalist, were important to him, the $77 billion in American aid paid to keep the Camp David agreements in force over the period of Mubarak's presidency.

In his last interview with Charlie Rose, mid-2009, he even replied to the first question, about whether he would run again, in English. Pre-scripted of course, including a lame joke that Rose obligingly laughed at, silently and mirthlessly. Mubarak said he wasn't thinking about that now, he was busy with the programme he'd been elected on, and 'all parts of the programme are going very well'. Hosni Mubarak, elected politician, hard at work. As interviews progressed and his interviewer moved adroitly onto sensitive subjects such as human rights, free elections and so on, his style would grow more lively and his face become a complete pantomime in and of itself: there was resignation to the folly of others, the what-could-I-do look, hands outstretched, mock surprise, the pre-prepared jokes and rhetorical questions which lead to My Answer, occasionally the look of a naughty boy caught off guard at the back of the class.

But his relationship was with foreign, specifically, US, media. Parts of the US interviews might even be replayed on state media, truncated and suitably bowdlerised, for what the interview itself betokened. Egypt is important! Look, here's the president being interviewed on CNN! The set-piece interview was an accoutrement, an adornment of modern Egypt. Mubarak frequently held press conferences when foreign statesmen and women came to town, but even then there was rarely a thrust and parry of question and answer that the Egyptian media would broadcast.

Mubarak didn't do real Q&A with his own countrymen. Why would he? He was simply following a pattern established by Anwar Sadat at the time of the Camp David agreements, when Egypt became a strategic US ally in the Middle East, with his generation of journalist superstars, Peter Jennings and Walter Cronkite. Before that, policy had been different, the Egyptian leadership guided by its pan-Arab ambitions looking towards the region rather than abroad. Gamal Abdel Nasser had been a media star in his own right, dominating the airwaves across the Arab world in the 1950s and 1960s with his weekly broadcasts on Sawt al-Arab, Voice of the Arabs. But it was a one-way flow. The Nasser era was to produce an Egyptian journalist of independent stature, Mohammed Hassanein Heikal, who has remained active to this day, hosting a popular show on Al Jazeera in his eighties and becoming a trenchant critic of the Mubarak regime. Heikal was more than a hack for Nasser. Often described as an adviser and confidant, he articulated his ideas and policies with a free hand. But Heikal's career in fact fell in two stages. There is the emeritus journalist of his later years, the thinker with enough experience and stature to speak freely. But his reputation was made by association with power, not scrutiny of it, as a spin doctor, an Alastair Campbell or Karl Rove. The fact he was able to combine this role with the editorship of *Al Ahram*, the Arab world's most august newspaper, for nearly twenty years speaks volumes for the nature of the relationship between media and power. It's as though Campbell had stayed at the *Daily Mirror*, become editor, but still virtually lived in Downing Street.

It remains the case that until the revolution Egypt had never seen full and frank discussion between politician and journalist on the airwaves.

And now here we were with Ahmed Shafik, prime minister, ex-head of the air force, fighter pilot hero of the 1973 war, challenged on air by a couple of writers and a businessman. If Aswany led the charge, Naguib Sawiris followed, not intent on attacking the prime minister but quite unafraid to speak his mind. At one point, the discussion still on the burning issue of the future of the security forces, Shafik was defending himself. Clearly we need to keep the state security force, he said. Who can dare to say that we shouldn't? A rhetorical question he expects to gain him the floor.

Except that Sawiris, next to him, puts up his hand and says 'I do.' Shafik goes back to a stock Mubarak-era argument: Every big country, every great power, has an internal intelligence service. Sawiris turns to Shafik, puts his hand on his arm, and says: 'Maybe you didn't have a whole lot of contact with the state security services before the revolution. But they were a complete parallel government that interfered with everything. Who gets the job. Who gets promoted. Who goes to the bathroom!'

He then relates a story about how OnTV had invited a member of the Muslim Brotherhood onto a show, only for the state security to phone them beforehand and tell them they would not be allowed to put him on the air.

Time passes. One of the joys of revolutions is that everything gets off-schedule. They've been on the air now for over two hours, it's coming up to two in the morning but still they keep going. Shafik is being buffeted left and right and just hasn't got the answers. Does he approve of the new appointment to the Arab League? What's the old foreign minister, Mubarak's mouthpiece, still doing in the government? That leads to an extended discussion about which ministerial posts are in the remit of the prime minister and which belong to the presidency, now the higher military council. Shafik again resorts to let's-be-reasonable. The thing is, he says, you know the high military council are busy right now and they don't have anyone who can deal with, say, Burundi – who have just signed up to a treaty about use of the Nile waters that Egypt, the increasingly parched downstream country, opposes. So the feeling was, why not let's just stick with expertise, keep the guy on for the moment?

How come there are still political prisoners? Why is emergency law still in force? Were you aware there was torture when you were a minister in Hosni Mubarak's government? What about oversight of the police? Shafik starts into a description of how new 'popular committees' are being formed which have both the police and the public on them. What do they call those things abroad? Juries? Well, only today they met in the Four Seasons Hotel . . .

'The Four Seasons Hotel?' asks Hamdi Qandeel, the other writer on the panel. Meaning that it's a bit of a rarefied environment to discuss police excesses that afflict the poorest regions the most. Like if you decided to hold broad community consultations about urban regeneration of the Bronx at the Ritz or the Waldorf.

'What, we have to discuss the hotel now?' says Shafik, exasperated.

But generally the tone mellows as the discussion goes on. There are policies and issues and disagreements on them, but that's all between reasonable men and women. Until just before the end. Aswany is back in full flow, asking about prisoners, and torture.

'This is a revolution in which many people died. The prime minister of Egypt should be a lot more interested in prosecuting the killers than in handing out chocolates!' – a reference to Shafik's comments during the protests, Mubarak still in power.

How long are you going to keep on about that? Shafik asks. Until there are prosecutions, Aswany replies. He's robust, in Shafik's face. Earlier, Shafik had begun with a homely little image of how we needed both hope and discipline for the future, because without discipline the plant cannot grow in the garden. Aswany is withering as he replies: It's not the man in the street who needs lessons from us about discipline. What I saw in Tahrir every day was that the protesters had enormous discipline. It was the Egyptian authorities who lacked it.

'You saw the video of the armoured personnel carrier running over civilians. What is your view as prime minister?' he asks Shafik.

'You're not going to lecture me about patriotism,' shouts Shafik.

'Don't talk to me about your patriotism,' replies Aswany. 'The man run over by the APC – isn't he a human being too?'

Now it's chaos. Shafik is shouting, really shouting, like in the worst kind of domestic. Aswany won't give ground, he keeps saying over again what Shafik has said is wrong. Shafik tries to explain away his comment about the chocolates. The only possible way to explain it would be by a fulsome apology, but he pretends it was a comment filled with concern for the sustenance of the protesters. But in context it sounds more like Marie Antoinette's let them eat cake. Nobody else can get a word in edgeways. For maybe a minute they are shouting like this. Yosri Foda actually gets up and moves across the set to try and persuade Aswany to back down. He barely succeeds.

The rest of the programme is recovery from this row. Everyone all bright and breezy, Reem Maged ends with a practical question about how to get yourself on the electoral roll. But somehow it feels like something has snapped.

Ahmed Shafik's resignation was announced the following day, along with his cabinet. He was replaced by Essam Sharaf, like him an ex-Mubarak minister but one who had joined the protests in Tahrir Square. The day after his appointment Sharaf appeared at the ongoing demonstration in Tahrir and announced he got his legitimacy from them, the youth of the revolution.

You could not say the OnTV programme had been solely responsible for that – the protesters had made the continuation of the Mubarak government a key issue from the day Mubarak himself had resigned. But it was glaring evidence of what that issue was and how it played. Egypt's chief executive had descended into a shouting match with, and lost to, a writer with a sharp tongue, introduced by Yosri Foda at the start of the programme as 'part of the conscience of Egypt'.

A week later, mid-March now, Yosri Foda and Reem Maged were back on the air in another political chat show that would again be a first in the history of Egyptian media. But this time it was announced in the morning newspapers, where OnTV took out large ads announcing that Mohammed El Baradei, who had won the Nobel Peace Prize for his work as head of the International Atomic Energy Agency, and then become an activist against the Mubarak regime, would be interviewed exclusively on the channel at eleven o'clock that night. This is pretty much prime time in Egypt.

The build-up made it clear that something was afoot. And sure enough, the first question Reem Maged asked after the formalities had been completed was: would El Baradei be standing for the presidency?

The answer was yes. But it took several goes to get it right. First he said he would declare his candidacy when the time was right. But Foda pushed back and said the time is now. El Baradei split hairs and said he was a legal man and couldn't officially declare his candidacy before the candidacy process was under way, and eventually Foda constrained him into repeating a formula that declared his 'intention' to become a candidate for president. In Canada or Germany, the fussing and nitpicking might have been annoying, a candidate being over-precious about specifying that she was only standing by popular demand. Here, in Egypt, it meant a new way of doing business. Foda tugged away at the point until he got total clarity, at one point confessing: 'We need this to be clear. All the rest of the programme is built on it.'

The interview lasted over three hours. It kicked off with El

Baradei's detailed position on the direct issues of the revolution. Egypt needs a completely new constitution because, although it might seem far removed, 'people need to understand that a large part of the corruption stemmed from a corrupt constitution'! They then moved on to a wide range of internal political issues: El Baradei described himself as a social democrat who believed in some public ownership, was against crony capitalism, and saw the next president's highest priority as providing the basic needs for all Egyptians: 'Democracy is not just voting and elections. The forty per cent of Egyptians who are below the poverty line are the source of the mandate for parliament. What are their concerns? Education, health, housing, work, a minimum wage, freedom of action for trade unions.'

And, finally, foreign policy. El Baradei, who started his professional life as a diplomat in Egypt's foreign service, said he had always been against the Camp David agreement and described Egypt's relationship with Israel as one of master and servant. Egyptian influence in the region had become a myth, he said, just look at all the issues that have cropped up recently: Sudan has split in two, Gaddafi next door in Libya is vowing to make war district by district, and Egypt is supporting a blockade of a million and half people in Gaza which defies all humanitarian reason. He was surprisingly strident in his positions, maintaining that the war on Iraq was not just a mistake but the result of clear deception by the American administration. Plus, he maintained, Hosni Mubarak had told him personally in his role as head of the IAEA that there was evidence that Saddam Hussein was trying to build biological weapons.

But the process was more engrossing than the substance.

Here was politics as normal, finally, in Egypt. A candidate setting out his stall. The presenters edged gently into personality and background questions, still couched in the third person deemed more respectful in Egypt. Would Dr El Baradei care to elaborate on the family status of his daughter and dispel rumours? Yes, she married in the Egyptian embassy in Vienna, according to *shari'a* law, and her husband is a Muslim. He converted to Islam? Yes, he converted. He is my son and a Muslim. What about suggestions that Dr El Baradei is far removed from the mass of ordinary Egyptians and may even look down on them? That's rubbish. I had to go abroad to communicate with Egyptians better. There was an orchestrated campaign against me.

Polite but insistent, Yosri Foda said: 'After you finished your term at the IAEA you came back to Egypt. There was a honeymoon period but then it all seemed to fall apart. Finally Hamdi Qandeel of the Association for Change issued a statement in which he said that you preferred to work on your own because you had your own working style.'

El Baradei replies he has always been a team player. 'We set out to gain a million signatures online and they mocked us and said it's only the virtual world. Now it's the regime which is virtual,' he said.

He comes across as someone with refreshingly little to prove, or to hide, as might only be natural for someone who has won the Nobel Peace Prize and reached a summit of international diplomacy. Asked if he would be prepared to become a minister in someone else's government, he says: 'I don't think so. There are many things closer to my heart than being a minister.' He talks about the difficulty he had at IAEA hiring Egyptians because of the broken education system, and points out how far behind Egypt has fallen compared with Spain, which it equalled in terms of per capita income in 1960, and South Korea.

At the same time, he is not above politicking. The interview was delayed an hour by Yosri Foda being summoned to the office of new prime minister Essam Sharaf, where he was given a wide-ranging interview live for two hours with Sharaf himself and his interior, finance, and other ministers. Coincidence? Hard to tell. But El Baradei is not above correcting the new prime minister on his choice of words to describe the counter-revolution, and mentions, in passing, that of course he recommended Sharaf to the High Military Council as one of two possible candidates to succeed Ahmed Shafik. Ministers and presidents phone him all the time – 'They're my friends.' To a cynic, his warm and handsome references to World Women's Day and how proud he was of his mother and sister and daughters demonstrating in the streets, and how we should be grateful to all Egyptian women, might also look like conscious vote trawling.

He declared that as president, his first news conference would be held from a slum, where he would formally apologise to all poor Egyptians for the state having failed them.

Repeatedly, Foda attempted to get him to comment on Amr Moussa, Egypt's former foreign minister and now secretary general of the Arab League, who is the other most viable candidate for president. Moussa has wide recognition in Egypt and considerable popularity as a result of his strong political positions against Israel at the time he was foreign minister.

Strangely enough, as El Baradei revealed, the two joined the foreign service as contemporaries and spent four years together in the same office, serving under Ismail Fahmy, then Egyptian ambassador to the United Nations, later to become foreign minister: 'We have been friends and colleagues for fifty years. We agree about a lot and we disagree about a lot.' Which didn't stop him criticising by implication Moussa's suggestion that Egypt, faced with a nuclear Israel, should threaten to withdraw from the nuclear non-proliferation treaty. Well, it's not tenable, he said. Any move would bring such a range of sanctions and other penalties down on us that we would not be able to sustain it. *Moussa was just playing politics*, is the implication.

Would Dr Baradei take part in a live televised debate with Ambassador Moussa? Of course.

In the end, El Baradei's major contribution is that he is a viable candidate for Egypt's presidency who doesn't need to win. When he says he will be happy simply with the honour of trying, he sounds credible. As such, he is going to raise the game considerably whether he wins or not. What we were seeing was Democracy 101 in action in Egypt, and it was a tremendous sight. Sometime soon a real election is coming to Egypt with at least two independent candidates, a watchful populace, and an independent media. None of which would have happened without the revolution.

PART THREE

Libya

15

Looking for Mercenaries

I was in Benghazi, Libya's second city, liberated from the tyranny of Muammar Gaddafi for a week now, and had sought out its poorest neighbourhood, Luheishi, to get a haircut. It is an old ploy. Like eating – slowly – whatever comes to hand, slurping tea, or getting your shoes shined. Any transaction that helps you blend into the street. And there are few things you can do with strangers as intimate, as conducive to shared confidences, as to bare your throat to their razor. Besides, I needed it, and a barber in the Middle East will shave you, clip and tweak your facial hair, give you a short back and sides and rub your shoulders and still give you change from five bucks.

I had diverted from Egypt because, just as I had been in Tunisia when Mubarak left Egypt, now I was in Alexandria when the east of Libya had risen up against the forty-year rule of Muammar Gaddafi and in the space of a week driven out his forces from a 600-mile stretch of the country. There was no way of knowing what would happen next. But sitting in Alexandria, with the 400-mile road to the border leading out of the city, there had seemed little choice but to go. A few days later I had ended up in Benghazi, Libyan capital for a long time and now the seat of the rebels.

Most of the barbers' shops in Luheishi had been run by Egyptians who even as I walked past their shuttered doors were at that moment headed back home through the border post at Salloum, 400 miles to the west. But one was open and staffed by young men from the neighbourhood. Luheishi has the reputation in Benghazi of being rough and *sha'abi*, working-class. The kind of place cabbies sometimes refuse to take you to, especially at night. And there were a couple of young toughs hanging around inside the barber's, all taut faces and jerky body language. But it was the middle of the day and everyone was sober and polite.

Wael was taking a long time with my haircut because he was busy explaining how he had been among the thousands of protesters who had overrun the Fadhil Bu Omar building, the headquarters of Gaddafi's dreaded *Katiba* security apparatus for the whole of eastern Libya, just ten days before. He would break off for hand gestures, the revolutionary guards levelling their rifles at them, them lobbing Molotov cocktails inside the battlements and baring their chests to machine guns.

Then this man wearing a military jacket walked in, searching for a socket to recharge his mobile. I watched him through the mirror as he took an empty seat between the others and lit a cigarette. I never learnt his name.

'He was there!' exclaimed Wael with a big grin. 'He was at *Katiba*. Weren't you?'

The vibe had changed. The new man nodded curtly at Wael's words but nothing about him seemed rebel. He had a thin, military moustache, was older, perhaps in his early thirties, and full of self-important bustle, ordering tea, fiddling with his phone. But surely Wael could not mean he fought on the other side? Over two hundred people died in that battle, not five miles away in the centre of town, including two of Wael's friends. They could hardly be exchanging pleasantries a few days later.

'Well I only fired in the air, and the Africans were behind me with a gun to my head,' said the other guy. 'I fled as soon as I could.'

So, yes, the other side. And still wearing fatigues. I wondered what the deal was but it didn't seem my place to ask. Military Man got up and went outside to stretch his legs for a moment.

'Fired in the air . . . gun to his head . . . fled when he could,' muttered Wael as he ran the shaver over the back of my neck, clearly disgruntled.

'What, you don't believe him?' I asked.

Wael started a little at my question and instantly changed tone and went all bright.

'Oh yes, of course I do. He is from the neighbourhood, we know him well. He's not bad like the others,' he replied.

Wael carried on cutting my hair while Military Man, back on the bench, talked about all the weapons that had been snatched from the army depots when the rebels overran them. And thousands of regular prisoners – criminals – released from jail overnight.

'That's the real danger,' he said, shaking his head woefully. 'Frightening.' Nobody said a word.

Later, one of the lads from the barber's shop invited me back to lunch at his house round the corner. Ali, just twenty, was repeating to his father Mahmoud the story of how the guy walked in and he and Wael had exchanged words, kind of, and how I found the whole thing hard to understand.

His father yelled: 'He had nothing to do with it!' A little shocking as Mahmoud was a gentle man, the overwhelming impression he gave being one of grief for a wife who had recently died, as Ali had told me. 'They didn't like Gaddafi! Nobody liked Gaddafi!' he shouted.

At that moment Mahmoud did not seem to care about the truth of the man's guilt or innocence. The story of the *murtazaqat*, Gaddafi's African mercenaries holding a gun to every Libyan head, were a release valve, a way for everyone to live together afterwards. All it took was one meddling outsider like me to plant a seed of doubt and a cycle of retribution could begin. And then who knew where it might end?

It put the obsessive nature of the search for the mercenaries in a new light. It was the supposedly ubiquitous presence of foreign mercenaries that gave Gaddafi's men a huge collective alibi, that allowed the rebels to forgive all but the most egregious cases of brutality among their fellow Libyans. Blame the outsider, it always works.

It also presented itself as the perfect antidote to tribalism, a different way to pitch Libyan against Libyan. The revolution was only a few days old but tribalism was suddenly a vexed question in the free areas. Clearly, it existed in some way. The very urgency with which literally thousands of banners and graffiti insisted that it didn't – 'No to tribalism!' 'We are all the sons of one Libya' – proved that. The deeper question was actually a simpler one – What was it? What did tribalism in Libya actually amount to?

Tribalism is a great hunting ground for the opportunist expert. Learn the names of a few tribes and where Gaddafi is from and you're good for a three-minute talking-head slot on most of the major news channels. Anyone would think you spoke the language, or had at least gone there. But the fact is that though tribal affiliations are clearly alive and well in Libya, the country has undergone a fairly typical transformation over the last two generations. Most people live in cities working in recognisable jobs of the modern age where they have developed other social networks – neighbours, workmates, classmates.

Gaddafi's regime had promoted tribal affiliation, rotating the coveted secretary posts on the popular committees by tribe, and now, backs against the wall, they, and in particular Gaddafi's son Saif ul-Islam, were warning the world that the country would descend into uncontrollable civil war by clan, Somalia-style. Opinion formers in the international media saw margin in the catastrophe scenario, and were pumping it.

There was really no evidence one way or the other. But it was hard to believe that concern about possible fissures in Libyan society was not making all the stories going round about African mercenaries grow taller.

Earlier, sitting in the courthouse in the centre of town with a colleague, we had met another of Gaddafi's fighters, a Libyan, who blamed the African mercenaries for everything he had had to do. We were sitting in one of the hundreds of small offices of the sprawling complex, on the second floor, overlooking a winter's storm on the Mediterranean 100 yards through the window, white-tipped waves crashing against the seafront, watching a team of prosecutors, mostly women, grapple with a caseload of possible war-crimes cases that was expanding by the minute. Clerks brought files and scribbled notes, whispered exchanges were followed by hurried exits. It was one of those revolutionary moments, beautiful to the reporter, where the new newsmakers are too polite and inexperienced to realise they should just kick us the hell out. Instead they offer us tea and biscuits and, because they don't want to deliver any African mercenaries to interview, give us one of Gaddafi's special forces instead.

He comes in with a blanket over his head. No photos, no name, he says, not even his age. One of the prosecutors leaves him in a side room with us and a couple of volunteers, rebels in their early twenties, dressed casual, with the ease of young men who know they are on the right side of history.

Our man takes his blanket off his head, revealing a shaved head, tired, slightly buzzed eyes, mid-twenties, both ribcage skinny and built. His voice deep and slightly cracked. Wired but with no sign of ill treatment. He is anxious to tell us how much he loves the revolution. Flashes a V-sign, picks up the pre-Gaddafi flag on the table and waves it. There is no pressure from his guards to do this since they, endearingly, have nothing to prove and are leaning forward to catch a kind of conversation they don't normally get to hear. The door opens and closes every minute or so, someone looking for someone else not here. Nobody yet knows who is using which room for what.

Talk us through it, we say.

'Nothing much to say,' he shrugs. 'Major General Abu Bakr

Younis saluted the forces of the revolution in the main square on the twentieth of February.'

But you, we ask. How were you taken?

'I wasn't taken,' he said, chin out, lips out. 'Nobody took me. I was there at the *Katiba* on the Friday. The Africans were at my back. A gun here.' He points to his temple. 'Then the *shabaab*, the rebels, they overran the camp. I changed into civilian clothes, took my gun, went home and stayed at home. Then I came here and handed over my weapon.' He nods to the guards, as though they should nod back.

He makes a show of bumming a cigarette off one of the heads that poke round the door. Every little ingratiation a complicity, a tiny step further away from the status of enemy. What did you do during the four days of fighting? we ask. He takes my pen to draw a diagram, showing how far back he was from the front line.

'I shot in the air mostly. But I shot someone in the leg. That's why I'm here. I came to hand in my weapon and confess,' he said.

Tell us about life in the revolutionary guards, we say. He talks of three years away in Tripoli although he is a local lad, from Benghazi, learning how to handle weapons. 'You can't step forward and use the Betrayer, just like that,' he says, clicking his fingers.

The Betrayer? Erm, machine gun, he says. Why Betrayer? Because if you don't know how to handle it, it can jump, fall on the floor and fire randomly or blow up. You wouldn't want to be there when that happens.

Did you ever meet Gaddafi? 'He came to the parade ground

twice. I saw him. But I didn't like him. He was a liar and a cheat. It was all bullshit.'

Why did you join? Because I didn't have a job, he says, genuinely surprised at the question. How much did you earn? He appraises his guard-friends. Oh I don't know, he says, 320, 380 dinars a month, something like that. The pay of police, or regular army, or an average civil servant, about $300. Even though we're hearing that the special forces and revolutionary guards and intelligence – the fellow travellers – make twice that.

Do the *murtazaqat*, the African mercenaries, speak Arabic? we ask. Oh no, he replies. Then how can they be telling you what to do? With the gun, he says, fingers to the temple again. But that's a yes–no option, I say. They can use a gun to make you carry on doing that thing you both already know they want you to do – like shooting into the crowd. They can't use the gun to make you understand new orders: retreat to this point, maintain radio silence, look to the left. How would the *murtazaqat actually* command Libyan forces? Erm . . . translators, he says. They use translators. A few.

We leave him after an hour. He's anxious to please and would talk all day. After all, the people who will decide his fate put him in the room with us. But his own personal story is already tightly formed. And ultimately, he's just some bloke who ended up in Gaddafi's special forces. We've got what we can.

Outside, I ask Azzedine al-Awami, one of the prosecutors handling his case, what might happen to him. He says the law provides up to three years in jail for cases of bodily harm like shooting someone in the leg – 'If we believe his story.' And if not?

'Under the old criminal code, which we are referring to,' he replied, 'premeditated murder carries the death sentence.'

The courthouse is packed and thronging with all kinds of activity. While Gaddafi men are being held and interrogated on the top floor and in some underground cells, so rumour has it, the first- and second-floor rooms are being seized by various committees. A Libyan American called Mustafa is wandering around introducing himself as press spokesman for the transitional government. There's intense protection at the front door of the building, a lot of young men ordering each other about as though they, also, are not really sure who is in charge.

The whole town is in this kind of tumult. Next door, at the old secret police headquarters, old 'graduates' have gathered to display their wounds and point to the cells where they were held, sometimes for days, sometimes for years, without trial or daylight. Above them a group of young men and women have made themselves into a press reception committee, handing out Free Libya press passes and assigning volunteers who speak English to incoming reporters.

Awami also arranges for us to meet some Africans who are being held on the top floor of the court complex. There's a throng at the entrance to the building, trying to get in for all sorts of reasons. Every so often a new African is brought in amid tumult, roughed up, sometimes bloodied.

Inside, though, the treatment we see is gruff but correct. We are shown into an empty room and shortly afterwards four young Africans are herded in, Ethiopians and Eritreans. We all sit on blankets on the floor while Awami takes the swivel chair.

They are all young construction workers, trying to save money. In a story I'm to hear repeated over the days, the Eritreans can't go home because they are part Oromo – part Ethiopian in other words, caught in the middle of another big man's quarrel, since Ethiopia and Eritrea are still at war. Awami explains their stories are being checked out. When they are confirmed, they will go free.

'He's already free to go,' he says, pointing to Ermias Degefa, an Ethiopian. 'Our investigations are complete. But he doesn't want to be back on the streets.'

Degefa nods. The Africans are all worried about being photographed. If their pictures get onto the Net as detainees – suspected mercenaries – they may never be safe again.

They're tired and stressed, probably not sleeping or eating well, or getting the chance to wash. Their life has just nose-dived and they know it. They have no jobs to go back to and their savings are gone. But they show no signs of abuse and are not cowed. Salah Jaber, from Eritrea, speaks Arabic and asks Awami directly why he can't phone his friends just to let them know he is OK. You can, says Awami, nobody's stopping you. But they smashed my phone when they took me in, Salah replies. Why don't you lend him your phone? I ask Awami, who is sitting on a swivel chair above us. He hands it over and Salah retreats to a corner of the room and makes a call.

So if these guys weren't mercenaries, who were? The main incidence seems to have been 150 miles east of Benghazi at the town of Bqayda, where Africans had been landed by the plane-load during the regime's brief attempt to squash the protests. Scores were killed and up to 150 taken prisoner and held in a school. Many of them, little more than teenagers, said they were not told when they were bundled onto planes that they would be going to fight. They were simply looking for work and had only found out what was happening when they got off the plane at the town's airport and had guns thrust into their hands.

This created a big reaction in Benghazi and all the other towns which had risen up against Gaddafi, provoking them to round up all the Africans they could find. There were tens of thousands, as Libya had routinely imported African guest workers to fill menial jobs, like the ones in the Benghazi court-house.

There is no definitive picture to be drawn, of course, but I am convinced that Azzedine al-Awami and the other prosecutors I met are committed to legal process. Later, accounts from other reporters and the Human Rights Watch representative give similar impressions. It's hardly pretty. But a new leadership is fast emerging from the ranks of Benghazi's lawyers, engineers, doctors and businessmen which is as constitutionalist as it is revolutionary. And at that moment, these professional elders have the ear of the street.

As I was to discover, in Libya, in fact, to be constitutionalist is to be revolutionary. For thirty years, since Gaddafi introduced the Green Book, he has cynically maintained tyranny through a combination of puerile, Che-like personality cult and a form of supposed anarcho-syndicalism. To be in favour of system, to support institutions with declared, and therefore circumscribed, authority, is to be against Gaddafi's system of no system. Against the Great Libyan Socialist Arab Jamahiriya *c'est moi*.

16

Looking for the Green Book in Libya

I've always loved chasing the obscure. So when, sitting at breakfast in the hotel in Benghazi, I discovered a thirty-year-old link to an ideologue of Gaddafi's Green Book amid an extended discussion of Plato's *Republic*, it was too much to resist. I had to try and find him.

I had been reading an anthology on Gaddafi's seminal work which I had recovered from a broken-open prison on the edge of town. Entitled simply *Problems of the Contemporary World*, the book was published in 1985 by the World Centre for Study and Research of the Green Book, the proceedings of a conference that had happened in communist Poland a couple of years earlier. The contributors were academics in Libyan universities. I browsed the table of contents, discovering a fairly random range of essay titles like 'Woman as a Commodity', 'Towards a New Sporting World Order', and 'Mediation and Alienation at Work'.

One title in particular caught my attention – 'On Democracy and the Popular Committees' – as I was beginning to hear from people something of the way the committees inserted themselves into every corner of public life. Written by a law lecturer called Ibrahim Abu Khazam from Gar Younis University, in

Benghazi, I was intrigued to find it opened with a page-and-a-half quotation from Plato's *Republic*. I later checked the text against Benjamin Jowett's English translation. It was abridged and paraphrased in parts but essentially true to the original.

Socrates and Plato's brother Glaucon are discussing the famous allegory of the dwellers in the Cave. Socrates is explaining that real daylight could be painful for the cave dwellers when they are brought to it, and they would find it easy to be confused and assume that the ghosts of the cave were more real than the glare of life above, outside the cave, from which they must at first shield their eyes. So we should take it step by step, Socrates continues. Keep the cave dweller at first in the shadows, then introduce him to reflections of things in water, then to the stars and moon at night, and finally to open daylight in all its glory. Glaucon, dazzled by the dogged lucidity of the Master, like all his interlocutors, affirms and interjects – 'exactly', 'absolutely', 'clearly', 'without doubt'. Only then, Socrates persists, will the former cave dweller look back on his state in the cave and his friends there, and think of himself as lucky by comparison.

And that, concludes Abu Khazam, is the state of the world today with regard to systems of government. We are all cave dwellers unwilling even to acknowledge the existence of sunlight. For although numerous thinkers have acknowledged the influence of Greek thought on the evolution of democracies in Europe and the United States, and some have even complained of the elision of the concepts of democracy and representative government, direct democracy remains a beautiful dream. The majority stay fixated on the phantoms in the cave, not daring even to conceive of direct government. From here, Abu Khazam leads us to discussion of the popular committees, and Gaddafi's grand concept of direct democracy.

The theory and ideology of the Green Revolution might seem abstruse, far removed from the death and bone-cracking we were seeing evidence of all around us.

The day before I had had to turn away, again, as a grown man, who had held himself together while relating the systematic torture he underwent for years, broke down when he got to the part about sexual abuse. Outside the courthouse there was a permanent sit-in with an entire wall displaying mugshots of hundreds of political prisoners believed to have been machine-gunned in Abu Salim prison in Tripoli in 1996. In Benghazi itself, along with thousands of amazed locals, we wandered round the vast *Katiba* complex where hundreds had been held. Gaddafi's repeated use of the word 'rats' in his TV appearances to describe the rebels took on special pungency when you saw the vast chambers underground, big enough to drive an entire motorcade down into. 'Rats' wasn't some random Mad Dog mouth-off. It was a calculated taunt by Gaddafi to his victims, like Hutu perpetrators sending messages through the Red Cross to Tutsi survivors of the Rwandan genocide, saying they can't wait to see them again, or Nazis on railway platforms drawing their fingers across their throats as the trains for Auschwitz pass through the station.

And of course it's quite possible that none of the men who beat, electrocuted, raped and killed thousands have heard of Ibrahim Abu Khazam, or the other contributors to the book. Many may not even be that familiar even with Gaddafi's Green

Book, though they will certainly have been called upon to pay obeisance to it at some stage on the path that brought them to the torture chamber, either in school, special forces' boot camp, or both.

But it would be a mistake to think because of that there was no thread that connects Ibrahim Abu Khazam and other apologists for Gaddafi with Abu Salim, the underground torture chambers at the *Katiba*, or Gaddafi's petrodollar-fuelled foreign adventures like the war in Chad, or Lockerbie, or all sorts of mischief across the Middle East. The fair-sized industry of intellectuals, Libyan and foreign, who flattered Gaddafi, held conferences and published books about the Green Book, and encouraged him in the vanity that his ideas amounted to a cogent global ideology competing with capitalism and communism, were as complicit, possibly more so, than many low-grade torturers who pulled a trigger, pushed a switch.

Funnily enough, I had been unable to find a copy of the Green Book itself. In just ten days it had vanished from eastern Libya, and even discreet enquiries in Benghazi's biggest bookshops yielded nothing. So I had to make do with this book of essays about the Green Book, bearing a stamp from the department of prisons library in Benghazi, found in the detritus of 4,000 prisoners stampeding out of their cells overnight. And its authors – were they fools, rabid ideologues, or fellow travellers? Was there something perhaps in the theory of political structures set out by Gaddafi, and elucidated by his coterie, that explained what had happened in Libya these last forty years? Was it even possible there was something to Abu Khazam's description of the *jamahiriya*, or communes, as the true heirs to the direct democracy of the Athenian Golden Age?

Abu Khazam begins by explaining that Gaddafi himself and his thought has been described as the *tajawuz*, 'transcendence', of the Libyan revolution of 1969, an echo of Nietzsche's view that the major achievement of the French Revolution was the chance for Napoleon to shine as Übermensch. Then he starts into a discussion of what the role of the committees is: 'The task of manufacturing the democratic citizen is both the goal of change and its mechanism,' he asserts. The system of communes – *jamahiriya* – introduced in Libya in the 1970s has essentially solved, or dissolved, what communists call the class struggle, he explains.

This means civic education should not be what it is in representative democracies, where it is merely to educate a populace in how to run for and hold office. Since the people already own and control everything in the *jamahiriya*, there is no longer any need to compete for power, and the committees should instead prepare the citizen to exercise it. In this sense, public life is much more efficient than in so-called democracies which are taken up with campaigning and elections. Everyone is a member of the commune, but the committees perform the role of guiding the citizens as a whole. They can do this because the members of the committees are themselves already democratic, says Abu Khazam.

He doesn't elucidate what it means to be a democratic man or woman, and this is the first warning signal. Democrat is something magical and transcendent, just as the ideologue Michel Aflaq expounded a concept of Baathism, adopted in

Syria and Saddam Hussein's Iraq, based on *ishq*, or passion, which was unexplained, beyond words, transcendent. The *jamahiriya* will be democratic because the committees that guide them are made up of Democratic Men and Women. The basis of the ideology is solipsism. That way lies madness.

A couple of days earlier, a friend of a friend driving us around Benghazi had explained how he had had problems in his job because of the popular committee there. There were committees in every institution of more than twenty people, said Khaled, not just government offices but the local branch of the bus company, a boy scouts association, the association that built and runs a mosque, a transport company, or as in his case, Agoco, one of Libya's major oil companies with perhaps 8,000 employees. The problem was you never knew exactly who was with the committee.

'There were usually five or six you knew by name,' Khaled said. 'But they were the easy ones. You had to understand who they were connected to. There could be twenty or thirty people in the company that were linked to the committee, but you would only ever know who if you made it a full-time job to find out. But then they would see you watching them and you could be sure something would happen to you before you got close.'

The committees cut across rank and department. You could be a senior manager mulling a major appointment when a junior member of staff would sidle up to you and let you understand, for the first time, he was a member of the popular committee in the company and had some advice to offer, said Khaled.

This ties perfectly with an important function of the committees, according to Abu Khazam's essay: that of advising on the 'objective circumstances' surrounding any major policy decision. Because – again – the inefficiency of the democratic process is recognised, he says, citing an argument redolent of Europe between the two world wars, when editorials in *The Times* of London talked about Herr Hitler giving a new sense of purpose to the German nation, and Signor Mussolini making the trains run on time. Dictatorship, as the rule of one man, is the most efficient form of government, then oligarchy, then partial, then full democracy. In the earlier European iteration of the debate, this brought with it the corollary that because dictatorship was most efficient it was, in some sense, most modern. In this sense at least, the argument supporting Gaddafi's *jamahiriya* is more evolved, since it seeks to temper the fantasy of a pure technocracy with at least a nod towards the desirability of building popular consensus and political will.

The cacophony of democracies, writes Abu Khazam, often leads to decision making that is legitimate precisely because it mediates between competing voices. But such policies won't necessarily be sound, or viable, unless they are also just, or rightly guided.

'This is where the popular committees find another justification for their existence,' he writes. 'Their role is in giving guidance to the political institutions who alone own decision making, and guidance in its simplest meaning, to explain the objective circumstances surrounding each decision point.'

If you're a devotee of political theory, it is possible to conceive of how direct, participatory governance might work in some contexts. The 'do-ocracy' used to run the annual Burning Man arts festival in Nevada, for example, where authority attaches to people as and when they simply assume responsibility for running this or that, is essentially a system of popular committees working at some scale. Over 50,000 people headed into the Black Rock desert in 2010 for the festival, many staying the entire week. America's leading dissident Noam Chomsky calls himself an anarcho-syndicalist, maintaining it is now the natural application of classical liberalism in advanced technological societies, where people no longer need to be treated like cogs in a machine, and decentralised federations of free associations are possible. And then there are the ancient Greek city states themselves of course, where the entire polity was run as a plenary of the citizenry, with all its functions as subcommittees.

There is an interesting debate to be had about if and how such thinking and practice could be broadly applied in the world today, for the many of us who feel in some way or other railroaded by political dispensations that were fixed when the nation state reigned supreme, admixed then with a heavy dose of top-down patriarchy, yet diluted now by the globalisation of Big Business. But all the modern conceptions at least emerge from societies where mass literacy, the rule of law, an economy distributed across many manufacturing and service sectors, governance based on taxation, and what might broadly be called a culture of respect for difference, are givens.

In Libya, this has played out instead as a parallel structure of ideological correctness that never assumes office, or responsibility, and is governed by a single interest group that cannot be called to account. The unpredictability that tabloid head-lines encourage us to associate with Gaddafi's personality is actually broader and deeper, a feature built into the political system itself.

The popular committees themselves are never elected. That would encourage strife and self-serving according to the theory. Instead, as Youssef, a clinician in a hospital in Tobruk, explained, they are led by secretaries whose 'ascension' is announced peri-odically. In larger committees, such as those that effectively govern cities and municipalities, the period of a secretary's tenure is more regular, perhaps three or four years. In smaller committees it can be randomly long or short.

And unlike the party apparatchiks that both the Nazis and the Communists deployed at various times to police state-run institutions for political correctness, there is no formal member-ship. Occasionally you might find, said Khaled, some time after you made your hire, that the junior colleague who'd decided to offer you guidance about the 'objective circumstances' wasn't even a member of the committee, or at least had over-represented his role.

So where are those people now? I asked Khaled. In your company, in Agoco, where are they? A couple of the high-profile people left but most of them are still there in post, he said. So who are they? I asked. I should point out that right then I had my notebook on my lap, in the front seat of his car.

What do you mean, who are they? Khaled asked, looking shifty. I mean their names, I said. What are the names of the people who were on the popular committee in Agoco? He mumbled something I didn't catch, though we had had no comprehension problems until then. Sorry? I asked. I don't know, he said, a little sullenly. I kept my distance. I didn't get involved. This from a man who had just spent a quarter of an hour in a tirade against Gaddafi. They seemed tentacular, these committees, hard to see but everywhere.

Down in Luheishi they had a robust view of them and the entire edifice of Gaddafi's direct democracy.

'He's always been about government directly by the people, how he's only an ordinary citizen. Whatever,' said Mohammed Ali Belhassan, acerbically. His family, totally non-political, found itself on the wrong side of the regime after his father, a regular soldier, had had the nerve to allow himself be taken alive in Gaddafi's ruinous war with Chad along the Aouzou Strip in the 1980s. Gaddafi refused to take back the hundreds of prisoners of war, calling them a disgrace to the country, and eventually, after intercession by the Red Cross, they wound up in Ronald Reagan's United States.

'Well now we've taken him up on it. All this you see, the young men directing traffic in the roads, arresting and taking suspected mercenaries for questioning, that's the popular committees. He told us we were sovereign and could do anything we want. Well what we want is for him to just fuck off,' said Mohammed or words, somewhat more graphic, to that effect.

I wanted to track down Ibrahim Abu Khazam. Was he still alive? The paper, after all, was written nearly thirty years ago. What did he *mean* by quoting from the *Republic*? Was it a flight of fancy that a man of culture, forced into obeisance of an uncouth leader, allows himself as a private act of defiance while accepting the pact with the Devil? He is after all, carefully elliptical in a number of places. He doesn't himself say Gaddafi is a genius, for example, he merely quotes others who do.

Was he a genuine believer? Or a false intellectual, a hypocrite who, like Winston Smith's neighbour Parsons in Orwell's *Nineteen Eighty-Four*, tries his hardest to convince himself of what it is in any case imperative to believe? Or was he any of those things then but has changed since? When I got back and showed the book to my nine-year-old daughter Ruby, and talked about who had written it and how, she immediately asked: 'Did all those people write those things about Gaddafi because they liked him or because they were afraid?' That was the essence of it. Who was, or is, Ibrahim Abu Khazam?

The courthouse was the place to start. Libya's new leadership was there, harassed by fifty foreign journalists and their newly acquired stringers. If Abu Khazam was still around, someone there would know. I imagined a neighbourhood that once passed for posh in Benghazi, out of the centre but before you hit the public housing projects, large villas spaced by large bougainvilleaed gardens, in one of which an old man, until recently important, shuffled around in synthetic slippers and a heavy dressing gown, tended to by loyal womenfolk, or sat listlessly channel-zapping a flatscreen TV, his life's work, half a shelf of panegyric like the essay I had seen, in a glass cabinet behind him under lock and key.

A group of lawyers shuffling papers at a table were unenthusiastic. They exchanged glances, stole glances at me, and discussed quite openly, because they assumed I couldn't understand, that Abu Khazam was 'not on our side'. Then the nearest one turned to me and said in English: 'He's not in Benghazi. That's for sure.' Proof he was still around, though.

I felt sure they knew more but didn't blame them for stalling. It was a pretty obscure thing to be asking about on Day 12 of Free Benghazi, and they had no real experience of journalism that didn't necessarily adopt the position of its subjects. I explained my self-appointed mission. One of them got it, the other three didn't. But she really didn't know anything, and the others, without actually being rude, had made up their minds they wanted no part of it. A guy at the Press Centre set up by the rebels looked nervous, and told me Abu Khazam's family weren't from Benghazi, and that he wasn't here.

The more people lied to me, or tried to talk me out of it, the more I became determined to find out where this guy was. Gar Younis University, where he had been a lecturer in 1985, was closed because of the revolution and in any case fifteen miles out of town. I went to the business centre in the hotel and, since he had been at the faculty of law, started looking through a Yellow Pages for lawyers in Benghazi. Maybe he had developed a law practice somewhere along the line. I jotted down a couple of names and phone numbers of what looked like major offices, because they had taken out ad space, and figured out where they were in town.

And then Google saved me. The Internet, which had been down for nearly two weeks in Libya since the fighting started, came back on in the hotel and I Googled Ibrahim Abu Khazam. And found that he had become president of Nasser International University in Tripoli. A slideshow on the university website showed him giving out various awards and speaking on a rostrum with a huge picture of the Maximum Leader behind him.

His career path yielded part of the answer to the question of who is Ibrahim Abu Khazam. He was at the pinnacle of a career in Libyan academia through his close association with the ideology of the *jamahiriya*. He still went to international conferences. You might have met him, paunchy, plate in hand, at the buffet of a workshop in a five-star hotel in Barcelona or Cairo or Dar es-Salaam, with a suite of arguments about the subject of the conference, willing, eager even, to claim his place in the global technocracy, while adhering to the party line in all matters relating to Middle Eastern politics.

Born in 1952, Abu Khazam comes from the Fezzan region of south-west Libya. At the time he wrote the essay I found in the prison yard, he had just finished a master's. He combined a rise through Libya's academic institutions with a career in Gaddafi's political apparatus. In 1986, after the United States bombed Libya and killed, among others, Gaddafi's two-year-old daughter, Abu Khazam was sent to Latin America to drum up diplomatic support against the Americans. Later, he served as 'director of the office of fraternal relations, Baghdad' – Libya's ambassador to Saddam Hussein's Iraq. All the while he kept publishing, building a profile as a political scientist, with books like *Constitutions and the Phenomenon of Dictatorship*, *The Galvanising Factors of History*, and *The Basics of Crisis Management*.

In August 2009, according to Wikileaks, Ibrahim Abu Khazam was a member of the Libyan team that met a high-level US delegation in Tripoli at a time when the United States was trying to deepen the normalisation of relations that had begun with the Iraq War of 2003.

It was a classic dialogue of the deaf. The Americans walked out when the leader of the Libyan delegation just kicked off with a peroration about direct democracy and the Libyan political system, and refused to stop to answer questions about why the delegation and working agenda had been changed. Foreign Minister Musa Kusa then intervened and reconvened a meeting for the same day in the evening. The Americans were trying to focus on human rights issues while the Libyans focused on the fact of a dialogue itself.

Reading the Wikileaks cable, I actually felt the opposite of what Julian Assange presumably intended, a sneaking sympathy for the American negotiators flown in from Washington. It must be hard to have a dialogue about human rights when the other side denies that Libya has any prisons, since the concept of prisons is reactionary, or any discrimination against women, since the country has signed an international treaty saying women are equal, and rejects the need for anything called civil society, since such organisations exist to promote distinct special interest groups whereas Libya is one, single and homogeneous society. A prepared press release was scrapped and both sides agreed not to publicise the talks.

None of these gems was attributed to Abu Khazam in the cable, and I wondered what had passed through his mind during that long, cantankerous day. Ritual rage at the Great Satan? A concern to say, or not say, the right thing in the presence of his peer group of senior Gaddafi apologists? Was the meeting an opportunity to shine, a minefield to be negotiated, or simply, at this stage of his illustrious career, a chore to be endured, part of what comes with high position, an entire campus as your playground and limitless foreign study tours?

Nasser International University's website yielded a phone number in Tripoli. But it rang out when I tried it.

Abu Khazam's name was on a list of speakers at the third annual Arab symposium on quality assurance in research, due to be hosted by his university later that month. He was on the board of trustees of the sponsoring organisation, whose board of directors also included Amr Moussa, chairman of the Arab League, former Egyptian foreign minister, and touted as candidate for president in the post-Mubarak era. I emailed the address given on the call for papers but didn't get a reply.

Resigning myself to the probability I would not be able to reach Ibrahim Abu Khazam, I returned to his essay. The book by now was well-thumbed. I'd probably given it far more attention than anyone in Benghazi prison ever did.

Abu Khazam finishes his essay by discussing political leadership. The problem with representative democracy, he says, is that it entails rule by a minority elite of elected officials. This contradicts, he explains, both the principles of majority rule and also the idea of equality. And yet, he continues, fear of dictatorship of the majority countervails fear of rule by a minority, and extreme concepts of equality in fact undermine notions of equality of opportunity as opposed to outcome. The argument is cogent and paced, preparing us for the denouement. This mess of argument and counter-argument applies only to representative democracies, Abu Khazam reminds us, since in a direct democracy there is no elite. Some might wonder then about the popular committees, he continues, since they are clearly – as yet – the whole of society. History is full of examples of populist leaders and groups who came to power with genuine intentions to serve the people but were transformed over time into tyrannical regimes which themselves had to be removed by force.

The trick, then, is to ensure that these committees never take office, so that they cannot become an elite, and to rely instead on leadership. Not the failed leadership of formal or constitutional authority, such as presidents or generals, nor yet a totalitarian concept that formally integrates personality cult, like *Führer* or *Duce* – and yes, he uses these terms in Arabic. No, the answer to providing direction is moral, not political, authority. A president can enjoin obedience to the rule of law, which presumably he has a hand in making. But it is the moral leader, the *qa'id*, who can achieve much greater things because his weapon is persuasion, not law, and usually by force of his personality.

Consider France at the start of the Second World War, he continues. Marshal Pétain had political authority, but it was De Gaulle, in exile and without office, who was the country's real leader. Abu Khazam laments lax use of the vocabulary of leadership, noting that Margaret Thatcher is considered Britain's 'leader' because she occupies the post of prime minister, whereas her very personality contradicts the idea.

It's not hard to see where this is leading us. Churchill and Egypt's Gamal Abdel Nasser were each in their way flawed personalities called to greatness by the times they lived in and the moments of crisis through which they steered their countries.

And then: 'Muammar Gaddafi is my final example of leadership. Not just for building his country, but perhaps also by the measure of the ideal living world, not just because he has taken part in a noble, national struggle, but also because he has sought to change the shape of Being. And I don't consider there has been a greater struggle than this for centuries.'

If this last passage sounds obscure, I believe it is meant to be. Abu Khazam has shown himself by now to be a smart and versatile thinker, and his career path suggests he knows how to finesse different worlds.

If you are Muammar Gaddafi, or Saif, or any of the inner circle, you might just gather that Abu Khazam has said that Gaddafi is the greatest living leader in the world today, and for centuries past. But if you are, for instance, someone at the Arab League or the United Nations, or any of the circles of international legitimacy and boondoggles to which an Abu Khazam might aspire, in fact he could show you, if he needed to, that he pulled his punches, using carefully calibrated meaninglessness. Gaddafi is a leader 'perhaps' for 'the measure of the ideal living world'. It is the struggle he is engaged in that is the greatest for centuries, not necessarily Gaddafi himself. Abu Khazam could hold his head up among the motley collection of academics assembled at that Warsaw University conference back in the 1980s, men and women dedicated to apologising for different tyrannies around the world. And he could still qualify for a UNESCO ambassadorship today.

He concludes by spelling out the characteristics of this moral leadership: oratorical strength, nobility of thought, an impeccable personal life given the intrusive glare of modern media, and a capacity to tolerate sadness. Because the true leader is always alone. Most of the prophets and leaders in history have embraced a form of life in which the ordinary joys known to most of us are absent. It is in this wretchedness that greatness is born. Indeed he ends by paraphrasing an incident that happened to Napoleon during his Egyptian expedition. The young consul's party came upon the statue of an ancient Egyptian ruler, mighty and still erect, unlike Ozymandias, but isolated in his greatness amid the modern decay and the Roman graffiti. 'How sad,' said one of the entourage, turning to the emperor-to-be. 'Yes,' replied Napoleon. 'As sad as greatness.'

So Abu Khazam, in a few short pages, has led us ineluctably, from a first-principles consideration of all forms of government, to the concept of direct democracy, to be inspired by the popular committees, to be inspired by the moral authority of the Brother, Leader of the World Opening Revolution in his role as the Great Inciter – these are all formal terms. But, as Gaddafi himself has never tired of repeating, he fills no office and exercises no formal authority. He enjoys influence only in so far as he is right, or, in Gaddafi's case, cool. Let's not forget that Gaddafi is a child of the Sixties. He took power in 1969, the same year as Woodstock, and his role models as he reached for international name recognition included Che Guevara and Carlos.

It is the enshrining of adolescence as a mode of government. It also predicts a formidable challenge for international investigators if they ever try to adduce legal-level proof against him for the many excesses and disasters he has 'incited'.

A few days after retrieving Ibrahim Abu Khazam's essay from

the front driveway of Benghazi prison, I toured the city's Green Book Institute. Every town and city in Gaddafi's Libya has had one, huge modernist monstrosities with a statue of the book itself standing proudly at the entrance. In the east, they were all put to the torch in the first hours of freedom. Picking our way through the rubble, the 100-seat auditoria and the socialist realist friezes on the walls, we came across scores of scattered little ID cards. They were membership cards for the library at the institute, a library dedicated to the glorification of a single book, published thirty-five years before by the man still ruling the country.

The back of the card reads: 'Knowledge is the natural right of every human being.'

17

Of Oil, Revolution and Complicity

Every hour or so, in free Libya, you hear this phrase: 'The richest country in the world and the poorest people in the world'. Statistically speaking, there's poetic licence on both sides of that equation. But it would be a harsh judge that denied its essential truth.

From the Egyptian border at Salloum to the city of Tobruk is nearly 180 miles. In each of the dozen small towns and villages we passed through, we peered up the side streets – not one was asphalted. Many Libyans are functionally illiterate. Walking through the streets of Bqayda one night, Libya's capital before Tripoli and still considered a town of some stature, a crowd of fifty people were gathered at a kiosk that normally distributes concert tickets, waving ID cards, trying to get stamps that would give them access to basic commodities at subsidised prices or for free.

When I asked the nearest man in the queue exactly what would be handed out, he said: 'I don't know. But whatever it is, we want it!' Public building projects in most of the cities of the east all but ceased in the 1990s. The modernist housing estates that the urban poor live in are twenty years old but already decrepit, cheap plasterwork crumbling, man-sized piles of rubbish, marauding packs of wild dogs, no paved pathways or car parks, large families crammed into small blocks. Libya seems like some weird combination of Middle Eastern rentier oil state – Asian construction workers, East European doctors – and African subsistence economy – divoted, muddy roads and street stands still selling tape cassettes.

You can hardly begin to imagine where Gaddafi's trillion petrodollars – current values – have gone.

So, one morning when a Libyan friend invited us to visit the oil company where he worked, I jumped at the chance. The Arabian Gulf Oil Company, Agoco for short, was one of the largest oil companies owned by the Libyan state, employing 8,000 people or more, by far the biggest single organisation in Benghazi. Khalifa actually worked in a medical services wing of the company, part of the extensive array of social services the company organised for its extended communities out of their headquarters in al-Keesh district, not far from the infamous *Katiba* building where Gaddafi's special forces had built their underground prisons.

Before the protests started, Agoco was producing 440,000 barrels of oil a day out of its fields in the south-west of the country, perhaps one barrel in every 100 traded on markets around the world every day, worth in the region of $15 billion a year. Agoco was at the heart of the engine driving Gaddafi's regime. A few days before I had been sitting with an Egyptian friend watching the Arabic TV channels. The rolling banners at the bottom of the screen showed oil spiking. The price of a barrel of Brent rose ten dollars within one cup of tea, and it was mainly fears that fighting in Libya would close off the country's oil industry to world markets that were pushing the hike. What would happen now Agoco, and other companies like it, fell under rebel control?

When Khalifa drove through the main gate flashing his employee's ID card, I had no expectation of what journalists call 'hard news'. I would be happy just to hang around in the offices for a couple of hours, talk to whoever was around, and get the feel of the place. As it turned out, though, we were to stumble over a market-moving story within ten minutes.

It was barely a week after the rebels had taken Benghazi but the company's headquarters were calm and orderly, in striking contrast to the rest of Benghazi: a sprawling complex of well-maintained office blocks unscathed by the recent fighting. The only evidence there had even been a revolution was an A4 printout in the reception area of the hospitality suite, to where we had driven, commemorating Mahdi Mohammed Ziu, employee and martyr of the revolution, who had played a key role in taking the army garrison when he drove his car, packed with home-made explosives, into the main gate.

Other than that it seemed like a smoothly running corporation. Well-trained receptionists staffed a phone bank at the entrance. We were shown through to a large lounge and sank into deep armchairs to wait for whoever had time to see us. Liveried waiters approached to ask what kind of tea or coffee we would like. The chaos of the streets outside seemed like a different world.

The contributed books on the shelves declared their allegiance to middle-aged middle England and America – thrillers by John Le Carré and Dick Francis, Wilbur Smith and James

Clavell, a popular science explanation of the causes and treatment of irritable bowel syndrome. It became clear that the hospitality suite was mainly for the use of expat oil executives.

A slim man wearing a jacket, V-necked jumper and tie introduced himself in good English as Hassan Bolifa, a senior manager and member of Agoco's management committee. What would we like to know? he asked – the same deliciously naïve attitude to media we had experienced with investigators at the courthouse.

Oil is actually my day job. I had taken three months' leave from my post at the United Nations advising on the public policy aspects of the industry in the Middle East in order to cover the Arab Spring. So faced with a senior manager, I immediately seized the chance to grill him about all aspects of the industry in Libya, from nerdy basics up – where the producing fields were, what recovery techniques are used there, pipeline and refining capacities and so on.

Bolifa went straight into an explanation of how the company would honour its commitments to international markets for shipments of crude oil. Two tankers were approaching Tobruk even as we spoke, he said, to take on 1 million and 750,000 barrels of oil respectively, worth some $200 million. Who's going to get the money for that? I asked.

'Good question!' Bolifa replied. 'The shipments are on the standard thirty-day or forty-five-day terms. We would hope problems between Benghazi and Tripoli would be resolved by then.' In other words, that the rebels would win, and management of Agoco and its parent company in the capital be reunified. And if not? 'My own suggestion is for the United Nations to set up and handle an account similar to the one for Iraq.' And if that couldn't be arranged in time? 'Right now, we need to send a signal to the markets that we are serious about doing business,' added Bolifa. 'Even to the extent of honouring agreements reached before the revolution.'

So Agoco, under rebel control, was prepared to pump oil that sent some $200 million flowing into Gaddafi's coffers to show the world it was business as usual? 'There is no embarrassment about this. Producing Libya's oil is a mutual interest between us and the international community,' said Bolifa.

Business across ideological divides is common in the oil industry. Hugo Chavez shouts little about the fact that the United States continues to be a major customer for Venezuelan oil. In Iraq, Saddam Hussein and his Kurdish enemies had a deal for years which allowed oil to flow through pipelines in the north of the country for export into Turkey, in defiance of UN sanctions. Libyan oil itself had long flowed to countries in Europe that decried the excesses of the Gaddafi regime.

But there was yet another complicating factor in Agoco's case, which we learned later from one of the expat technicians hanging around in the suite. Once you've started producing oil in a field, it's hard to stop overnight without causing permanent damage to the reservoirs. Agoco's fields were quite old, which meant that a lot of the initial pressure in the field which drove oil up to the surface spontaneously had dissipated. The company, with its international partners, used submersible pumps in some fields and water injection in others – pumping huge amounts of water into the hydrocarbon-bearing strata of rock to make the oil, which is lighter than water, rise to the surface. Many of the internationals who were employed on these enhanced recovery techniques left the fields in the first days of fighting.

Agoco, in fact, had employed best practice and simply offered them the choice of leaving. Hundreds had made epic trips across hundreds of miles of the Sahara, their jeeps crawling over sand dunes at ten miles an hour, and God knows what ensued if they broke down, rather than wait and see. I was to meet Britons, Algerians, Libyans and Vietnamese, on boats, in hotels and in immigration areas who had fled the fields in the early days of the uprising, although most of the fields are deep in the desert and were not touched by either side.

All that led to a sharp drop-off from normal production levels.

Nevertheless most of the fields were still ticking over. Even now, Agoco was producing 180,000 barrels a day from residual pressure within the fields and some skeletal continuation of enhanced recovery. But the oil, produced deep in the Sahara Desert, hundreds of miles south of the coast, needed somewhere to go. From the wellheads, it was being pumped as usual into the pipelines, 500 miles long, that connect the fields to the export terminals at Tobruk and Ras Lanuf. But now, nearly two weeks after the fighting started, the pipeline was chock-full and so were the limited storage terminals on the coast. Some other executives told me storage tanks at Tobruk were close to their 5 million barrel capacity.

Agoco, in other words, desperately needed to offload some oil, almost regardless of who got the money. The company had scoured the world's shipping markets to find any kind of tankers prepared to come in the current turmoil. It wasn't even certain the tankers could be insured against damage and loss on the markets.

This story was screaming to be told. Back in the days when I worked for Reuters news agency, I would have sweated blood to get to a phone line and pump it out on the wires as a one-line bulletin – 'Agoco managers – tankers near Tobruk to ship 1.7 million barrels'. The import of Bolifa's casual train of conversation was that the rebels controlled one of Libya's largest oil companies and were keen to do business with world markets as usual. At a time when a major open revolt had been going on for ten days in one of the world's largest producers and nobody had any direct input from the industry on the ground, this could make the price of oil dip by as much as a dollar per barrel, maybe even more. Billions of dollars could change hands in deals based on this one piece of information, delivered by Mr Bolifa in between fond reminiscences of his pre-Gaddafi childhood, and graduate studies at George Washington University, against the backdrop of a flatscreen TV showing football highlights on mute.

But we now had nowhere to take this story because neither I nor my French colleague Sara Daniel worked for a real-time news outlet. Later, we watched with a mixture of awe and stupefaction as a pack of journalists followed our trail from the hotel to the Agoco hospitality suite and the company's management called an impromptu press conference.

Knowing what the main story was, I was able to observe at first hand the distorting effect of the breaking-news view of the world. Faced with the press conference format, the managers suddenly became didactic and uninformative when minutes before they had been open and concise in response to questions. They weren't trying to conceal, they were simply conforming to their impression of what a news conference should be. Early on, a passing reference to past management failures provoked a prolonged search from the journalists for an exposé. They grilled the Agoco managers on what previous management had done wrong, who was to blame, who was in control now, what their connections to Gaddafi had been and what their plans for the future were. By the time we left, nobody had asked how much oil was being produced or where it was going and none of the managers had thought to say. Eventually I ran into the Reuters correspondent late in the afternoon and just gave him Bolifa's phone number and the story. He rang, confirmed, and ran the story.

Bolifa and his team exemplified the weird and wonderful fact that behind almost every long-standing dictatorship such as Muammar Gaddafi's or Saddam Hussein's stand phalanxes of competent technocrats – oil executives, civil engineers, perhaps even army officers – who are fundamentally decent men just doing their duty as they see it, without wishing harm on anyone. Through sanctions, air strikes, coups d'état and outright war, they go to work out of professional pride and simple patriotism.

Given the chance, they had organised a coup inside the company as the wider uprising in Benghazi unfolded, getting rid of the old director Saad Abdel-Wanis. But they took great care to frame it with due process, persuading Abdel-Wanis to resign rather than be marched out of the building, replacing him immediately with a management committee to avoid a power vacuum, and respectfully informing the National Oil Corporation in Tripoli of events on the ground. 'It was not like a big revolt. He was very understanding,' Bolifa said.

The speed and decisiveness of Agoco's recognition of the new political order had been remarkable. The company declared its support for the revolution within hours of the city falling, and one week later commercially produced banners three metres high sponsored by the company festooned buildings all over town, urging everyone to keep the city clean and avoid random acts of vandalism.

Like many of the Middle Eastern oil companies, Agoco runs an extensive network of social services for employees, and communities in the areas where it is producing, all the more important for being set against a background where service provision by the Libyan state is pitiful if it exists at all. It acts as a centre of excellence. These services were kept going where possible.

Later, when international intervention occurred, the burning question was whether it had happened because Libya was an oil state. Chavez said it most nakedly: 'They want to seize Libya's oil. Once again the warmongering policy of the Yankee empire and its allies is being imposed.' But many shared the suspicion in quieter or softer language. The Iraq war had created a default assumption among large sections of international public opinion of hidden agendas, disingenuous public debate and 'blood for oil'.

On the surface, the Libyan intervention was very different to that in Iraq. It was mandated by a UN Security Council resolution, and the Arab League supported a no-fly zone. Nevertheless, there was no getting round the fact that it had been pushed along by the Western powers, notably France, Britain and the United States.

There is also a rich seam of technical information about Libya's oil industry which favours conspiracy theory. Just like Iraq, Libya is in the unusual position of being both oil-rich and yet considerably under-exploited as oil prize.

At 43 billion barrels, it has the highest reserves in Africa and something like 2 per cent of the world's proven reserves. But isolated for many years by UN and American sanctions, investment was very low and the pace of exploration only started to pick up after the first international bidding round in 2005 following Libya's reintegration into the international community. Several new fields have been discovered. Some companies say they can produce crude oil for a dollar a barrel, one of the lowest extraction costs in the world. Repsol and Total are stepping up production from the Marzuq Basin while BP has completed a survey off the coast that was regarded as groundbreaking in the oil industry for its unprecedented deployment of sophisticated 3D visualisation techniques over 70,000 square kilometres, an area the size of the Republic of Ireland. Survey ships installed huge supercomputers to carry out primary data processing on board, and new offshore drilling and production is expected to follow. Most of the new production is of the same grades of 'light' and 'sweet' oil, for which Libya is famous in the industry, crude oil that is easily and cheaply refined into petroleum, unlike the heavy and sour grades that are increasingly coming on line as a result of the rising scarcity of easy oil. And that's before you start to look at natural gas and Libya's perfect positioning to pipe it to the growing European market. There's no question that, at the end of the age of easy oil, Libya represents potential for growth second only to Iraq and perhaps Russia.

Ultimately, though, a conspiracy theory would require torturing the evidence. First, the most likely impact of a no-fly zone was to prolong the stand-off between Gaddafi and the rebels, whereas an 'Oil First' strategy would favour decisive victory by either side. Second, of the two sides, the Gaddafi regime is a known quantity to global markets over four decades, whereas the rebels are entirely unknown. The scale and depth of commercial relationships has varied according to the political weather, but there has never been a time under Gaddafi when Libya has not been as engaged on global oil markets as it was allowed to be. The list of companies doing business in Libya in early 2011 reads like a Who's Who of Big Oil, including BP, Shell, ExxonMobil, Total, ConocoPhillips, Occidental, Statoil, Repsol, Eni, OMV, Hess and Marathon. Third is the issue of proportionality. The loss of Libyan oil to world markets would be serious but not catastrophic, especially since Saudi Arabia offered to step in as swing producer to replace its 1.5 million barrels a day exports. Against that has to be factored the financial and political cost of another Middle Eastern neo-colonial war.

Of course, a diehard conspiracy theorist could argue that those planning to take over Libyan oil underestimate the cost, as the Bush and Blair administrations so clearly did with Iraq. But this is harder to maintain in 2011 than in 2003.

Nevertheless, if it just niggles too much that the first intervention in the Arab Spring, driven by Western powers, should happen in Libya, there is another, subtler way to scratch that itch. It is about oil because it's about Gaddafi, and in the most fundamental sense Gaddafi wouldn't be Gaddafi without oil.

The UN Security Council resolution was, technically speaking, humanitarian, directed only against the way in which Gaddafi chose to repress the protests. But this repression was always inherent in the nature of Gaddafi's regime. In addition, the degree of momentum that could be built to support it depended largely on his own foreign adventurism. With one or two opportunistic exceptions, nobody on the international scene would be sorry to see him go. Gaddafi is not just a common-or-garden dictator like two dozen others around the world, or even one who has acquired notoriety but only operates within his own borders, such as Robert Mugabe in Zimbabwe. He is a petro-dictator.

It is oil which has determined the nature of Gaddafi's regime. The length and degree of his hold on power, and his foreign adventures, would have been unthinkable without Libya's oil wealth. Over the years, his assassins have struck in Hamburg and London, Scotland and Cyprus, killing not just players but innocent civilians of twenty nationalities. He has verbally, and probably financially, backed Louis Farrakhan in the United States and the IRA in Northern Ireland. Militias have waged war on his petrodollar from Beirut to Ndjamena, Kinshasa and Kivu.

Inside Libya, the regime used petrodollar patronage to buy compliance. Like many oil states, Libya has a state-dominated economy. IMF statistics suggest the state employs at least a million of the 1.8 million workforce, or over 55 per cent, and the dream of most young Libyans entering the workforce is still the government job, or *wazifa*. In this they show no difference from the cultural expectations of their Egyptian and Tunisian neighbours. The difference is, the oil-rich Libyan state can deliver.

Several people described how in 2007–8 the government responded to the world food crisis by raising basic civil servant salaries something like 60 per cent. A teacher in Tobruk went from 210 dinars a month, or $190, to 340 dinars, or $300. But as elsewhere, a government job is not only about salary. It is about status and benefits, in particular, access to subsidised loans and mortgages. Interest rates on these dropped and borrowing limits rose at the same time as the salary raise.

For sure, the Libyan welfare state is subject to heavy expectation pressure: 'A twenty-year-old dreams of getting a government job,' said Youssef, a medical orderly from Tobruk. 'And maybe, if you're extremely lucky, a loan to buy a small car.' And economists will probably soon map how critical stresses in the economy in the twelve to twenty-four months before the revolution – the peaking of the oil price after a five-year boom and the global downturn – helped prepare the ground for it. One graffito on a wall in Benghazi read: 'Gaddafi leave so I can get married', a reference to economic stagnation delaying the marriage age, as young men could not build the careers and resources they needed to start a family.

But that's in the immediate run-up to the revolution. The longer-term view, the big picture, is current accounts surplus rather than deficit, year in year out; an immigrant workforce numbering over 10 per cent of the local labour market; and a sovereign wealth fund, the Libya Investment Authority, that has used ingenious financial engineering and minority sharehold-ings to circumvent sanctions and build a global portfolio worth perhaps $70 billion, with stakes in everything from banks in New York and Hong Kong, to real estate in Britain, petrol retailing across Europe, hotels across the Mediterranean and parts of Italian fashion houses.

Oil is what makes Gaddafi Gaddafi. Just as it is a large and inseparable part of what we really mean when we talk about Ahmadinejad, Chavez, Putin or Saddam Hussein, their person-alities and ideologies, their impact on the world. Or Osama bin Laden come to that: the ideology of al-Qaeda birthed in the easy millions, sense of command and closeted xenophobia afforded by being heir to a Saudi construction empire. This is not to be deterministic. There are, of course, dictators without oil and oil without dictatorship. But it is oil that often fuels the perfect storm, allows the dictator to project further, last longer, and never grow up, a sort of malign Peter Pan.

This is one of the biggest reasons why the political economy of Libya, and therefore its revolutionary dynamic, is different. In Egypt and Tunisia, the Arab nationalist paradigm at inde-pendence, of the all-providing state running a central command economy, slowly imploded under bad management and lack of accountability. In an overall environment of scarcity, the institutions of state then began to be used for extortion and bribery. Officials used the state to steal from the people but, like any parasite, they needed to limit what they took in order not to kill the host. Even at their most predatory, the regimes needed a textured state and society to prey on. They were in that sense civil dictatorships.

In Libya, the same lack of accountability prevailed, but in a state formation that was much less developed to begin with and which didn't run out of money. If you overlook the grand larceny of a trillion petrodollars at source, straight out of the wellhead, resource flows still trickled down from the top. It was easier for Gaddafi to buy well-armed loyalty both by pampering his regular armed forces and by recruiting the normal host of competing security services. And unlike resource-poor countries there was no imperative to encourage enough private-sector growth to steal from. All of that stuff sounded good, and it might be fun to talk to the IMF from time to time about privatisation. It gave sheen to Libya's Noughties re-entry into the international community. Fundamentally, though, Libya's economy and society, just like its politics, could be all Gaddafi all the time.

Petrodollars bought social engineering, in the form of wedding grants paid to Libyans to marry African nationals and build an entire social stratum owing its very existence to 'Muammar'.

It also paid huge blood money, systematically.

In Benghazi, residents told me of a human rights organisation run by Saif Gaddafi. If your relative had died in Abu Salim prison, you could go to this organisation and sign a paper which exonerated the authorities from any liability, implied that your loved one was in some way responsible for his own death, and walk away with $170,000. In the district of Luheishi one house was pointed out where the family had two torture deaths, signed, and immediately bought the large compound on the back of it.

As I travelled round eastern Libya, taking in the enormity of what the Gaddafi regime had wrought over the last forty years, a chilling thought occurred. The Libyan leadership had not been trapped, like Ben Ali in Tunisia or Mubarak in Egypt, by a political economy that was ever tighter as the population grew, resources shrank and there were tough decisions to make about how best to keep military and technocratic elites happy. Gaddafi and sons had enough money to turn the tap on or off, according to inclination. Saif's agency could drop $170,000 for every corpse dumped in the prison morgue, while its patron gave interviews to satellite TV in his polo-necked jumpers. The Libyan government could raise salaries by something like 60 per cent overnight, whereas its neighbours in Egypt would struggle mightily to fulfil a pledge made during the protests to raise public sector salaries by 15 per cent. If the Libyan people suffered economically, it was because the regime wanted them to. While the other regimes fell into behaviour patterns that were venal, selfish and arrogant, Libya's appeared, quite simply, whimsical and cruel.

So if the no-fly zone was not 'blood for oil', do we in the West bear any complicity for Gaddafi's petro-dictatorship?

I met Trevor from Middlesbrough at the Agoco headquarters, waiting to be evacuated on HMS *Cumberland*. Mid-fifties, balding skinhead, overweight, he was one of the company's expat workers and my first thought was to wonder if he had contributed, or read, any of the Le Carrés or Wilbur Smiths on the shelves behind us. What was it like where he had been? I asked.

'Yeah, not so bad, you know,' he said in Geordie sing-song.

'The locals got a bit excited and trashed a few buildings at first, but then they teamed up with the police, like, and guarded the pipelines and refineries. It seems OK now.'

So why are you evacuating? I asked. 'Well it's the end of me shift. Twenty-five days in, seventeen out.'

He told me he had been working in the Libyan oil industry for thirteen years. What's that been like? I asked. 'Well it's changed a lot.' There was a pause and I wondered where he was going with this. 'In the beginning you couldn't even bring in a pocket calculator, could you, Ernesto?' he said, turning to a Portuguese colleague for confirmation. 'They had no supermarkets, you had to bring in everything yourself.' He then told me what kind of music system he had, how you could get booze although Libya was dry, and what British TV channels you could get by satellite. He had obviously found some way of making it work for him. He worked for a contracting company, not directly for Agoco or any other Libyan company. That meant he had Libyans as clients rather than bosses.

In other words Trevor was a regular bloke, with normal preoccupations, engaged in making a living. The fact he's spent time working in the oil industry in Libya is pretty much irrelevant. If you were to start into how he's abetted Gaddafi, he would reply that if he didn't someone else would, find some glaring inconsistency in your own lifestyle, and you'd end up at an impasse with Trevor and 99 per cent of humanity on one side, and you and a few unbearable fanatics – and rogues probably – on the other.

On the other hand a few days later I met Mike, a senior oil exploration engineer, and he had a different story to tell.

A couple of years ago, he had been working with a foreign company in Libya, he said. He declined to say who it was other than to specify that it wasn't BP, his current employer. The company did a large deal with Libya's National Oil Corporation, working out profits and cost recovery, and all the other dozens of revenue streams that make oil industry accounting so fraught, on the assumption that oil cost $45 a barrel. Libya's share of revenues was maximised below that price. If it rose above it, the oil company would gain most or maybe even all of the windfall.

Now there was a moment that year when the price of crude oil on world markets dipped below the $45 mark, falling to $38 a barrel in February after it had hit an astonishing peak of $147 the previous summer. But it rapidly rebounded, and major international institutions such as the World Bank later averaged prices at over $70 for most grades of crude across the year. Moreover the rebound was predictable, as was the new normal of $70 to $80 a barrel, created off the back of a five-year boom. Talk of peak oil and deep offshore drilling was widespread, and it was industry consensus we were nearing the end of the 'easy oil' era. Finally, more crucial than any particular price point was whether the contract, a long-term arrangement for development of a new field, built flexibility of terms into itself so that it did not have to be renegotiated every time the market dived or spiked and one or the other party felt short-changed by existing arrangements. These kinds of mechanisms have become standard in recent years, and would certainly have been within the knowledge horizon of a negotiating team like the Libyans, where there has been an oil industry for sixty years.

The natural conclusion is they short-changed the state to profit the foreign company, and themselves with a kickback. Mike was startled when I put it to him in those terms, and I should mention that he had no hand in negotiating it. But he had himself mentioned the deal in the context of a discussion about corruption within oil states and ways to minimise it, as an example of the kind of thing to be avoided.

The major beneficiaries of this deal were Gaddafi and his family on the one hand, increasing their store of purely private largesse – the yachts and planes and football teams – and the company's shareholders on the other, adroitly tax- and time-smoothed, presumably, by clever accountants, to attract as little attention as possible.

But a lot of oil is produced in deals that are similarly and deliberately opaque, and the dictatorships that sit on one side of these deals are not profit maximisers, at least not within the formal terms of the contract. Is it possible that we were all benefiting marginally from this opacity? That even as we belly-ache about rising petrol prices and politicians hurry to assure motorists that they will be protected, Big Oil and dictatorships they do business with collude to keep the price of oil lower than it should be to the end consumer? That we are all, by fractions of cents and pennies, complicit in the blood money paid to the victims of Abu Salim?

18

Yes, It's Facebook!

Strangely enough, it was in Libya, the least connected of all the countries, that I came down finally on one side of what might be called the Great Facebook Debate. I was in a clinic in Benghazi talking to a Libyan doctor, Hisham Gheriani, who had returned from Vancouver to help with rebel wounded once the fighting had broken out. He spoke fluent English with a charming Irish brogue, having studied in Dublin, and his wife was currently working in Limerick, my ancestral home town.

How did you keep in contact with back home when you were in Ireland and Canada? I asked. Well, he said, it helped a lot when people started using the Internet here. When was that?

'You could really start to notice the difference about three or four years ago,' he said. 'People were coming online. And you could see what they were thinking and talking about back home.

'I've never been very political and it was hard to find reliable news as such. But people shared stuff, links and so on. Like Satoor.' Who's Satoor? I asked. 'He's a cartoonist. He makes fun of Gaddafi.' How long has he been around? 'Oh quite a time, but he's got big in the past couple of years.'

I had noticed the name Satoor, a nom de plume that means

'meat cleaver' in Arabic, on one of the posters hanging in the courthouse, the de facto seat of the rebel governing council. That afternoon I went back to look at it. Gaddafi shouting into the phone, looking scatty, his hair sticking out from under his fezzan. A speech bubble comes out from the receiver. 'You've got less than one *Katiba* left.' *Katiba*, the word for security encampment, rhymes in Arabic with *daqiqa*, the word for minute. So Gaddafi is being interrupted by a pre-recorded system message to tell him time's up. Next to it was a slogan that read: 'We knew the path of freedom with the Cleaver and we have liberated it.'

The Internet also explained another thing I had been struck by. The creaky, awkward explosion of self-expression that was happening in the rebel areas.

A young man stands in the middle of the road in Tobruk performing for the passing traffic. He wears a Gaddafi mask and points his fingers to his temple as if he has a pistol and is about to shoot himself. It was in the days after the quick liberation of the east and the rebels were entertaining the fond idea that, Gaddafi being so unstable, he might just see the course of history coming his way like a tidal wave and put a bullet in his head. Or someone else would do us all the favour. A day later, there was a printout of the same image on a wall in Benghazi.

And then the Jewish thing. Slogans on every wall saying Gaddafi is Jewish or the son of a Jewish mother. At first it seemed like more of the rank anti-Semitism that has pervaded so much of Arab political culture, for long and complicated reasons, in the last two generations, and it never occurred to me to think about its provenance. But the story kept coming, differently inflected and spliced, embedded enough that it was clearly older than the revolution itself. A schoolteacher in a small town tells me the Green Book is full of twaddle because it's 'an Israeli book'. A taxi driver in Bqayda relates a long story about a Libyan studying in Bulgaria who was murdered there by Gaddafi agents because he talked about having proof Gaddafi was Jewish. It was on the Arabic satellite channels, Hassan, the driver, says.

And so it was. But first, Israeli TV, which had interviewed two Israeli women in 2009 who claimed to be Gaddafi's cousins through his mother's mother. Whether it is true, and why it would be any kind of a deal if it were, is a whole other story. The point here is that in a digital world the Arabic channels could somehow hear about the two-minute breakfast TV interview on Channel Two and could find the clip, subtitle the Hebrew in Arabic, and rebroadcast it. And then it made the rounds as a YouTube link and Facebook page. Where it still is for anyone who cares to look.

Figures for Libyan Internet use are minimal and probably unreliable. The World Bank's data bank shows an estimate of 5.5 users per 100 people in Libya in 2009 compared with 20 in Egypt and 33 in Tunisia. Wireless data sticks using USB hubs had just come onto the market in the country when the revolution broke out and the regime started to close down the Internet.

But that's not the point. Every user is a potential rebroadcaster to their own, real-world, social networks, and when Internet use is overwhelmingly concentrated among the young, as it is in Libya and most other low Internet penetration countries, there's minimal duplication in the bush telegraph system. Each youngster becomes the news agency for his or her immediate family.

Gaddafi has been in power in Libya since 1969. But it wasn't until forty years later, in the late Noughties, that he could be pilloried and defamed by his people with impunity. The gods may make mad whom they wish to destroy, but for humans it's enough to mock them.

Which brings us to the Great Facebook Debate. During and after the revolutions in Egypt and Tunisia, pundits spent many broadcast hours on all TV channels debating whether these were Facebook revolutions. In fact, it was one of those weird media debates where the natural dynamic of proponent and opponent was thrown off because most of the guests were keen to voice their qualifications and reservations, and there was often a strain to create the kind of civil disagreement talk shows strive for. The Internet was quite important but not very important. It didn't create the revolutions, which were about real things like jobs and police brutality. What 'important' meant was never really defined. It's just that the Internet and social networks like Facebook were, well, important but not very important, or maybe even very important but not all-important.

A lot of this hesitancy had its roots in a lucid and cogent book just published called *The Net Delusion*, by Evgeny Morozov, a Belarusian opposition activist turned Internet scholar. Taking on supposed cyber-Utopians such as Clay Shirky, who'd written a book with the grand title *Here Comes Everybody*, Morozov argued that the belief the Internet was an unadulterated force in favour of freedom and democracy, as propagated by many but particularly the US State Department, was dangerously naïve. Dictators loved the Internet, he claimed, because it allowed them to spy on people and feed them disinformation better. Plus, the Utopians were too affected by their home environments, secure democracies with ubiquitous broadband, and could not understand just how few people in countries like Belarus, or Iran, actually had access to the Internet, and therefore how marginal the Internet actually was. So much had been made of Iran's 'Twitter Revolution' in 2009, wrote Morozov, yet there were fewer than 20,000 Twitter users inside Iran. Most of the Iran channels on Twitter had been clogged up at the time by well-meaning but mindless messages of good wishes, in English, from foreigners with no stake.

Morozov doesn't deny the Internet has its uses, and it's not as though it's going to go away. He himself has a background as an Internet activist and continues to work in the field. His arguments are subtle and well-researched: authoritarian regimes from China to Venezuela are learning to spin rather than censor. The very frictionlessness of the Internet risks creating 'slacktivism' rather than the concerted and disciplined organisations needed to overthrow dictatorship, where joining a Facebook group becomes a substitute for real action. Media is more often used as soma than as a means to provide missing information.

Nevertheless Morozov's book, which received a lot of media attention, suffered the same fate as the 'cyber-Utopianism' it sought to challenge. It got dumbed down. It succeeded in planting the idea that it is naïve to believe that the Internet must automatically be transformative. But, as relayed by various experts on talk shows and panels on both English and Arabic channels, that turned into a fairly inarticulate feeling that the Internet and social networking platforms could not have played a decisive role in the revolutions because, well, human beings and Arab societies are just deeper than that.

And yet they had played that decisive role. The Internet's role in social protest does not begin, and is not limited to, Where shall we demo this afternoon? There's a whole great big Before of personal expression – 'This regime stinks and I have to tell the world'; solidarity – 'Oh my God you feel that way too!'; even embarrassment – 'Gosh, it seems like everyone thinks the Big Man is rubbish' – which, depending on the degree of tyranny and the state of civil society, could take many years to build up. Maybe in some countries those preconditions have existed for a long time. But where they don't, as in the North African countries, the Internet has been essential in nurturing them. Once you have the Internet, it's like a big *Psst* in your ear. However serious the oppression and your very real fear of the regime, you can never actually *believe* them again, and you know it's the same for nearly everyone else. Gradually, it becomes hard even to pretend to believe them.

'I honestly think Wikileaks had something to do with our revolution,' Nabil, a professor at Kairawan University, had told me back in Tunisia. Towards the back end of 2010, a series of cables from the US embassy had been released which showed what the Americans really thought of their ally Ben Ali, talking of the endemic corruption and the excesses of the ruling family.

'It's not that people didn't know the facts already,' said Nabil.

'But now it was in front of us, in our faces. We knew that the Americans knew. And we knew that they didn't think a lot of Ben Ali, whatever they said in public. The regime was oppressive, but now there was a new feeling alongside the normal ones of fear and self-preservation. Humiliation. It had become humiliating to have a president like Ben Ali.'

Morozov neatly dismantles the idea that the Internet consistently and reliably facilitates real-time communication between the people who matter, empowering their operations. The real picture is a lot messier and more ambiguous once you factor in the bad guys, he says, and he's right. But in this preparation stage it is another, and opposite feature of the Internet that is crucial – not its real-time transience but its permanence.

Satoor has been publishing for years, and the rumours of Gaddafi's Jewish origins have probably been circulating for longer. But it's the Internet that has given them potency, and makes them live in the present. As long as that clip exists on YouTube, that cartoon is just a link away, it is part of the environment here and now in which you or I as Libyans think about the Gaddafi regime. Nothing ever gets lost.

It's also graphic and visual. Egypt's protest movement was revitalised by the two images of Khaled Said. Libyans and Tunisians began to lose their fear when they saw Gaddafi and Ben Ali visibly mocked in cartoons.

'The image has become all-powerful,' Hiba Zakaria, an Egyptian blogger and Internet researcher, said at a conference in Cairo. 'When television came it brought the image and the image-dominated text. But with it the television brought greater control, because of the high costs. There was only one source for television. Now the Internet and social networking have brought images back, but without control.'

During the protests in all three countries, the regimes have tried to disrupt the convening power of the Internet and mobile phones by simply throwing the switch. In Egypt, for example, the Internet was cut on 26 January for the best part of two days, which was the period in which the demonstrators grew from a surprisingly large spontaneous crowd of 50,000 people or so in Tahrir Square on Tuesday 25 January to an unstoppable force of hundreds of thousands, or maybe even a million across the country, the following Friday. Proof, say the naysayers, that the Internet could not have been essential. How could Facebook matter if the protests grew most when it wasn't available?

But that is to misunderstand the forces of precedent, imitation and critical momentum. The hundreds of thousands who came on the second and third days only came because of the 50,000 who came on the first day. And they had come, in numbers defying even the organisers' expectations, because at least 800,000 Egyptians had the chance to find out directly about the demonstration in Tahrir via the Facebook page *We Are All Khaled Said* set up by Wael Ghoneim, and millions more of their friends through them. Revolutionary protest, like fire, is not a static and linear phenomenon. 25 January alone unleashed enough energy for the protests that followed to be the biggest in Egypt's history, even if the end result, the removal of Mubarak, was far from certain until the last minute.

Even in Libya, with its exiguous Internet access, the revolution was sparked by a day of anger announced for 17 February on Facebook. In the end, protests started earlier in the east of the country when Gaddafi's men arrested Fathy Terbil, the human rights lawyer, and shot relatives come to protest for him.

Visuals also played a part in real time. Because everyone was aware of the constant battle for image, myths were created in real time. In Egypt the cross and the Qur'an held aloft in Tahrir Square. In Tunisia, as we saw in Sidi Bou Zid, protesters rushed home from battling the police to upload their struggles, or see if anyone else had.

Satellite stations were playing what can only be called 'highlights' of the protests every night. If time speeds up in revolutions, the instant feedback loops of digital media sped it up again. On 21 February I walked into an empty restaurant in Cairo and found the serving staff watching some revolution highlights on OnTV. Crowds were waving huge banners and it all looked like generic Tahrir to me, but then I hadn't been there. 'This is from ages ago,' said a waiter, idly. Ages, I asked? Yes, you know, the first days, he said. When I pointed out to him that the first days, and his 'ages ago', were in the last week of January, less than a month before, he didn't really see what I meant. He'd already lived it dozens of times on TV.

If the Internet played a major role in the run-up to the revolutions, it is already a crucial factor in the new dispensation. In Tunisia and Egypt, Facebook pages are routinely set up to support or denounce not just top-level politicians but district governors, town mayors, even heads of schools. In Tunisia, particularly, where there are an estimated two and a half million Facebook users, such pages are effectively the country's first free and fair votes with known results about anything.

But it will be not just the immediacy but the permanence of the Internet which matters in an ongoing political process.

In Tunisia, the return of the leader of the Islamist party Rachid al-Ghannouchi a few weeks after Ben Ali fled was met with both trepidation and intense interest by wide segments of society. Would he support democracy, stand for president, demand *shari'a* and the veil for women? Ghannouchi is near the end of a long journey from hard-line Islamist roots towards the political mainstream, but many distrust the evolution.

'He can enter politics with his new positions,' said Ayman, my medical student friend. 'But if he tries to claim he was never extreme, it is all there. All his early speeches from thirty years ago, in full, not the edited versions his supporters like to publish. I believe he could never be elected president because of what he did as a young man. And now we can see that.'

In Egypt, similarly, the growing debate about the nature and extent of police brutality will probably be influenced by documents such as Omar Afifi's book. A former career policeman, Afifi fled Egypt for the United States in 2008 after publishing a book called *How Not To Get Whacked on the Back of Your Neck*, written in question-and-answer format as a kind of guide to citizens' rights. The authorities banned it almost immediately but then he republished it on the Internet, where it stayed as the first real testament to the pervasive nature of police brutality from an insider. Even though the revolution has now opened up the publishing environment, who knew what, when and how far you could get in the police force without getting your hands dirty are live questions likely to be influenced by this and other self-publications on the Internet. Not to mention the local versions of Wikileaks, Tunileaks in Tunisia and in Egypt a site called State Security leaks, where supporters of the revolution are publishing documents they say show corruption and brutality.

In Tunisia, some human rights campaigners are interested in collecting testimony for transitional justice by video self-deposition. The first interior minister after the revolution installed a team of young surfers specifically to gauge public opinion by their interactions on social networking sites.

So to go back to the question of how important the Internet has been to the revolutions in Egypt and Tunisia, and Libya's ongoing uprising. Abstract definitions of the word important aside, they simply couldn't have been imagined and planned and carried out without it. The Internet is neither the cause nor the instigator of the Arab Spring. But it continues to be its single most important tool, blackouts or no.

The Net Delusion is a passionate plea for respect for the complex realities of environments in which the Internet is deployed, the need for empirical research, and above all not to simply stop thinking because we're talking about technology. Technological Determinism, the idea that technology overrides all other factors, is the great bogeyman.

And yet if it is true that Technological Determinism is mistaken to assert or assume the pre-eminence of technology as a general principle, it is equally true that – *sometimes* – there are moments when the change in the nature of the tools and technologies available does become the decisive difference in a situation, even if that situation is most naturally viewed, and lived, as a complex human and sociological construct, of vital importance to everyone, not just the geeks who proselytise for the new technology. *No printing press, no Reformation.* In fact as history marches on after the event, and the technological innovations that catalysed the development live their life cycle from innovation to ubiquity and often obsolescence, their role becomes harder to see, maybe invisible. *No literacy, no monotheism.* And paradoxically, many of those who insist on the primacy of the real, the physical and the human over the digital and the virtual fail to take into consideration complex social and psychological dynamics such as long-term motivation, self-worth, peer-group approval or pressure, and embarrassment. *No oil, no world war.* But it is the cumulative heavy impact and interaction of the Internet on each and all of these and other human and social factors which means that in the case of Egypt and Tunisia we can say yes, these are Facebook revolutions. *No mass media, no totalitarianism.* It is a view that starts the clock ticking at the moment a self-defined group of activists wants to organise a protest, missing the years before and after. *No Internet, no . . .* we don't have a name for it yet, but when it comes it will be as big a historical development as monotheism or the Renaissance.

The revolutions in Egypt and Tunisia have been such moments. The question of why and how the Internet could play such a key role in Egypt and Tunisia, how the regimes were caught unawares, how years of monitoring Internet traffic and bloggers failed to translate into more effective repression, is one that scholars will doubtless ponder for a long time. But from the ground it is clear that it is the case.

And this is just the beginning. Egypt and Tunisia are the

first countries in which the Internet played a crucial role in creating a new political dispensation. It would be strange if that reality didn't play out in some way we can barely as yet predict. If we stop projecting, thinking of the Internet as it has happened for us, and admit the possibility of what geeks call 'technology leapfrog', it is possible that Tunisia and Egypt may create paradigms of Internet-based democracy that are world firsts, and that we will follow.

19

Untold Treasure

Once I hit the crystal-blue waters, I knew I had made the right decision. An entirely unexplored and totally preserved Roman road lay three metres beneath me as I trod water. I could see it, and the pattern of the Ptolemaic harbour that had subsided into the sea in a fourth-century earthquake, with the naked eye. I could dive down and nose my way around streets and the foundations of buildings that had lain untouched for the last 1,500 years. Looking back to land, olive groves and pine forest stretched up from an empty, spectacular coastline to a plateau some five miles inland. It could have been Calabria, or Croatia, or Thrace, with one difference. There was nobody here. This was the pre-modern Libyan coast, the Med before tourism hit it.

The whole landscape, as I knew from the drive down, was littered with untouched Greco-Roman sites.

The land part of the port of Apollonia, if it had been in Spain or Italy would have drawn a half-million tourists a year. Leptis Magna, Libya's biggest site of classical remains, has got onto the international tourist map after the country was delisted as a terrorist state and a tentative thaw in relations with Western countries came about. At only seventy-five miles out of Tripoli it's a comfortable day trip, as is Sabratha, forty miles west towards the Tunisian border.

Instead, like the early Orientalist painters, Roberts at Petra or Holman Hunt in front of the Sphinx, I encountered only flocks of sheep and goats as they wandered through the temple to Apollo, and had to give a couple of wild dogs a wide berth by the ancient theatre. The entrance to the site, in fact, had been locked and a small boy had had to run off and fetch the keys from the director, who was at home having lunch.

It might seem frivolous to beg off Libya's uprising for an afternoon to go to the beach and tour ancient sites, but I've always been of the opinion that one of the best ways to get to know a place is to have as much fun as possible in it. And it had just been too good to resist. The battered tourist guide I got from a Benghazi bookshop had shown the old coastal resort of Soussa, just an hour north of the town of Bqayda, which was already on my route. There were two major ancient sites there, the guide stated, which belonged to the ancient Libyan Pentapolis, a cluster of five cities. Apollonia is the port established to serve Kyrenia, a city built by Greek colonists in the sixth century BC on the plateau above the coast, and which later became the seat of a philosophical school, the Cyrenaic philosophers.

I had originally intended to head down there at lunchtime, lounge around the sites in the afternoon, and put up in the only hotel in town, the Manara. But when I got there the hotel appeared uninviting and empty of guests, apart from a couple of women in full face veil or *niqaab*, curiously walking unaccompanied round its garden. I hesitantly asked the receptionist if they had rooms available.

'Of course. But you might want to stay at the Pearl up in Bqayda. They're much better,' he replied, with disarming honesty. Would you at least have any fresh fish in the restaurant? I asked. There were a few small boats moored up in a harbour at the back of the hotel. Bqayda, he replied, shaking his head, as if he'd already answered that question. You'll get what you want in Bqayda.

A day trip, then.

I headed on to the port site. Once the boy had returned with the key I entered. Without any signs or any literature available I had to guess blind what I was looking at. I had enough classical background to distinguish Doric architecture, Greek rather than Roman influence, and to hazard a guess that the garish 'new' marble columns stuck in the middle of the old temple, with crosses etched into them, were probably a Byzantine church. But I was operating largely blind and began to understand how these sites must seem to locals who have no background in them. Vaguely impressive and nice to have around, like a favourite piece of old furniture. But worthy of respect rather than enthusiasm, and not so precious that you might not borrow bits, from time to time, to buttress a wall or help you with your extension. Still, at least Libya's isolation meant it probably hadn't fallen prey to professional antiquities thieves.

By the time I had finished wandering around, the director himself had turned up. Breik al-Koweini was a small man, perhaps sixty years old, with twinkling light-green eyes. He had been born down the street but went off to Benghazi to study for high school and university, where he graduated in 1974 in archaeology. Then he had returned home and held the same job ever since, as director of the site at Apollonia. He gave me an impressive verbal tour of the site as we sat on beds with suspect blankets in the guardroom and a couple of guards brewed sweet tea on a gas stove on the floor, covering its various stages from early Greek to late Roman antiquity, and then those barbarous Byzantines – and here there was just a hint of mischievousness – who lopped the heads off the statues of the pagan gods and wrecked the temples as a sign of devotion to their one, true, Christian God.

The site seems very large and like there is still a lot of work to do, I said. Did he get any help from foreign colleague archaeologists?

'Of course,' he replied. 'Do you know Graham?'

Some back and forth elicited his surname. Barker. Graham Barker. I asked which university he might be from. We went back and forth between Liverpool, Manchester and Cambridge, before settling on Cambridge. 'He comes almost every year. And Jean Sylvain from the Sorbonne.' I guess it's all relative. Mr Koweini thought he had a lot of help because a small team turned up every once in a while. Meanwhile he was sitting on a site which if it were in Italy would be attracting perhaps half a million visitors a year.

He had had what might be described as a threadbare career as an archaeologist these last thirty-seven years. He had employed the young men from his extended family to help him dig up a Panathenaic-type stadium one summer, at $10 a day. He stashed Greek and Roman jewellery away from the dilapidated museum in a number of safe houses, not to steal it but to protect it. The same Manara Hotel that had suggested I look elsewhere for a room and fresh fish had been built in 1993 when a developer trashed a colonial-era Italian villa that had stood there. Mr Koweini had had to beg for a reprieve of two weeks to retrieve what he could from the Ptolemaic burial site that was revealed underneath it.

'I really had to hurry,' he recalled. 'Once again I could not get any funds from the government. They did not seem to be interested in our glorious past. But I got my friends and family together again. We managed to move eighteen coffins to the museum before they brought in the bulldozers.'

It was a glorious spring day, full sun, and I had already been bursting to get into the sea when Mr Koweini told me about the ship. In the ancient harbour, just a couple of hundred metres out to sea now, was a Greek ship sunk in no more than four metres of water. Would it be possible to swim out there? I asked. Oh no, he replied, and my heart sank. Perhaps I could come back when it was warmer, he added. I realised then that his biggest concern was my safety, and went to work on him. How warm the water was compared to Brighton, I said. Why it was already warmer here than with us in the height of summer – which is possibly even true. He began to reminisce from his childhood, about how the British at Benghazi would go swimming at any time of the year. They just seemed to have different skin, he mused. Yes, well, I began, pinching my own forearm, and did some more wild boasting about cold-water swimming. How once I swam into a snowstorm, another time across a bay, another time across the mighty Thames in London. In the end he just turned to me and said, as though he had never been of a different mind, 'Well would you like to change next door, then?'

And so, on the first day of March, I negotiated my way down a bluff just by the old Byzantine palace, which had spent the last thousand years politely, unobtrusively decaying, collapsing into the sea foot by foot, and clambered over the wreckage of Greco-Roman buildings, now left to the mercy of the Mediterranean, into the water. I waded out along the great, smooth slabs of a Roman road until I was out of my depth. And then I swam towards the old harbour. Excited by the prospect of a wreck you could dive without aqualung, I spent half an hour looking for telltale eddies that might give away the presence of the Greek ship, just beneath the waves.

Had I been able to find the ship I confess I would not have been able to resist having a poke around. I later found a refer-ence to the site in a guide from Abercrombie and Kent which stated that 'for obvious reasons, snorkelling and diving are prohibited'. And yet there I was. This feeling of accessing your own patch of history, its intimacy, was thrilling, intoxicating, the more so for being unexpected. Had Alexander walked these streets, lying a bare three metres beneath me? Apollonia was already three hundred years old when he headed deep into Egypt's Western Desert, not so far away, to cut the Gordian knot at Siwa. It was entirely possible. Had Alcibiades or Alkidas tramped up and down them a hundred years before, desperate for support for Athens or Sparta during the Peloponnesian War, the ancient Greek experiment with total war? Three centuries later, did the quartermasters of the town, now a Roman colony, nervously check their stores, and ship's masters anxiously watch the horizon, trying to read the signs of the death throes of the republic in the traffic of triremes passing one way then the other to Alexandria, where Marc Antony and the boy Octavian fought for Egypt? While, just over here, in this pile of rubble that I could almost stand on, a callous young man of good family sat oblivious, drinking bad wine and writing bad verse in honour of his latest infatuation with a Syrian slave girl? What lay beneath these gently lapping waters was an endless virtual cycle of question and answer, each round bigger and more engrossing than the last. And it was all there for the taking.

But I couldn't find the ship so I carried on to the harbour. There were a dozen berths for ships, cut with amazing precision into hard rock, and I realised that despite a degree in Classics I knew next to nothing of the mechanics of Greek seamanship. The berths were small, the average trading ship crossing the Mediterranean then being perhaps no bigger than a businessman's play yacht today, but without the outboard motor. Natural rock formations with a small opening in the middle afforded year-round protection.

Sitting there on the salt-lashed rocks, looking back at the tiny scale of the Greek town laid bare against its landscape, and on the other side the unbounded sea, it was impossible not to be intensely aware of the resilience of the ancients. These were not at the time considered precarious outposts, any more than New England was from England through a century and a half of voyaging across the Atlantic by sail. They were an integral part of the Greek world. And yet maintaining that connection presumed a constant pitting by man of himself against greater forces, the sea, the winds, the supplies brought by the previous year's harvest. There were many shipwrecks, people aged quickly and died young. The Romans were so nervous about the sea that they called the Mediterranean *mare nostrum*, Our Sea, as if its force were a god to be appeased by appropriation. But life still seemed good, on the whole. Not for the first time, I wondered what the Greeks and Romans would have made of a culture of Sky Sports, war by videogame, endless petty indignation and mass obesity.

When I got back to shore, tingling, it was late. Mr Koweini gave me a letter of introduction to his colleague up at Cyrene, muttering darkly about his relative youth and inexperience – he was only fifty. I got back in the car and snaked up the hill again, past three separate necropolises, to reach the ancient city just as it was starting to turn dark.

Cyrene was even more extensive than Apollonia, the major city of the old Libyan Pentapolis. Founded in 630 BC, it flourished in Ptolemaic times, from the third century BC on, and limped through to the end of antiquity, although by the fourth century AD Ammianus Marcellinus was referring to it as largely abandoned. According to the Bible, it was one Simon of Cyrene that a Roman soldier pulled from the crowd in Jerusalem to carry the cross for Christ up to the Mount of Olives after he was too weak to do it himself.

The site was already closed by the time I got there, so I committed my second act of cultural vandalism of the day and climbed over the walls. For about ten minutes I had the entire city to myself until a jogger ran past, hurdling the fallen columns of a Hadrianic temple as he did so. The city stands just at the neck of the final pass up onto the plateau leading back to Bqayda, glorious green slopes lying beneath it and the Mediterranean stretched far below. Then the jogger ran back to tell me that the driver wanted me to know there was a madman with a knife on the loose coming this way. The way he carried on jogging himself suggested a different story to me, that Hassan the driver, who had not been too keen on stopping again before getting back to Bqayda, was trying to hurry me along. So I stayed put, walking through the colonnades, admiring the huge mosaics in the baths, embedded in open view, and shooting a quick film with my pocket flip camera. Sure enough, as I came to the main exit there was the line of gods and goddesses all with the heads neatly chopped off, as Mr Koweini had said. Those naughty Byzantines! There's a twenty-minute film on YouTube if you search for 'A tour of Cyrene'.

I couldn't help wondering what the whole of Jebel al-Akhdar could be like given just a little peace and stability. Two hundred miles of lush Mediterranean hills, forests and meadows and cypress-tree-lined avenues, barely explored and with less than a million people in them. The area is so undeveloped that just before Benghazi I clocked about thirty miles on the main road, running parallel to sandy beaches a half-mile away, without a single paved road down to the sea. Even now, in the middle of the war, it would make a fabulous week's cruise, coming down from Malta to Derna just next to the Egyptian border and working your way west to Benghazi then up again.

I also thought of Mr Koweini, trying to engage his extended family on his various digs in order to save untold ancient treasures, and how a friends society could help him. A sort of new and unassuming people-to-people diplomacy to replace Gaddafi's grand-standing buyout of poor African dictators. Infinitesimal but real.

20

Back Home, Egyptian Style

Tens of thousands of Egyptians were leaving for home and I needed to join them. I was in Bqayda, the ancient capital of Libya, but needed to be in Alexandria, 500 miles along the coast. I cut short, as politely as I could, the hotel receptionist's story of his part in the revolution, and headed towards the shared taxi stop.

The shared taxi, or *servees*, is one of the Middle East's glorious institutions. It's not the tilting overloaded bus lurching down rutted tracks of filmic imagination in India or Africa, groaning with authenticity. It's something altogether more comfortable and intimate, five to eight of you in a spacious old Mercedes more often than not, lolloping along. Cigarettes, sweets and suspect bits of home cooking are freely passed round, there are frequent stops for tea, prayers and relief, and, nearly always, conversation flows freely, Middle Easterners being generally far more adept at that kind of human relation than buttoned-up Westerners.

A bunch of travellers were hanging out in a cafe next to the stop. When they heard where I was from they were naturally curious to chat. We talked about the revolution and football while sipping sweet white coffee. The man sitting next to me, a weary forty-five, reminisced wistfully about how as a boy he had lived next to and played with a little European boy called Johnny who belonged to a family working in the oil industry. One day he had come home to find the family gone, part of the fairly rapid emigration of expat families as Gaddafi's hold on power, powered by a virulent strain of Arab nationalism, strengthened in the early 1970s. When he asked to stay in contact I handed him my notebook and pen, expecting him to write his phone number. Instead, when he handed it back, I found he had neatly inscribed it in neat cursive as follows: 'Nasir al-Tajouri, a Libyan soldier deprived of all his rights by the regime. He loves the English and the Americans and I hope that our friends know that a close friendship binds us together.'

The fare, when the car was full, was twenty Libyan dinars, or about $17 for the 140-mile trip to Tobruk. We skittled along, out of eastern Libya's wonderfully fertile Jebel al-Akhdar region and into the desert. Three people did most of the talking. A chain-smoker in the front passenger seat who I named Marlboro, the driver, and an Egyptian Bedu beside me from Marsa Matrouh, the main town along Egypt's western coast. Matrouh did most of the talking but for half an hour I could hardly understand a word, not even where one word stops and another starts, so thick was his Bedouin dialect. This must be what Arabic sounds like for my mum, I thought, all guttural clashing and glottal stops. At one point Matrouh took his passport out of his pocket and thrust it into my hands. It showed him to be from the Awlad Ali, the region's largest tribe, and thirty-seven years old. But I still have no idea what the point was.

Gradually, though, like a fade out and in in a film, the new scene came into focus, and I could begin to sense the drift of the conversation.

The Americans might land, their ships had six thousand troops on them, Marlboro man said. Cabbie said the best time to have been alive for an Arab was the 1950s and 1960s, the era of our grandparents. That is when there were heroes. Then the talk converged around 'Muammar', as Gaddafi is universally known in Libya, even among those who would like to kill him. You just never knew what the man was going to do, never! We pass through a checkpoint where soldiers wave us through quickly, and there is a seasoned debate about the calibre of gun mounted on the armoured vehicle straddling the crossroads. It was certainly a 14.5 cannon, the consensus ran, but was it loaded? Popular attitudes to the army, or rather those units of it in the east which had joined forces with the rebels, were deeply mixed. Rumours were rife of army units being gradually desupplied by headquarters back in Tripoli, as part of a long campaign to run down the strength of the forces in the east. At the same time the change of sides orchestrated by Major General Abu Bakr Younis held the distinct air of opportunism.

The most excited moment was actually talk about the weather. Look, look, Matrouh yelled and pointed to the left. The lake's got water in it! The heaviest rains in perhaps twenty years had fallen in the previous two weeks, not wispy, fleeting showers you might stick your tongue out at to taste, but solid, drenching downpours that stuck your clothes to you. Now the Jebel al-Akhdar was a riot of green, and even this lake, which I gathered had been dry for many years, was suddenly on the full side. The waterline reached as far as an old beached ship which had stood parked in the middle of the desert for years. Marlboro floated off into how his father had taken him there as a child. Matrouh said he had been coming and going on this route for fifteen years and never seen anything like it. It was a harbinger of hope.

The radio was talking about a new transitional council which was handing out portfolios. Abdel Fattah Younis would be minister of the interior. Is he from the Mzein clan? Matrouh asked the Libyans. He was.

As we approached Tobruk, new half-completed apartment blocks snaked further and further out to meet us coming in on the road from Benghazi. One apartment block had a large 'Obeidat. Reserved' spray-painted on the wall, implying public housing was being allocated by clan.

Matrouh talked about his search for work. He was in construction. His boss in Benghazi had laid him off but referred him to another boss in Bqayda. But when he got there the man had nothing for him and had referred him to another boss in Tobruk. If he didn't find anything there he would go home for a while and figure out what to do.

Matrouh was a strong, bold man with one metal tooth set off against otherwise even rows, and a hairline glued to his scalp. He could have been typecast as hero in one of the gushing black and white films Egypt produced in the Fifties and Sixties after Nasser's Free Officers Revolution when all was hope – the *fellah*, peasant, who puts backbone into his fellow villagers to resist the machinations of the feudal landlord and his vile seductress daughter. I knew he was illiterate because he handed the passenger on the other side a scrap of paper to read for the phone number. But he talked a mile a minute and was a natural, unstoppable storyteller.

Saudis are the hardest people to work for, he said. They keep changing on you. It seems like they want to wrong-foot you on purpose. I was in Saudi Arabia for eight years but there was never a Saudi I could call friend. The boss would never pray with you. And twice, they wanted to send me away without paying me, he said. Twice. We were left to understand that, somehow, he had found ways of taking what was his. The Libyans listened sympathetically, and after he got out, just before the town to track down a potential new job, Marlboro said: 'There's a man who knows what's what.' Matrouh had a way of commanding respect.

The changeover at Tobruk took three minutes. We pulled up at the *servees* point on the edge of town. The cars on one side of the dusty highway head west to Benghazi, and on the other side east to the Egyptian border. Pop your bags out of the trunk, dodge the traffic, pop them in another trunk and away you go. There was already another car waiting for its last passenger – me. From Tobruk to the border another 140 miles and $15.

My two fellow passengers this time were Abed and Reda, Egyptians in their mid-twenties. They'd been working out at Barda, a small town where Saif Gaddafi had built a tourist resort. They were college graduates but were working on building sites. Why did you have to leave? I asked. There's no fighting out there, everything's normal again. But things are more complicated than that, Reda explained. Enough people on the site, other nationalities like Africans, had left that those who

remained couldn't do their job, since all the different special-
ities were intertwined. Plus, it seemed, a lot of money for projects and businesses in the east was tied up in the national
banking system, and other institutions, such as government
departments and the oil corporation, which were based in
Tripoli. With the country still split in two, there was a cash-
flow problem. Reda and Abed would have to go home to Buheira
province in the Nile Delta.

When he found out I was writing a book, Reda wanted me
to give the 'right picture' of the Arabs. What's that? I asked.
'Not like the Jewish news agencies do,' he said. There *aren't* any
Jewish news agencies, I said, a little exasperated, you might just
as well talk about Jewish clouds or Jewish tables. So what about
those reporters who are sacked for saying bad things about the
Jews, then? he asked. I realised he was talking about cases like
Helen Thomas and Rick Sanchez, US journalists who had to
quit because of controversial comments about Jews, Thomas
because, in 2010, she had suggested Israeli Jews could simply
go home to Europe and Sanchez because he implied that Jews
controlled the US media establishment. We truly live in a world
where a little learning is a dangerous thing. I wondered how
the nuance of those stories appeared once they had been ground
through the lens of Arabic satellite TV.

Reda's world view was remorselessly reductive, and depress-
ingly passive. Despite the fact his country had just experienced
the finest moment in its modern history, a peaceful revolution
by the people against a police state, all from within, he was all
about America's influence on the world, Israel's influence on
America, and how everyone hated the Arabs. Will America allow

Gaddafi to keep the oil industry? Will America allow the Egyptian revolution to succeed? Get with the project, I harried him. It really doesn't matter what America thinks. Why don't you tell America what to think? I wondered whether, if Reda had been in Egypt during the revolution and gone to Tahrir Square, he would have seen things any different. Meanwhile, he was looking at me as though I was an alien.

So what about Palestine? he said. What's your explanation for the fact that the British gave Palestine to the Jews? Well I believe there are three main reasons, I said. First, the British, like all the European colonial powers, were racist and thought nothing of carving up other people's land. Second, the Zionists were European, and so understood how to influence international opinion more effectively than the Arabs. And third they, the Zionists, were totally committed to their ideal, and had spent fifty years already building it – trade unions, universities, town councils, kibbutzes. Reda was not satisfied with my admission of ancestral moral guilt. Why did everyone else agree to persecute the Arabs? he said. What is it about the Arabs?

It's not about the Arabs, I replied. Did you know that at the same time Palestine became Israel the British also screwed up another colonial secession, India? Two million people died in the fighting between India and Pakistan. There have been twenty Palestines around the world in the sixty years if you want to talk about human suffering. It's just that they don't form part of your narrative the way Palestine does. I know it may not be much consolation, but the Arabs are not uniquely persecuted. They're just averagely persecuted. You'll have gathered I might have been overheating by this time. Something in Reda's view of politics as self-pity by other means was galling.

Abed in the front sat this out, grinning, as did the Libyan driver. It's quite common in political discussions in the Middle East for the majority to sit back and enjoy. When there was a lull, though, he popped his head round the headrest and asked me if I could get him a visa to Britain. Very hard, I said. It's either relation by blood or qualifications. The best thing you can do if you want to get to Europe is to practise your English in these three months. Yes but, yes but, yes but, he came back, as if hoping that when he asked the question again the answer would be different. And then asked me if I had any female relatives he could marry. And was only half joking.

So it would be fair to say I was a little ratty by the time we hit the border. As we paid off the driver, an Egyptian officer barked at his detachment and they all came running towards us – to give us all regulation soft drinks, one of the little gestures of initiative and confidence that were cropping up in Egypt in the days after the revolution. Then I headed into immigration, relieved to have a polite excuse to part company with Abed and Reda. There were thousands of people from every nationality that had worked in Libya: Nigerians, Vietnamese, Pakistanis, Bangladeshis, Thais, Ghanaians, Sudanese, Filipinos, Sri Lankans, Koreans.

The scene at the Egyptian border was nothing like the pictures I had seen on TV from the border with Tunisia, where a major humanitarian crisis was developing. Knots of Africans sat on large packs playing cards. Young South Asian men strolled past the many administrative buildings, arms draped carelessly over each other's shoulders. There was a lot of boredom, fatigue, and probably no small measure of long-term anxiety. But no signs of desperation. The foot soldiers of globalisation are used to waiting, sleeping where they sit, and generally going short.

Relief workers were beginning to arrive, staff from the United Nations High Commissioner for Refugees and various red crosses and crescents. I walked past a tall American I had seen on TV the night before giving an interview to Al Jazeera English. Most of the third nationalities seemed to be grouped at the border post itself. It looked as though the Egyptian authorities would keep them there until their own authorities made arrangements.

A young Egyptian army captain, when he heard that I was British, escorted me out of the hall, I thought to a different desk. But it turned out he had been asked to take me to a delegation from the British embassy parked in a Range Rover, a couple of friendly ladies from the Home Counties and a man in his fifties with a shock of white hair, army trousers and a pressed designer shirt who sat in the driver's seat. He looked suspiciously fit for a man his age. He used my first name relentlessly – the ladies had already marked it down in their register of returnees. I knew it would somehow be impolite to ask him his. He spread a map out on his knees and asked me how many soldiers I had seen in the rebel area, where, and how well armed they looked. I parried and evaded. The ladies handed me back my passport and I set off back for the main hall where the Egyptian immigration officers waved me through in record time, one punctiliously writing in my passport that I would have to pay for a visa on exit as they had now run out at

Salloum. A quarter of an hour later I was out on the road again, hauling my bag across no-man's-land.

On the Egyptian side, row upon row of minibuses were lined up, waiting to pick up fares to Alexandria or Cairo. Crossing the border I had entered a different world. The spaciousness of Libya, 6 million people in a country three times the size of France, gave way to the crush of Egypt. Hawkers were walking up and down selling everything from lighters to sandals to revolutionary souvenirs. Minibus drivers were arguing about who should park where. It was the kind of crowd you have to gird yourself up to throw yourself into.

I was just on the point of doing that when I heard an ecstatic shout: 'Johnny! Johnny.' Reda and Abed were sitting on the kerb nearby. They jumped up and mobbed me as an old friend.

'We missed you,' said Reda. 'Abed kept saying "Where's Johnny, where's Johnny?"' Instant affection is another of the tropes of travelling in the Middle East. Just add tea and mix. Sometimes the skein of hospitality is stretched so taut that someone is declaring his undying friendship within an hour of meeting you and then asking for your phone number. I'll never forget the time a Jordanian taxi driver, after twenty minutes, complained that I was going to forget him when I went back home. 'You'll forget me, won't you, Johnny?' he said. 'Yes!' I replied impishly, just to see what would happen next. Luckily, he laughed uproariously. Paradoxically, of course, I haven't forgotten him.

It would be too rude to try and shake them off now. So we teamed up to try and find a minibus. Reda, Abed and I became a team facing the world at Salloum border post.

And what a world it was. For the next two hours, we negotiated with minibus drivers. We got in and out of a single bus
three times because we couldn't fix a price – 'Whatever you
like to pay, sir', 'There is no god but God. Just tell us!' At one
point, the driver came to blows with someone in the back of
his minibus I had taken to be a fellow passenger, waiting like
us for a full complement, but who it turned out was a driver
from a bus nearby who saw that we were having trouble reaching
agreement and had sneaked in to try and steal our custom.
Then there were the fights outside, at least two of them 'Stop
thief's, with a man running out front, another behind, and the
crowd as mercurial judge and jury, growing so packed that at
times they were jammed against the side of the bus we were
waiting in and rocked it. At one stage we had agreed a price
with the driver but he couldn't then manoeuvre the bus out
past the other buses parked in front. By the time he found the
other driver we realised that we had different understandings
of what was agreed, and so went back to negotiating again. But
he couldn't concentrate on talking to us, being more drawn
instead to arguing with the driver who had blocked his exit.
Everyone seemed to be shouting at everyone, Reda and Adel
impugning the drivers' collective good faith, one of them tugging
Abed on the arm to tell him how, since they came from the
same province, they were virtually kinsmen.

In between were periods where I sat looking at the religious
stickers inside the van – 'Pray to the Prophet', 'Cleanliness is
the guard of the faith', 'Whatever God wills'.

At another point, we had actually agreed the price and driven
out a couple of miles along the road, when the driver wanted

to go back to pick up one of his friends. There was a traffic jam ahead so we said OK. He parked the bus at the rear of the queue heading back towards Libya, got out, and clean disappeared. But this is Egypt. Other cars and buses began to appear behind us and it was clear that within a couple of minutes we would be boxed in.

He'd left the keys in the ignition so I hopped into the driver's seat to swing the minibus round out of the press at the crossing itself and park it by the side of the traffic lines. The driver came running, at full tilt, out of nowhere, out of his mind with rage. Understandably, I guess. The minibus is not only his living, it's his pride, an aspect of his manhood. Some random foreigner just starting it up unasked probably feels little short of sexual harassment. Nevertheless, words were exchanged. He would have hit me if I hadn't caught his arm. A crowd forms, the instant jury. An old man persuades them to my case and they tell the driver to apologise. He does, but doesn't mean it. I too have my pride and decamp in what I hope is a dignified huff, Abed and Reda trailing behind me. The old man who took my side then offers us a decent rate in his own minibus and we are off at last. More civilised this time. We pick up a mother and daughter who live just a couple of miles down the road but have no transport. When we drop them off, they insist on buying us tea in the cafe. All hope of reaching Alex by dark having gone, we relax, happy to be out of the throng. It's going to be a long night anyway, what's the point in hurrying?

There are a couple of words, not perhaps unique to the Egyptian dialect of Arabic but most commonly in use there. One is *zahma* – pressure, crowd. The other is *dowsha* – hard to translate into English as it stands almost exactly in between argument and fight – voices raised, maybe some shoving, a symbolic blow or two.

What I had just experienced for half an afternoon was what millions of ordinary Egyptians live day in day out, *zahma* and *dowsha*. You become part of it, you have no choice if you want to go anywhere, get any kind of job, make ends meet. And it's upsetting. It's not just striving and hard work, the fact that it could take hours and be utterly exhausting to do something as simple as get on a bus to Alexandria. Very few people here, like anywhere else, mind struggling if they can see their way clear to that making a difference in their lives and in the lives of those they love. It's the fact that under the constant struggle for survival you risk being humiliated, losing your dignity, your *karama*, maybe being hit by a bus driver or, conversely, having some weirdo drive your bus off. Not enough opportunity has been created so it's the law of the jungle, whether you like it or not. In a very real sense this is what the Arab revolutions have been about. Expressed at a high level, they are about human rights and freedom and elections. But the same sentiment is working at a more everyday level. People want to live decent lives. To work certainly, to struggle perhaps – but with *karama*, dignity.

We drove on from the border post. Salah, the driver, told me how he had spent three years of his life as a conscript in the huge army encampment we were passing, bored out of his mind. There was just nothing to do, he said. They'd put us on the parade ground for an hour in the morning, and then maybe another hour of exercises. And that would be it for the day. No

TV, no radio to speak of, no place to go, food always the same. The first few weeks I would sometimes cry, literally from boredom. Then I think I went into some kind of haze. For two years. I've never smoked hashish. Plenty of the lads did but it's against our faith, I would never do it. But sometimes I wonder if those two years were like being on hash. I woke up when I got back to Alex. He spoke without rancour, almost with resigned amusement, as though that was what life brought. The same way someone else, a European or an American, might describe being crapped on by a pigeon or falling into a pond.

We got as far as the town of Salloum, about ten miles beyond the border, when we found the road closed. Forty cars, buses and lorries were queuing in front of us at the entrance to the town, on the single road hugging the coast to our left. Ten minutes, twenty minutes, half an hour, and I decide to get out of the bus to see what's up. Reda and I walk down the gentle hill to the front of the queue of cars.

About fifty people, boys and men of the town, have set up a barricade across the road, demarcated with small boulders. Some of them are sitting neatly in a line across the road while others are chanting in front of a small police post to the side. This is a fabulous laboratory for Egyptian democracy, I say to Reda, advancing towards the crowd. It's one of those protests, continuing after Mubarak has gone, which are 'special interest actions', the subject of concerned columns in newspapers warning about a collapse in the public spirit fostered by Tahrir Square. Reda meanwhile is tugging at my arm, counselling me to hang back. Advice I choose to ignore. It's not that kind of protest.

What's up? I ask. An elderly man, clearly a ringleader as the police report would have it, steps out of the chanting crowd and embarks on a long and complicated story about a local police officer, Major Someone, who is, at different times in the conversation, tearing up travellers' passports or preventing humanitarian aid going through to Libya. The sit-in has been organised by townsfolk, he says, to protest against police brutality.

By now the queue is a hundred vehicles long.

That may be so, I say, but I just want you to know there are maybe a thousand people backed up waiting now. Including people like African workers who haven't eaten or slept properly for days. I'm sure you've heard of the troubles at the border. You may have a good cause – I don't say you haven't. But all those people – I sweep dramatically with my hand – are innocent of any of your complaints. With freedom, I conclude pompously, comes responsibility.

'There is no freedom! There is no freedom! There is no freedom!' he yells straight in my face. So how come you're shouting that at the top of your voice and blocking a major highway to a thousand people? I ask. Where are you from? someone else is asking me. Britain, I reply. When the ringleader hears this he starts dancing, swirling round, some age old anti-colonial song about dastardly generals I've never heard, that the crowd takes up. It's all very febrile, hugely entertaining in a kind of Pythonesque manner. Within seconds, I've become an object of mild derision to the small crowd and someone else taps me on the shoulder to say – You're the ones who started all the trouble. You gave Palestine away! *What?* I reply.

I come down here to inform you that your action is inconveniencing maybe a thousand innocent bystanders and all you can find to say in reply is that I carry the passport of a country that did something somewhere else half a century ago? Colonialist! Colonialist! he chants cheerfully in my face. There's clearly no use so I start to move out of the crowd. Well all I can say is, this is childish behaviour, I say as my parting shot. Well he's a child, says one of my adversaries, pointing to – a child.

Reda and I walk back up the hill to the truck, past an army checkpoint, Reda muttering it would take a hundred years for democracy to work in Egypt because 'they' – people like the protesters – are 'backward'.

I pass the time of day with the young officer lolling about with his men. 'We're hardly going to run them down. They'll stop when they stop,' he said. You felt as if he wanted to roll his eyes but was too disciplined. Not for the first or last time I silently thanked the vision of the Egyptian army in holding back, allowing the protests, and the revolution of the popular will, to triumph without violence. Messy and bothersome it might be, but nobody was going to be killed or injured today, and another few inches of progress may have been made towards democracy taking root in Egypt.

Now, at last, we really were rolling, the long motorway stretching out 400 miles ahead of us to Alex. We settle in, jamming our packs into the corners of the seats to use as cushions, passing round biscuits and water and dates. But there's another wobble when an older passenger says that the Egyptian border authorities are handing out stamps to confirm the re-entry of workers thrown out of work by the upheavals. Neither Abed or Reda bothered to get the stamp, so won't be eligible.

It'll be like Iraq, says Hajj Metwalli, the older man, referring to the expulsion of a million Egyptian workers from Iraq during the 1990–1 crisis and war over Kuwait. Some people got up to 60,000 pounds then, he adds excitedly – what would have been nearly $20,000 then. But you'll need the stamp to prove you came out, he says, waving his.

Reda and Abed are confused. Who exactly's going to pay us? asked Reda. Our employers? No, says, Metwalli, the state. The Libyan state. From which I gather that the idea is that the new Egyptian government will approach whoever ends up on top in Libya and, relying on the fact they, the Libyans, will continue to earn far more petrodollars than they can possibly spend, will gently but insistently suggest they support the brotherly revolution in Egypt and be good neighbours by reimbursing the million or so Egyptian workers who lost earnings as a result of the Libyan revolution. Given the current workload of the Egyptian government, this seems more like that rare thing, a bureaucratic initiative, than actual state policy. But tempting none the less to Reda and Abed as they sit on our minibus, hurtling away from their chance to cash in. In the end, though, they can't be bothered to go back and we carry on speeding into the darkness.

I looked out of the window as the light faded, pondering the question of what it is to live in an ugly world. Housing developments were dotted all the way along the road, here and there, most of them block-like structures thrown up with a good deal more graft than care. Thin walls, painful angles, naked lighting if at all, drab as drab can be. Of course Egypt has some world-famous buildings and locations: Luxor, old Cairo, Aswan, Sharm al-Sheikh – tourism Egypt. And life is good for the moneyed classes, no question of that. But many, perhaps most, of its people live in environs that are not just poor and dirty, but ugly. One complex we pass has six rows of five apartment blocks, laid out in a perfect rectangle. Each block, uniform sand yellow, is six storeys high, and each floor, by the looks of it, had four small apartments. Doing the maths, that comes out at 720 apartments. In Egypt, average occupancy could easily reach five people per apartment, so that would mean close on 4,000 people living in a block of an apartment, in a block of a building, in a block of a development, in the middle of nowhere. No shops to hand, no workplaces to be seen, no organic growth of any kind as yet. That would come in time – it was a new development. But then it would more likely than not be against plan, implosive, corroding. And with it all, a drabness that could make you cry. A friend described how, on arriving at Cairo airport and driving round the ring road, seeing very similar kinds of housing projects, she had felt it was 'like India, but without the colour'.

I was startled from this reverie by Abed shouting down his phone. 'What? We've talked about this before. Go home. We've talked about this. Go home now! We'll talk when I get back.' He comes off looking mad.

Who was that, I said. My lady friend, he replied coyly. Why were you shouting? Because she answered the phone in the street, he said. What? I reply. You can't be serious. It's not good for women to do that, he says, she shouldn't talk on the phone in the street. It's against our customs and traditions, he adds. That's codswallop, I reply, you're just making that up. No, Reda intervenes earnestly, it really is our customs and traditions. You've had a mobile phone for, what, ten years, and you want to tell me there are customs and traditions? I know what he means – that somehow an interpretation of the religious injunction to be modest translates into women not talking into their mobile phones on the street – but am choosing to be obtuse to make my point. She's your girlfriend, right? Abed nods. And she knew it was you. No, she didn't, he says, becoming animated, it's not my normal number. She didn't know it was me at first. So the woman's real crime, it seems, is that she answered a call from a number she didn't recognise and talked to a man for a few seconds without being certain who it was – although it turned out to be her boyfriend. Abed looks knowing now he's brought in the point that she didn't know the number, like he's just put himself beyond reproof. Unbelievable, I say. Poor girl. Abed smiles smugly. Later he's on the phone to at least one other woman, flirty and coy, and I haven't forgotten his earlier attempt to marry my daughter, or sister, or whoever else I have available.

Some passengers have got out and I have a bench to myself. I lie down and retreat for a while into the space offered by MP3s, relishing the incongruity of music to place. The Blue Scholars, a Seattle jazz-rap band, as we pass Marsa Matrouh. Then random play brings Meatloaf and Alan Jackson, a country and western singer I downloaded once on a trip to Bible Belt America – *Where were you when the world stopped turning?*, an 11 September dirge. Abed and Reda are making call after call and I notice something I've seen before. Although they were born and raised in Egypt, have been in Libya less than two years, and are calling their Egyptian friends and family, their speech is loaded with Libyanisms – *towa*, now, *al-hoosh*, home, *al-gad*, there. Rather like, as teenagers, those of us who summered in the States could be guaranteed to come back with some choice expressions. Talking foreign is glam, helps you stand out.

About an hour short of Alex, smelling something familiar, I sat up. Reda was rolling a joint, crumbling some hashish into an empty Marlboro tube that he had caressed free of its tobacco, which lay in a heap on some paper in front of him. Abed was looking on keenly. Reda had bought the lump in Bqayda for about $7. He said it was going cheap because rebels had found a big stash when they overran police headquarters. And carried it on him through the border crossing, which I found hard to understand. He either knew something I didn't about Middle Eastern borders or had a radically different way of assessing risk-to-reward ratios. So much for traditions and customs, I thought. But said nothing. I was feeling all talked out.

It was nearly ten when they dropped us at the *servees* station on the edge of Alexandria, and we went our separate ways, Reda and Abed off to Buheira province where friends and family were waiting up, me into the centre of the city, old Alexandria, the only bit foreigners usually visit.

With only a light bag, I wandered nearly a mile down the road from the stop, in a busy shopping district, eager to soak in this other Alexandria, which approximated the rest of Egypt better. The shops were still open, families were out, and vendors pushing carts. Lots of everything wherever you looked – mobile phone shops, clothes shops, big families crammed into small cars, neon lights in sagging rows strung across the street, or from one building to the next or over a shop front, cafes with men sitting out at cheap metal tables on cheap metal chairs. It could have been anywhere.

Eventually I hailed a cab and got in, asking the driver, a devout young law student earning extra cash, what part of town we were in. Agami, he said.

Agami! I had come here at least once a month for two summers back in the early 1990s, with my friend Mohammed. His family's beach home was 100 yards from the sea. In the mornings, we'd go down barefoot, me to swim, Mohammed to wind-surf, to a beach that was empty every day except Fridays. Now I could only tell where the sea and his house must be, over to the left, by the fact I knew we must be heading due east towards the centre of town. This choked-up high street must be where we had come from time to time to buy provisions from shops, which stood back then with plenty of land between them.

In Egypt, anyone over thirty is an oral historian. As we crawled along a street I could not recognise, I thought about Egypt's millions of migrant workers, men like Reda and Abed, Salah and Matrouh, that I had travelled with that day, and wondered if even at that moment, as they arrived home to relax in the bosom of their families, any of them were finding the world had changed up on them again.

Epilogue

There were a few hopeful weeks early in 2011 when it seemed the entire Arab world could fall to people power as Egypt and Tunisia had, in a matter of weeks. We now know that it won't play like that. As I write, there are four other countries in major crisis – Libya, Syria, Bahrain and Yemen – and stirrings in Morocco, Algeria, Jordan, and Oman. The regimes in these other countries have not been caught off guard as those of Zine el-Abideen Ben Ali and Hosni Mubarak were. To some extent the remaining autocrats must spur each other on, taking heart from every protest quelled, each day that passes across the region without further regime change. The innocence and wit of people power has been overshadowed by two old demons of the Middle East rearing their ugly heads: sectarianism, whether real, or fabricated by the regimes, or really fabricated by the regimes; and foreign intervention, as a Western-enforced no-fly zone in Libya turns into humanitarian and possibly financial and military support for the rebels.

When what was suddenly made simple has become complex again, and uncertain, it's tempting to fall back on those safe old clichés about the Middle East.

That it's a region bound by history, blinded by an obscurantist faith and gagged by special forces snipers. It's tribal, ornate, rhetorical and Byzantine. A mindset us moderns can't comprehend. Opaque, *Syriana*-like, full of unseen hands and vested interests. Above all, feel-bad – again. For a brief moment it felt like joy was in the mix there, but now it seems as if it's reverted to type. Endless suffering. Swathes of unreason. Some of the good guys beginning to look like they've got skeletons in the cupboard, or at least their heads in the clouds. And some of those vested interests uncomfortably close to home – as in a mile down the road at the nearest petrol station.

But don't be fooled by all that. It is true that the snipers are staking out rooftops daily, in the suburbs and bustling centre of Damascus, in the southern Syrian town of Daraa, here and there in towns along the Mediterranean coast. They are men who can shoot dead unarmed protesters from the safety of distant rooftops through their scopes, go home to ruffle their children's hair and eat a hearty supper and come back the next day for more – because you just know some of them are keeping their own tally. Just as it's true Saudi soldiers are stationed across the sweltering heart of the Bahraini capital Manama, a foreign intervention that somehow sneaked under the radar, determined to prevent, God forbid, a Gulf democracy. Thousands have been killed since Mohammed Bouazizi set light to himself that December morning. And it's clearly not over yet.

But the very complications that have set in since the easy victories of January and February should warn against general assumptions about the region as a whole.

There are some easy short cuts to explain why the revolutions should have succeeded in Egypt and Tunisia so quickly while they ran into resistence in Libya and Syria, Yemen and Bahrain. There's the fact that in January all this came out of the blue and the first two regimes were caught napping. Then there's the positioning of the Egyptian and Tunisian armies above politics, and the relative homogeneity of their societies which meant that Ben Ali and Mubarak ran *civil* dictatorships, with pretensions to ideology that were only ever tepid at best. By comparison, Syria's regime ran a full-on one-party rule for decades, as befits a former Soviet client, with travel bans, schisms, some lingering doctrinal resonance in the ragged remains of Michel Aflaq's Baathism, and a puritanical disregard for human life. Bahrain's ruling family by contrast spent decades smothering possible dissent over the sectarian basis of its rule with what passes for love in political economy, economic growth and modernism, malls and bars and well-run luxury car dealerships. While in Yemen the country split, then reunited, then imploded into multi-dimensional conflicts, oscillating wildly between tribal politics, nascent democracy, deep tradition and anarchy, edging almost as close as it is possible to go to becoming a failed state without actually being labelled a failed state.

But these are only place holders. The game is still very much in play and the broader point is that we are mistaken to think so often about the Arab world as if it were one, undifferentiated block.

If you are born a Bahraini, the GDP on your head is 20 times greater than that of a Yemeni friend, and you are likely to live 13 years longer. If you are a woman, you will be twice as likely to be working as your Syrian sister, and she, in turn, is twice as likely to be literate as her Yemeni sister. Countries in the significant neighbour category if you are sitting in Damascus include Turkey, a country with aspirations to join the European Union while in Sanaa, the Yemeni capital, they include Somalia, whose chaos has already propelled something close to half a million refugees across the Red Sea into a Yemen whose resources are already under severe pressure. If you are Syrian or Yemeni, you try your damnedest to get a job somewhere else, and to get there by human trafficking networks if you have to, night boats and forged passports and bundles of cash stashed on your body. But in Bahrain it's the other way round. More than three out of four people in the local workforce are foreigners, and if you travel to Europe or North America, you are more likely to be doing a masters with a couple of credit cards in your wallet than driving a mini-cab or helping out on a friend's market stall for cash under the table.

All three countries are mainly Arab and Muslim. And the timing of their popular unrest is clearly no coincidence – they share enough peer status to influence and be influenced by each other and the rest of the Arab world. But they also have configurations within a vast range of sectarian, historical, political, economic, social and cultural permutations at least as varied and singular as Finland, Bulgaria and Portugal within Europe.

But not only is every society different. To get caught in the day-by-day news flow – rebels retreat at Brega, Bahrain accuses Iran of stirring up its Shia population, this ex-minister goes on trial in Egypt, residents say that Syrian town is under siege

– is to risk missing the larger change which has already occurred, and is irrevocable. The floodgates have opened across the Arab world. Change, real change, has come so thick and fast it has blown the decades of stupefying stagnation that preceded it clean out of our minds. We ring our hands over the remaining autocrats who cling so desperately to power, unsure when they get up in the morning whether they are going to stall, kill or make concessions. But it is already a massively different world from the one that prevailed for two generations, virtually unchallenged, up to the end of 2010.

Ali Bouazizi and Khaled Said's brother Ahmed, among many, have proved the power of witnessing via the Internet, and that will never be taken back. Anis al-Shoaibi in Sidi Bou Zid, Abdallah al-Souissi in Kairawan and Ismail Alexandrani in Alexandria are just three among millions who have proved the courage of their convictions, whether it was against the snipers, phalanxes of riot police with their shields, or the torturer's cosh and chains and electric shocks under a strip light in a room that daylight does not enter. That sense of *karama*, of honour regained, likewise, cannot now be taken back.

Egypt, particularly, will anchor the Arab revolutions, resuming its role as the Arab world's centre of gravity. New political leadership in Cairo may no longer expect simply to command the attention of the region in the same way as it did when Gamal Abdel Nasser's voice crackled across the airwaves every week on Voice of the Arabs radio station in the 1950s. This is the channel-zapping age and that oratorical style will not stand. But Egypt's strategic weight, its role as the Arab world's pop-culture capital, and the millions of its citizens who work in other countries of the region could provide ballast to the Arab democratic ideal.

Tunisia can play a useful supporting role. Maybe even run out front in terms of the pace towards transition, with its 3 million Facebook friends, its 3 million diaspora in Europe and its powerful *exception tunisienne* for the role of women in the Arab world.

If these two countries can transition to democracy the pressure elsewhere in the Arab world will only continue to build.

If. If in Tunisia protesters like Anis get settled enough to marry and feel like they have found their place in society. If Abdallah gets some nod from justice at the treatment he received. If Abdik doesn't become so bitter he starts directly inciting violence in his rap, or does something drastic.

If in Egypt policemen like Colonel Mohsin are made to behave or leave, and if the lawyer Mustafa Ramadan finds a path too in the democratic process. If Hassan al-Misbah opens the doors of Space Net to generations more of ragged-trousered Internauts and Ahmed and Hisham the bloggers learn to take just a little bit of the edge off when they talk to common folk. If Hani and Salah carry on pretty much as they are, and Ali the Shoeshine gets a little hope and ambition, just a little. If Ismail Alexandrani is right about faith becoming a part of politics without seeking to dominate it. If Yosri Foda and Reem Maged are allowed as political talk-show hosts to become part of the conscience of the nation as Alaa al-Aswany is. If Mohammed El Baradei stands for the presidency and makes a good fist of it, win or lose.

As for Libya, they just need to end it, not just with victory, but with magnanimity.

The West has so far failed to engage with these revolutions in anything like a commensurate manner. There is already buzz around the US Congress about cutting aid to Egypt because Israel doesn't like the turn its foreign policy is taking, reconciling the Palestinian factions and talking of normalising relations with Iran. It may well be that such an aid programme is no longer appropriate, or would need to be restructured for new Egyptian priorities. But to cut it as some kind of punitive measure, emanating from Israel, would only confirm the worst suspicions.

Meanwhile Europe has been flaccid. The EC delegation's website in Cairo lists thirty-four news items from the time Hosni Mubarak left office on 11 February up until the moment I write this. Twenty of them are statements by Catherine Ashton, the nearest Europe has to a foreign minister. In one of them, she talks about the need to assist Egypt's economy in general terms with no numbers attached. The only new funding announced is grants of up to 40,000 pounds sterling for artists to produce works relating to the Revolution.

But this should be Marshall Plan stuff. Maybe something is in the works, but if so the lack of high-profile flagging to date is already indicative, and it is likely to be a tepid bureaucratic version of boldness. A 50 per cent expansion of the current 150 million euros a year assistance, perhaps, when we need a 500 or 1,000 per cent rise. Even a billion euros a year would amount to only 3 per cent of Portugal's bank bailout. Egypt needs two or three million jobs in a hurry to persuade the people at large – Ramadan the concierge, Ali the Shoeshine and the 30 million or so people who live below two dollars a day – that the revolution and democracy are about bread on the table as well as freedoms. Politicians are likely to grandstand fabulous figures of loans at summits in the months and years to come. But as usual with such declarations, the devil is in the detail and it remains to be seen how much of the headline figures is really new money, and how fast and flexibly it will be deployed. The history of development funding is full of bold promises that have never been honoured, as I saw for myself in three years in Afghanistan. Perhaps more important than notional sums are institutional arrangements. When we hear of new departments, or entirely new organisations, of significant numbers of smart and ambitious public servants tasked with helping Middle Eastern economies to develop, that will be the time to start taking the rhetoric seriously.

It's not as if the other Arab autocracies are the only remaining source of instability in the Middle East. Israel still occupies the Palestinians, who do not have a state. Iran, like America, still fiercely believes in its own exceptionalism, its role as a regional power. There's still the same uneasy alliance between Gulf oil and American military projection. Egypt and Tunisia represent 100 million people living along the shores of the southern Mediterranean who now, for the first time, have a chance to become free, pluralistic societies, and to inspire their neighbours – or not.

It would be mind-bogglingly short-sighted to dither or equivocate. We have already seen the economic migrants start to come in leaky boats as the old regimes' sea-patrol systems went into abeyance – some 25,000 people in the first three months after the fall of Ben Ali and Mubarak. It's a trickle that could easily turn into a steady flow. Scores of young men only stopped their accounts of the protests and their role in them to ask me if I could get them a Shengen visa, or complain about how much an application to go to the States costs – just on holiday, mind!

But to be honest I have met so many brave, passionate, courteous and modest people in the last few months that I don't even like to present the case from a viewpoint of pragmatism, or enlightened self-interest. The Arab street is alive like never before. And I don't mean bustle – it's always been bustling.

I mean fresh with ideas and debates, with a new ability to breathe freely, and even, sometimes, with the quiet buzz of hope. Like a thunderstorm has drenched off years of dust and there's a cool breeze blowing but also a touch of static still in the air.

The men and women of the Arab world deserve all the hope they can get. To anyone who has seen these revolutions, this is a Berlin Wall moment.

At that moment of victory, when the wall goes down, you do want to hug the person standing next to you.

Acknowledgements

Many people were very generous with their time in sharing their lives and talking about the momentous events of January through March 2011 across North Africa.

I would particularly like to thank the following: Anis al-Shoaibi and Aida Bouzidiya in Sidi Bou Zid, Hamed Bechir and Abdallah al-Souissi in Kairawan, Moufida Belghith and Rajaa el-Abbasi in Tunis, Ismail Alexandrani, Mohammed al-Dakhakhny, Ahmed Said and Mohammed al-Shawqi in Alexandria, Patrick Werr in Cairo, and Khalifa al-Faituri and Sara Daniel for their companionship in Benghazi. Of course, despite their help I alone am responsible for any inaccuracies and wayward opinions.

Special thanks go to Robert Twigger for encouragement and conceptual guidance and to Internews, who do such tremendous work with journalists across the region. Class 3D at Berlin Metropolitan School helped me retain the inspiration of the Arab Spring by being first audience for a children's version on my blog at http://delepaak.wordpress.com

Thanks to Natasha Fairweather at AP Watt for taking me on, Susan Watt at Quercus for choosing to launch her new list with this book, and Steve Cox for copy editing with sympathy, precision and verve.

Most of all I would like to thank my wife Steph for her combination of loving support and acute observation, and Roobs and Juju just for being there, and making me want to make them proud. I hope they both read this one day.